An Introduction to International Macroe

Also by Graham Bird

CLASSICAL WRITINGS IN ECONOMICS
INTERNATIONAL DEBT, Vols I and II (*with N. Snowden*)
COMMERCIAL BANK LENDING AND THIRD-WORLD DEBT
CONTEMPORARY ISSUES IN APPLIED ECONOMICS (*with H. Bird*)
ECONOMIC REFORM IN EASTERN EUROPE (*editor*)
IMF LENDING TO DEVELOPING COUNTRIES: Issues and Policies
INTERNATIONAL ASPECTS OF ECONOMIC DEVELOPMENT (*editor*)
INTERNATIONAL FINANCIAL POLICY AND ECONOMIC DEVELOPMENT:
   A Disaggregated Approach
LATIN AMERICA'S ECONOMIC FUTURE? (*with A. Helwege*)
MANAGING GLOBAL MONEY
THE INTERNATIONAL FINANCIAL REGIME (*editor*)
THE INTERNATIONAL MONETARY SYSTEM AND THE LESS DEVELOPED
   COUNTRIES
THE QUEST FOR ECONOMIC STABILISATION: The IMF and the Third World
   (*with Tony Killick, Jennifer Sharpley and Mary Sutton*)
THIRD-WORLD DEBT: The Search for a Solution (*editor*)
WORLD FINANCE AND ADJUSTMENT: An Agenda for Reform
THE IMF AND THE FUTURE: Issues And Options Facing The IMF
INTERNATIONAL FINANCE AND THE DEVELOPING ECONOMIES

An Introduction to International Macroeconomics

Theory, Policy and Applications

Graham Bird
Professor of Economics
Surrey Centre for International Economic Studies
University of Surrey

Third Edition

First edition 1987
Reprinted once
Second edition 1998
Reprinted once
Third edition 2007

Published by PALGRAVE MACMILLAN
Houndmills, Basingstoke, Hampshire RG21 6XS and
175 Fifth Avenue, New York, N.Y. 10010
Companies and representatives throughout the world

PALGRAVE MACMILLAN is the global academic imprint of the Palgrave
Macmillan division of St. Martin's Press, LLC and of Palgrave Macmillan Ltd.
Macmillan® is a registered trademark in the United States, United Kingdom
and other countries. Palgrave is a registered trademark in the European
Union and other countries.

ISBN-13: 978-1-4039-4004-9
ISBN-10: 1-4039-4004-5

This book is printed on paper suitable for recycling and
made from fully managed and sustained forest sources.

A catalogue record for this book is available from the British Library

A catalog record for this book is available from the Library of Congress

10   9   8   7   6   5   4   3   2   1
16   15   14   13   12   11   10   09   08   07

Printed and bound in China

To my family

Contents

Preface

The objective of this book has always been to explain international macroeconomics in an uncomplicated, accessible fashion, in order to shed light on global economic events. Because of this approach, it has proved itself to be valuable not only to students concentrating on economics who want to see how theory can be applied to the real world, but also to students taking courses in international relations and international political economy, who want to acquire an economic perspective on the world without having to read highly technical textbooks designed for upper-level undergraduates in economics.

In international macroeconomics it is easy to lose sight of the wood for the trees. This third edition, as before, presents complex issues in broad and straightforward terms but in a way that still manages to capture the essence of what is going on. Although the book contains a significant and rigorous theoretical section, the theory is always viewed as a means to an end rather than an end in itself. The end is to better understand how key aspects of the world economy work, and this is reflected in the structure of the book, which moves from theory to policy and applications.

There are quite a few differences between this edition and the second edition, published in 1998, and the changes I have made affect all three parts of the book. In Part I, and largely in response to requests from students, I have added a brief exposition of the *IS–LM* model as an appendix to Chapter 2. This has allowed me to edit and reorganise the contents of the main chapter. It also means that the book does not rely so heavily on prior knowledge. Chapter 4 now contains a slightly longer discussion of intertemporal models of the balance of payments, although the basic structure of the chapter remains intact. An extra chapter (Chapter 6) has been added to Part I to deal with theories of currency crisis. Such theories were embryonic at the time of the first edition and were in their infancy (or perhaps adolescence) at the time of the second edition.

In Part II of the book, the chapter on stabilisation policy in an open economy has been edited in some places and extended in others, while the one on exchange rate management and policy has largely been rewritten, particularly to say more about the choice of exchange rate regime. New chapters have been added to deal with remaining issues relating to balance of payments and capital volatility. The chapter on global macroeconomic management has been omitted in this edition, and been replaced by one on the international co-ordination of macroeconomic policy. This seemed to be an appropriate modification in the light of the issues covered and contemporary debates at the time of writing.

Part III of the book has been changed substantially. It now contains five chapters rather than three, and again, this is in large measure a response to feedback from users of the book, who emphasised the appeal of the applications section. In addition to a chapter dealing with the oil crisis in the 1970s and the Third-World debt crisis of the 1980s, there are chapters covering economic and monetary integration in Europe, including the introduction and early years of the euro, the economic crises in emerging economies during the 1990s and early 2000s, and the current account balance of payments issues faced by the USA in the mid-2000s, in conjunction with the broader question of global economic imbalances. Given the continuing involvement of the International Monetary Fund (IMF) in many developing and emerging economies, the chapter dealing with the IMF and macroeconomic policy has been retained but significantly rewritten.

The changes made to this edition have been designed to keep the book up to date in terms of both theory and applications. The opportunity has also been taken to extend the exposition of some ideas that were perhaps too succinct in the earlier editions. However, while this has meant that the book's overall length has grown, I have tried to keep this expansion within manageable proportions. I hope that, by clarifying some parts of the analysis, it may be a case of more being less. Certainly, compared with other textbooks on international macroeconomics, the third edition is still a slim volume. By being relatively light on the details of theory, but heavier on policy and applications, it fills a niche and continues to offer a blend of international macroeconomics that is not easily available elsewhere.

In addition to the acknowledgements made in the first two editions, I would like to thank Gherardo Girardi, who raised a few questions relating to some of the early material, and this caused me to be rethink it. In preparing the manuscript for publication I have also been helped greatly by Sirathorn Dechsakulthorn (who allowed me to call her BJ). She has the endearing habit of regarding any task as being 'no problem', and this has made my life much easier. A sabbatical leave from Surrey University gave me the chance to work on the new edition, and Claremont McKenna College was kind enough to invite me to spend time in California as a Visiting Professor. I would like to thank both institutions.

As with the previous editions, this one is dedicated to my wife, Heather, and my children, Alan, Anne, Simon and Tom. They know how much they all mean to me, so I shan't embarrass them by telling them in the preface of a small textbook on international macroeconomics!

Introduction

This book attempts to provide a non-mathematical introduction to the macroeconomic analysis of both the open economy and the world economy. Such analysis is appropriate for a number of reasons. First, all economies are, at least to some extent, open; they have trading and financial links with other economies. Second, what holds for a closed economy may not hold for an open one. Dropping the closed economy assumption from simple macroeconomic models is a strategic step which may even reverse the policy conclusions reached. Third, while it is important to see how the operation of an open economy differs from that of a closed one, it is also important to examine the operation of the world economy – or a substantial part of it – as a whole. Many macroeconomic problems are shared across countries and it is therefore relevant to ask whether these problems and their potential solutions should not be dealt with at a more aggregated level than that of individual countries. Furthermore, does it follow that what is right for an individual economy in isolation is right for the world economy?

Of course, none of this is very new. A great deal has been written over recent years – and indeed not so recent years – about open-economy macroeconomics, although perhaps rather less has been written on the macroeconomics of the world economy.[1] Much of what has been produced, however, has been quite mathematical and technical. Yet the issues raised are sufficiently important to warrant dissemination to and discussion by a wider audience which, while it may be happy to look at diagrams and to follow some elementary analysis, feels uncomfortable with too many formulae and equations. The purpose of this book is to provide just such an exposition. Of course, the simplification of theory has costs as well as benefits. The principal cost is a loss of analytical precision and rigour, although there can be legitimate debate over just how high a cost this is.

The book's purpose is not only to work through a certain amount of economic theory, but also to relate the theory to problems of macroeconomic management and policy formulation at both the individual and world-economy level. Theory is then not presented for its own sake, but rather as a means of assisting in the realisation of basic macroeconomic policy targets. As such, it is hoped that the contents will be of some interest to policy-makers as well as to students of economics.

The book presumes some basic understanding of macroeconomics but does not require any significant mathematical capability.[2] It could be used for first- or second-year undergraduates, either as a course text in its own right or as a supplement to other more conventional macro-economics textbooks. It could also be used as a complementary source on courses which provide a more descriptive and institutionally based treatment of international financial economics.

The book is written in a rather terse style and there is a noticeable absence of subtlety. The reasons for this are, first, the desire to avoid the book becoming over long and to explain the basic ideas in international macroeconomics as crisply and efficiently as possible. With more comprehensive textbooks it is often possible to lose sight of the wood for the trees. Besides, with long chapters it is sometimes difficult to keep the momentum going. Second, it is hoped that readers will be encouraged to read the book actively rather than passively; in other words, they will have to work carefully through the arguments and may have to dip into other textbooks in macroeconomics to fill gaps in their existing knowledge that is taken for granted here.

The layout of the book is as follows. Part I examines the macro theory of the open economy. Chapter 2 sets up a basic open-economy model which, in essence, simply augments *IS–LM* with a balance of payments component. Chapter 3 decomposes this model and focuses on the current and capital accounts of the balance of payments. Chapter 4 examines the various approaches to analysing the balance of payments and the causes of payments problems, while Chapter 5 looks at the theory of exchange-rate determination. Part I is brought to a conclusion by Chapter 6, which examines theories of currency crisis.

Having amassed these analytical building blocks, Part II examines policy. Chapter 7 sets the scene and briefly examines balance of payments policy options in broad terms. It discusses structural adjustment and the politics of policy choice. Chapter 8 examines macroeconomic stabilisation policy in the context of an open economy, concentrating on monetary and fiscal policy, with Chapter 9 focusing more narrowly on exchange-rate policy. Chapters 10 and 11 discuss international capital volatility and the international co-ordination of macroeconomic policy, respectively.

International macroeconomics remains in a rather strange condition. Simple models which focus on the short run and which largely put to one side many of the recent 'advances' in macroeconomic theory such as rational expectations, efficient markets, and inter-temporal optimisation, remain remarkably resilient at explaining many aspects of the real world. Indeed, they frequently provide both a clearer and more accurate guide than do the more 'advanced' models which theoretical purists prefer. Simple models continue to supply an expedient way of understanding many global macroeconomic events and therefore yield a higher intellectual rate of return. That this book ignores some modern theoretical macroeconomic work does not only therefore reflect its introductory status, but also the fact that incorporating these newer ideas does not significantly improve our ability to explain the world economy. Indeed, in many cases the newer theories are at odds with the empirical evidence. While making do with a basic model which contains theoretical shortcomings may not be ideal, it may be the best we can do for the present.

Part III of the book sets out to show that the simple model constructed earlier does indeed provide a useful framework within which to analyse aspects of the world economy. It gives us a worthwhile analytical tool kit. Chapter 12 examines the oil crisis of the 1970s and the debt crisis of the 1980s in the context of the *IS–LM–BP* model. Chapter 13 seeks to explain the near collapse of Europe's Exchange Rate Mechanism (ERM) in 1992 and the subsequent move to the euro. Chapter 14 turns attention to the sequence of crises in emerging economies during the 1990s and early 2000s. Chapter 15 uses balance of payments theory to better understand the enduring current account deficit in the USA and related global economic imbalances. Finally, Chapter 16 examines the choice of macroeconomic policy favoured by the International Monetary Fund (IMF). In each case, the applications are intended to bring the analysis to life and to show that it is relevant to the real world.

Part I

Theory

2 An Open-economy Macroeconomic Model

Introduction

One of the principal trends in economics over recent years has been to place considerable emphasis on the need to examine the various inter-linkages that exist between economies, and to move away from models that concentrate on the operation of closed systems. Of course, this is not to argue that conventional macro analysis ignores such interlink-ages; indeed, many of the older textbooks in macroeconomics and international economics include discussion of concepts such as the for-eign trade multiplier. But the presentation of this and related material as 'open-economy macroeconomics' is a more recent phenomenon.

The purpose of this chapter is very modest. It is simply to investi-gate in a fairly unrefined fashion the major implications for macro-economic analysis of opening up an economy and allowing for trade and capital flows.

Closed-economy macroeconomics tends to focus on the principal domestic behavioural relationships such as the consumption function, the investment function and the demand for money function, and then proceeds to build these into an overall model of income determination; open-economy macroeconomics considers, in addition, import and export functions and capital movements, and then examines how the process of income determination changes as a result of these additions.

From Simple Closed- To Simple Open-economy Models

Most students of economics at the intermediate level are familiar with the standard closed-economy models as represented by the Keynesian cross diagram, the equivalence of actual saving and investment, and, at a rather more sophisticated level, the *IS–LM* framework.[1] For those who are not, the *IS–LM* model is explained briefly in an Appendix to this chapter. For a closed economy without a government, the reduced form for income determination is derived as follows:

$$Y = C + I$$
$$C = a + cY$$
$$I = \bar{I}$$
$$Y = a + cY + \bar{I}$$
$$Y(1 - c) = a + \bar{I}$$
$$Y = \frac{a + \bar{I}}{1 - c}$$

where Y is national income, C is consumption, c is the marginal propensity to consume, a is a constant component of consumption and I is private investment.

In the case of an open economy, where there are imports (M) and exports (X), the reduced form is modified in the following fashion:

$$Y = C + I + X - M$$
$$M = mY$$
$$X = \bar{X}$$
$$Y = a + cY + \bar{I} + \bar{X} - mY$$
$$Y(1 - c + m) = a + \bar{I} + \bar{X}$$
$$Y = \frac{a + \bar{I} + \bar{X}}{1 - c + m}$$

As compared with a closed economy, the multiplier for the open economy has an additional term in the form of the marginal propensity to import (m), and is:

$$\frac{1}{1 - c + m}$$

What we discover is that the open economy has an extra source of expenditure injection, namely exports, into, and an extra leakage, namely imports, from the circular flow of income.

Implicit in the above analysis are the assumptions of constant prices, idle capacity and a passive monetary sector. Income can therefore respond in real terms to increases in expenditure without prices (including exchange rates) or interest rates changing.

Another key feature of this model is that, largely because of these assumptions, it is through changes in income, and induced changes in imports, that changes in the balance of payments on current account occur. The opening up of the economy also requires us to amend the conventional national income accounting identities of the closed economy. Thus instead of:

$$Y = C + I$$
$$S = Y - C$$
and $$I = S$$

we get, with an open economy:

$$Y = C + I + X - M$$
$$Y - C = I + X - M$$
$$S = Y - C$$
$$S + M = I + X$$
and $$X - M = S - I$$

Withdrawals still equal injections, but withdrawals now include both saving and imports, and injections include both investment and exports. Similarly the balance of payments may be seen as reflecting the difference between domestic saving and domestic investment.

The analysis may be further refined by adding a government that spends (G) and receives tax revenue (T). Then:

$$X - M = (S - I) + (T - G)$$

This accounting identity then suggests that, once we can explain variations in domestic private savings, and domestic investment, as well as changes in taxation and government expenditure, we can also explain variations in the current account of the balance of payments. Unfortunately, domestic saving and investment have proved to be quite difficult to explain, with simple theories often failing to fit the facts.

The basic relationships discussed above affecting saving, investment, imports and exports, but excluding the government sector, are represented graphically in Figures 2.1a, 2.1b, 2.1c and 2.1d. These relationships can be combined to give Figure 2.2. As this figure has been drawn, point A shows a situation where there is equality between domestic saving and investment and therefore perfect balance between imports and exports.

From a situation such as point A, equilibrium may be disturbed if either the $S - I$ or the $X - M$ relationship shifts. Let us assume, for example, that autonomous expenditure falls. $S - I$ then shifts upwards to $(S - I)^*$ and a new equilibrium is created at point B in Figure 2.3, where there has been a fall in the level of income, and the creation of

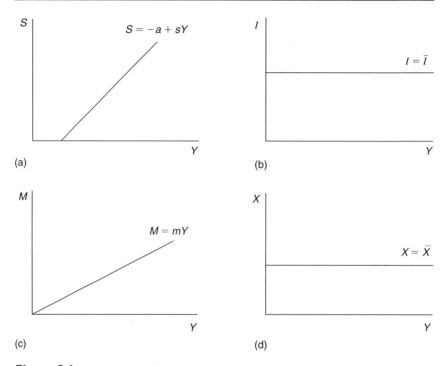

Figure 2.1

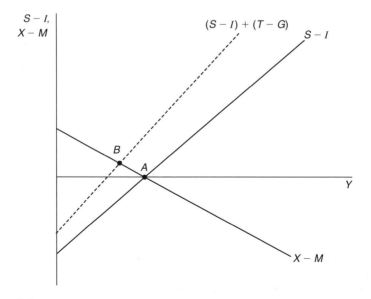

Figure 2.2

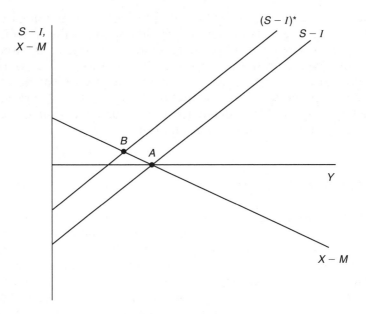

Figure 2.3

excess domestic saving as well as a payments surplus. The fall in income has been brought about by the multiplier process and is the means by which saving and imports decline. The fall will continue until leakages (i.e. $S + M$) have fallen by the same amount as the initial fall in injections.

If, on the other hand, $S - I$ had shifted downwards to the right, Y would have increased until the excess of domestic investment over domestic saving equalled the excess of imports over exports.

Figures 2.2 and 2.3 could be augmented (as shown in Fig. 2.2) to include a government sector, where $G = \bar{G}$ and $T = tY$, with t being the marginal tax rate. Then $S - I$ is replaced by $(S - I) + (T - G)$ and a new equilibrium is established (point B in Fig. 2.2).

What have we established so far? We have seen that simple Keynesian analysis, which concentrates on the real sector of the economy, may easily be modified to allow for international trade with exports constituting an extra injection into the circular flow of income, and imports constituting an extra leakage from it. However, although the inclusion of trade clearly makes for more realism, the model still suffers from a number of deficiencies. Two important ones are, first, that there is no direct reference to the monetary sector, and second, that there is no reference to the capital account of the balance of payments. Shifts in the $S - I$ schedule could, however, be associated with changes in the rate of interest. A standard presumption is that increasing interest rates will lead to greater savings, as people respond to the larger incentive to defer current consumption, and lower investment, as fewer projects now appear profitable. In these circumstances $(S - I)$ will shift upwards and the current account of the balance of payments will strengthen at the same time as national income falls. However, the monetary sector and the capital account are better accommodated by presenting an open economy version of the *IS–LM* model.

IS–LM and the Open Economy

Figure 2.4 illustrates a conventional *IS–LM* model, which is derived in more detail in the Appendix. *IS* shows the combinations of national income and interest rate which give equilibrium in the real sector of the economy (with planned investment equal to planned saving). *LM* shows the combinations which give equilibrium in the monetary sector with the demand for money equal to the supply of money. Point E therefore shows a combination of income and interest rate at which there is simultaneously real and monetary sector equilibrium. But what about the balance of payments? Can the *IS–LM* model be modified to include the current account and the capital account? Figure 2.5 is simply an *IS–LM* diagram augmented by a balance of payments relationship.

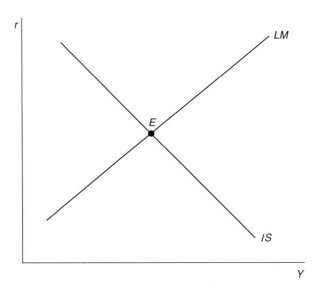

Figure 2.4

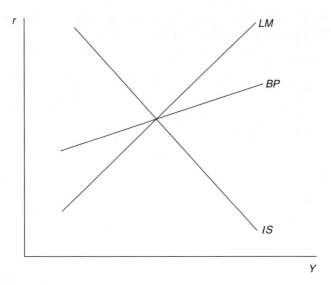

Figure 2.5

The theory behind this relationship is that, as income rises so imports also rise, and, with exports constant, the balance of payments on current account 'deteriorates'. In order to maintain overall payments equilibrium an offsetting capital inflow needs to be generated by raising the domestic rate of interest. The *BP* line in Figure 2.5 therefore has an upward slope, with its slope depending on the value of the marginal propensity to import and the degree of capital mobility. The higher is the former and the lower the latter, the steeper will be BP.

Chapters 3 and 4 look in more depth at the trade schedules and the theory of capital movements which underpin the above model, while the section of this chapter on 'Prices in the Open-economy Model' says something about the inclusion of prices into the analysis. However, before moving on to this we need to say a little more about the concept of the foreign trade or open-economy multiplier, and about the fact that, with open economies, economic developments in one economy can, at least to some extent, be transmitted to others.

The Foreign Trade or Open-economy Multiplier

We have already noted how the nature of the expenditure multiplier will change as we move from a closed to an open economy. We discovered that the significance of openness for the value of the multiplier depends on the size of the marginal propensity to import.

To reinforce our earlier analysis, the foreign trade multiplier may be derived in a slightly different fashion. Thus:

$$S + M = I + X$$
$$\Delta S + \Delta M = \Delta I + \Delta X$$
$$\Delta S = s\Delta Y$$
$$\Delta M = m\Delta Y$$

therefore

$$s\Delta Y + m\Delta Y = \Delta I + \Delta X$$
$$\Delta Y(s + m) = \Delta I + \Delta X$$
$$\Delta Y = \frac{\Delta I + \Delta X}{s + m}$$

and

$$\frac{\Delta Y}{\Delta I + \Delta X} = \frac{1}{s + m}$$

Certain features of this analysis may be drawn out:

(i) Provided that the value of the multiplier exceeds 1.0, an autonomous increase in exports will increase income by an amount greater than the initial increase in exports.

(ii) The value of the foreign trade or open-economy multiplier depends on the values of the marginal propensities to save and to import. The higher the values of these leakages, the lower will be the value of the multiplier.

(iii) Just as there is a 'paradox of thrift' in the context of the closed economy, so, in an open economy, an increase in the propensity to import may fail to generate an equivalent increase in actual imports.[2]

(iv) An autonomous change in exports will not lead to an equivalent change in the balance of payments, since it will induce a change in income and thereby a change in imports. The balance of payments will strengthen by only a proportion of any given increase in exports.

(v) From the viewpoint of one specific economy, an autonomous change in domestic expenditure will, to some degree, spill abroad. At the same time, changes in expenditure which have their origin abroad will have an effect on the domestic economy.

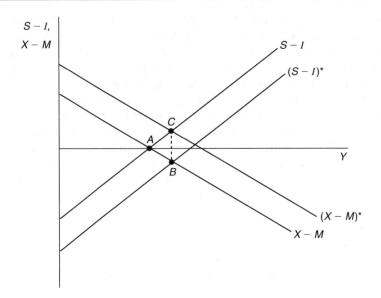

Figure 2.6

(vi) A change in any component of autonomous expenditure will have the same effect on income but will have different effects on the balance of payments. Starting from point A in Figure 2.6 an increase in investment, and therefore a rightward shift in $S - I$, leads to a deficit in the balance of payments (point B), whereas an increase in exports, and therefore a rightward shift in $X - M$, leads to a surplus (point C).

Two key features associated with the analysis of the open-economy multiplier are, first, that changes in the current account of the balance of payments are shown to be influenced significantly by changes in the level of national income. And second, that economic disturbances can, in principle, be easily transmitted between economies.

The Transmission of Changes in Economic Activity between Economies

The process through which fluctuations in economic activity may be transmitted between countries may be illustrated by means of a simple general example. Let us assume that we live in a two-country world. Now imagine that there is an autonomous increase in expenditure in country A. Income in country A therefore expands and this induces a rise in imports from country B. A rise in country A's imports is the same thing as a rise in country B's exports, and this leads to an increase in income in country B by a multiple of the increase in exports, depending on the value of country B's multiplier. The increase in income induces a rise in country B's demand for imports, or, in other words, country A's exports. As a result country A's income increases and so on.

This example illustrates the fact that where national economies are linked to one another by trade, changes in one country's national income will have repercussions for the national incomes of trading partners, which, in turn, will feed back on the national income of the country where the initial change in expenditure occurred. It is by this sort of mechanism that booms and slumps are transmitted between economies.[3]

The mechanism may be illustrated by using the diagrams intro-duced earlier. In Figure 2.7, a rightward shift in $S - I$ in country A leads to an increase in income and a trade deficit. In country B exports rise and $X - M$ shifts to the right. Income increases and the balance of payments on current account moves into surplus. However, the rise in

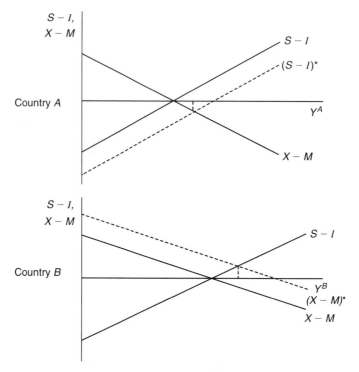

Figure 2.7

income induces an increase in imports such that country A's exports increase and its $X - M$ schedule shifts to the right. Eventually the situation will settle down with each country's rise in income depending on the value of the open economy multipliers in the two countries.

It would appear at first sight that we have unearthed a powerful mechanism by which fluctuations in economic activity are transmitted around the world. However, its strength rests crucially on a number of factors. First, the chain of reactions outlined above does not continue indefinitely since the value of the marginal propensity to import is less than one and the value of the marginal propensity to save is greater than zero. Second, the smaller is the marginal propensity to import of the country where the disturbance is initiated, the less will be the extent to which it spills abroad and the greater the extent to which it is bottled up in the initiating country. Third, the larger is the marginal propensity to save, the smaller will be the value of the multiplier and the smaller, therefore, will be the change in income associated with any autonomous change in expenditure.

These factors may combine to limit the potency of the transmission mechanism. Returning to the above example, a high marginal propensity to save in country A will limit the extent to which income rises in response to the increase in autonomous expenditure, while a low marginal propensity to import will limit the extent to which the expansion spills over to country B. In country B a high marginal propensity to save will again keep the value of the multiplier down and a low marginal propensity to import will minimise any feedback effect on country A.

The strength of the transmission mechanism is, of course, also exaggerated by concentrating on a two-country world. In a world with many countries and a fairly even spread of import sources, the effects of expansion or contraction in one country will be more widely dispersed. Also, if the initiating country is small, the repercussions on other economies are likely to be similarly small.

Some Reservations about the Simple Open-economy Model

It would be unwise to expect too much of the simple model we have constructed so far and it may therefore be sensible to itemise some reservations about it. We have already noted that it embodies very simple foreign trade functions and concentrates on changes in income without saying anything about prices in general or exchange rates in particular.

To these deficiencies we may now add the following. First, in the real world, transmission effects may occur not only through trade flows but also through the financial sector with rising interest rates, for example, having global consequences (see Chapter 6). They may also occur through changes in the prices of key traded goods such as oil. Second, the size of the trade effects will depend on the structure of a country's trading relationships. Some countries may not benefit from expansion elsewhere if they produce goods that have low income elasticities of demand. Third, the existence of multinational enterprises may distort the above analysis if a proportion of export earnings is repatriated. Fourth, the effects of falling income on import demand following a decline in export earnings may be offset by decumulating reserves or by borrowing.

During the course of this book something more will be said about most of these deficiencies of the basic model. In the next section, we turn to say a little about incorporating prices into the analysis.

Prices in the Open-economy Model

The analysis up to now has assumed constant prices. How restrictive an assumption this is depends on how rapid inflation actually is. With relatively low rates of inflation constant price analysis may not be too unrealistic. Even so, it is relatively easy to incorporate prices into the open-economy model.

The simplest, and not necessarily least appropriate way of doing this is to change the specification of the *LM*, *IS* and *BP* relationships so as to allow them to be affected by the price level. At the same time it is also necessary to identify the process through which inflation is generated. Again, a simple solution is to assume that changes in the price level within an economy depend on the difference between aggregate monetary demand and the full employment level of real output.

Diagrammatically, if *IS* and *LM* intersect to the right of this full employment level of output, shown by line *F* in Figure 2.8, the price level will rise, with the rate of increase depending on the extent of excess demand. The rise in prices will increase the nominal demand for money or, what comes to the same thing, reduce its real supply. *LM* will therefore shift leftwards. Meanwhile, if consumption and saving are related to the value of real cash balances, inflation which erodes the value of real balances will reduce consumption, increase saving, and shift *IS* to the left. *IS* may also shift to the left if inflation has an adverse effect on business expectations and reduces investment.

The location of the *BP* schedule may also be influenced by inflation. An increase in a country's price level, relative to that of its competitors, implies an appreciation in the real exchange rate. This, in turn, will tend to reduce exports, increase imports and cause a capital outflow in

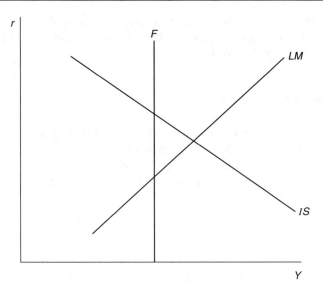

Figure 2.8

expectation of a nominal devaluation designed to restore the old real rate. To offset these effects on the balance of payments a higher rate of interest will have to be offered. Inflation thus causes *BP* to shift upwards. The loss of competitiveness will also reduce overall expenditure and will shift *IS* further to the left. The model will eventually attain a form of quasi equilibrium where *IS* and *LM* intersect somewhere along *F*, for in these circumstances prices will cease rising and the *IS*, *LM* and *BP* schedules cease shifting.

Of course, each of the effects of inflation discussed above as well as the inflationary process itself may be analysed in much greater detail. But for our purposes the benefits probably do not warrant the extra costs in time and space. The important points for us to grasp are the manner in which inflation may be incorporated into the model and the assumptions underpinning the particular fashion in which inflation is incorporated. Clearly, different models relating to the causes and effects of inflation are possible. More sophisticated analysis would need to examine these alternatives.[4]

One aspect of the inflationary process in the context of an open economy which it is important for us to note at this stage, is that domestic inflation may be affected by what is happening abroad as well as by the level of domestic demand. Both foreign demand and cost pressures may have a role to play in this regard. In the case of cost-induced inflation from abroad *IS*, *LM* (and possibly even *BP*) may shift even though there is no excess domestic monetary demand. We shall return to say more about inflation in the open economy and the world economy later in the book.

Concluding Remarks

The purpose of this chapter has been to show how simple analysis of the closed economy may easily be modified to incorporate a country's dealings with the rest of the world. The discussion has even revealed how, albeit at an unrefined level, inflation may be included into the model. However, as with most simple models, as many questions have been raised as have been answered. One key question relates to the nature of the balance of payments schedule that has been introduced. The next chapter investigates the analysis underpinning this schedule by looking at both its current and capital account components. Before that, the following Appendix to this chapter provides a brief summary of the *IS–LM* model for those who are unfamiliar with it, or need to be reminded.

Appendix

Notes on IS/LM

The *IS–LM* model sets out to integrate the real and monetary sectors of the macroeconomy. Although not exempt from criticism both in terms of its details and its fundamentals, the model is still widely used and provides a well-defined analytical framework.

The IS Schedule

As its name implies, the *IS* relationship brings together both the investment (*I*) and saving (*S*) functions. It shows all the combinations of the rate of interest and level of income at which planned investment is equal to planned saving; it thus shows equilibrium in the real sector of the economy.

To Derive the IS Relationship

1. Investment is related to the rate of interest (*r*); as *r* falls, *I* increases. The other things influencing investment, such as business expectations, will cause the investment schedule to shift (see below).

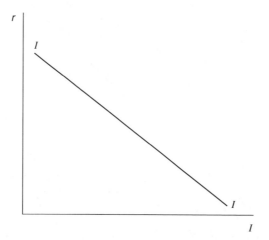

2. Saving is positively related to r; the higher the rate of interest, the greater the inducement to save.

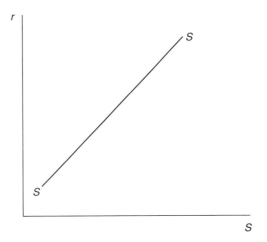

But saving is also positively related to income; $S = Y - C$ and $C = cY$, so $S = sY$. Thus the schedule just drawn relating saving to the rate of interest will shift to the right as income increases and to the left as income falls.

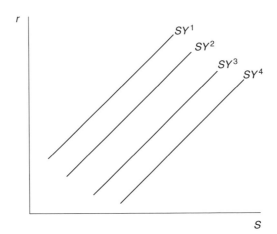

3. For equilibrium in the real sector, the condition has to be met that planned investment equals planned saving ($I_p = S_p$). Putting the saving and investment schedules together, we get:

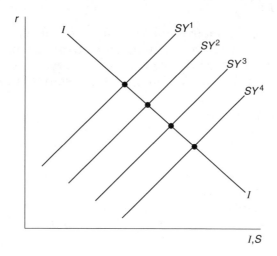

This diagram plots out a series of points at various levels of income and the rate of interest at which $I_p = S_p$. Representing this on one diagram, with r and Y on the axes, we get:

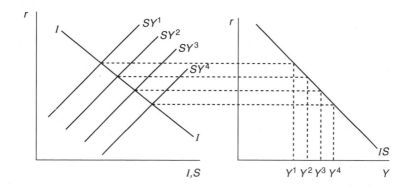

This diagram – the *IS* schedule – sketches out the combinations of r and Y at which $I_p = S_p$. It slopes downwards to the right since, as r falls, I increases, Y grows and saving expands.

We shall return to examine certain features of the *IS* schedule in a moment, but first let us move on to derive the *LM* relationship.

The LM Schedule

The *LM* schedule combines the demand for and supply of money functions. It shows all the combinations of the rate of interest and level of income at which the demand for money equals the supply of money. It thus shows equilibrium in the monetary sector.

To derive the LM Schedule

1. The demand for money is assumed to be made up of two components:
   (a) the transactions/precautionary demand for money as a medium of exchange; and
   (b) the speculative demand for money as an asset.
   The demand for money is therefore a function of both the level of income and the rate of interest.

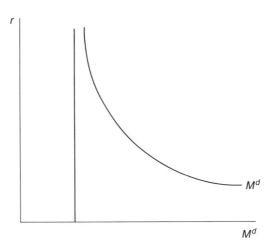

2. As income increases, so the demand for transactions and precautionary balances also increases, to maintain their proportional relationship with *Y*. The demand for money function as a whole will therefore shift to the right as income increases, and to the left as income falls.
3. Given the supply of money, shifts in the demand for money schedule will cause changes in the equilibrium rate of interest since, as

income increases, more of the given money supply will be demanded for transactions and precautionary purposes, and less will be available to meet speculative demand and will have to be rationed by an increase in the rate of interest; that is, the opportunity cost of holding money. Similarly, a fall in income, with a given money supply, will induce a fall in the rate of interest.

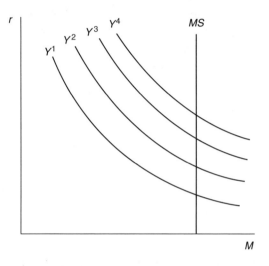

Once again, we can transfer this information on to a diagram with r and Y on the axes. This diagram shows the combinations of r and Y at which $M^d = M^s$. The diagram thus traces out the LM relationship.

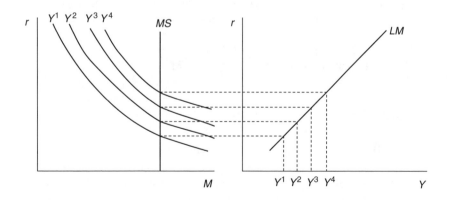

LM slopes upwards to the right since (with a given money supply) as income rises, the transactions demand for money rises and therefore the rate of interest rises as well.

IS–LM *Together*

We now have two diagrams representing equilibrium. *IS* shows equilibrium in the real sector of the economy, whilst *LM* shows equilibrium in the monetary sector. Thus along *IS*, $I_p = S_p$, and along *LM*, $M^d = M^s$. Clearly, where *IS* and *LM* intersect, both $I_p = S_p$ and $M^d = M^s$. Thus:

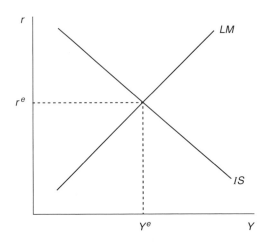

At $r = r^e$ and $Y = Y^e$, $I_p = S_p$ and $M^d = M^s$, and at this rate of interest and income level, the economy is in both real and monetary equilibrium. Note, however, that there is still no reference to employment, prices and the balance of payments, so even this broader interpretation of equilibrium is still quite narrow.

There is a great deal that can be derived from the *IS–LM* construct. But for the moment, two questions are of immediate interest:

1. What causes *IS* and *LM* to shift?
2. What determines the slope of *IS* and *LM*?

Shifts in IS and LM

IS shifts as a result of:

(i)   changes in investment caused by factors other than the rate of interest – for example, changes in entrepreneurial expectations; and/or
(ii) changes in the average propensity to consume.

Broadly speaking, *IS* will shift to the right as aggregate demand ($C + I$) increases, and to the left as aggregate demand falls.

Let us examine this on a diagram, concentrating on a rightward shift in *IS*. Imagine that there is a rightward shift in the investment schedule:

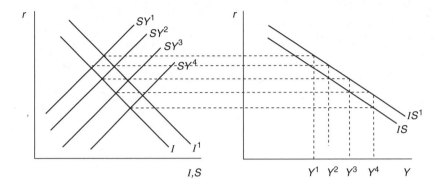

A leftward shift in the family of savings schedules is illustrated below by the shift from SY^1 to SY^* at a specific level of income Y^1, although the entire set of savings schedules shift left.

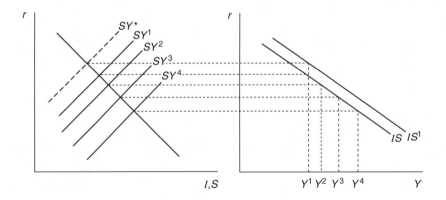

LM shifts as a result of:

(i)   changes in the money supply; and/or
(ii) changes in liquidity preference, (the demand for money).

LM shifts to the right as the money supply rises and/or the demand for money to hold falls at a given income level.
LM shifts to the left as the money supply falls and/or the demand for money to hold rises at a given level of income.
   Let us show a rightward shift in *LM* on a diagram.

An increase in the supply of money:

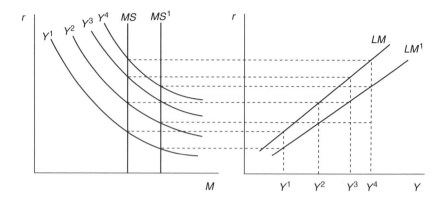

A fall in liquidity preference (just shown at income level Y^1):

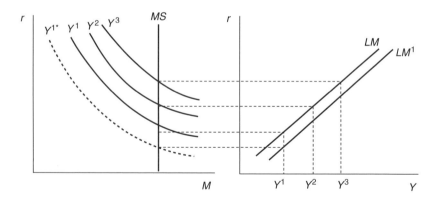

The Slopes of IS and LM

We have already seen that IS slopes downwards to the right, but what is the degree of this slope? The degree of slope will be influenced by:

(i)   the marginal propensity to save; and
(ii) the elasticity of investment with respect to the rate of interest.

(i)   The smaller the marginal propensity to save, the flatter will be the *IS* schedule, while similarly, the larger the marginal propensity to save, the steeper will be the *IS* schedule.

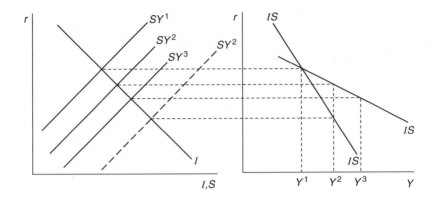

(ii)   The more elastic the investment schedule, the flatter will be *IS*, while similarly, the more inelastic the investment schedule, the steeper will be *IS*.

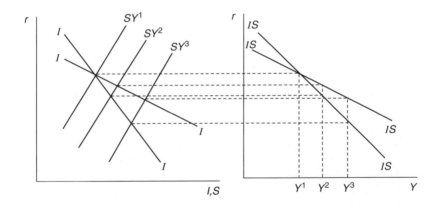

   We have already seen that *LM* slopes upwards to the right; the slope of *LM* depends on the interest rate elasticity of demand for money. The more elastic the demand for money, the flatter will be *LM*, and similarly the more inelastic the demand for money, the steeper will be *LM*.

   The slope of *LM* also depends on how the demand for money function shifts as income changes. If the transactions coefficient falls as income expands, *LM* will be less steep than if the coefficient is invariant or rises as income rises.

   The slope of *LM* will also be affected by the slope of the money supply schedule. A steeper money supply schedule will result in a steeper *LM* schedule.

IS–LM *in Disequilibrium*

How will the economy behave in disequilibrium? The following diagram illustrates.

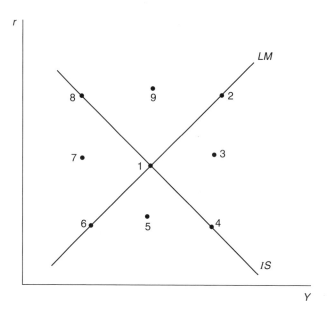

At
1    $I_p = S_p,\ M^d = M^s$
2    $I_p < S_p,\ M^d = M^s$
3    $I_p < S_p,\ M^d > M^s$
4    $I_p = S_p,\ M^d > M^s$
5    $I_p > S_p,\ M^d > M^s$
6    $I_p > S_p,\ M^d = M^s$
7    $I_p > S_p,\ M^d < M^s$
8    $I_p = S_p,\ M^d < M^s$
9    $I_p < S_p,\ M^d < M^s$

Let us see what will happen in some of the disequilibrium situations.

At point 8:

$I_p = S_p$
$M^d < M^s \to r\downarrow$
$\to \uparrow I > S \to Y\uparrow$
$\to S\uparrow, M^d\uparrow \to r\uparrow$
$I\downarrow S\uparrow$

At point 2:

$M^d = M^s, I_p < S_p \to \downarrow Y$
$\to \downarrow S$ and $M^d\downarrow, r\downarrow$
so $\downarrow S$ and $\uparrow I$

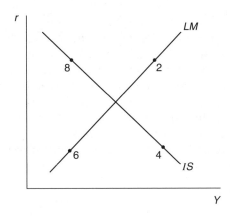

At point 6:

$M^d = M^s, I_p > S_p$
$\to \uparrow Y \to \uparrow S,$
$M^d\uparrow \to r\uparrow \to \downarrow I, \uparrow S$

At point 4:

$I_p = S_p, M^d > M^s \to r\uparrow$
$\to I\downarrow, (S > I) \to \downarrow Y \to \downarrow S$
$M^d\downarrow \to \downarrow r \to \downarrow S$ and $\uparrow I$

However, the *IS–LM* model is comparatively static in nature and not well suited to tracing out dynamic changes.

Some Deficiencies of IS–LM

IS–LM analysis as presented so far is open to a number of criticisms. These include:

(i)   It is more appropriate for analysing the short-run behaviour of an economy than its long-run properties.

(ii) It assumes that there is a constant price level, and that there is therefore no need to distinguish between real and nominal values. If inflation is included in the analysis this will influence the nominal demand for money, the real supply of money, the real value of savings and, possibly, investment. As inflation occurs, both the *IS* and *LM* schedules will therefore shift. But how will they shift, and what will cause inflation in the first place? The answers to these questions require *IS–LM* analysis to be integrated with the labour market and the production function.

(iii) It focuses on a closed economy.

From IS–LM to Aggregate Demand and Aggregate Supply

Aggregate demand and supply analysis provides another way of analysing macroeconomic ideas. It is a natural extension of market demand and supply analysis, but may also be derived from the *IS–LM* model once this has been augmented to include prices.

Aggregate Demand

As prices rise, the nominal demand for money rises (the real supply of money falls) and *LM* shifts to the left. The real rate of interest rises and investment falls. At the same time, consumption tends to fall, as people attempt to restore the real value of their savings. *IS* therefore also shifts to the left. As a consequence, *Y* falls as prices rise and the aggregate demand (*AD*) schedule slopes downwards, from left to right.

The *AD* schedule will shift as its determinants, other than the price level, change. Expansionary changes will shift it to the right and contractionary ones to the left.

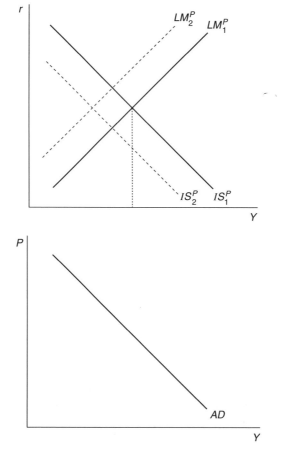

Aggregate Supply

The aggregate supply (*AS*) schedule is derived from analysis of the labour market and the production function. As the price level rises, real wages fall and the demand for the labour schedule shifts to the right. As a consequence, employment and output both rise. The AS schedule therefore slopes upwards to the right.

Where output changes for some reason other than a change in the price level, such as a change in productivity, the *AS* schedule will shift.

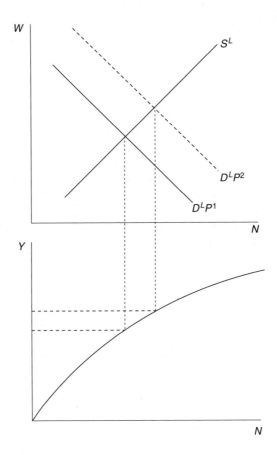

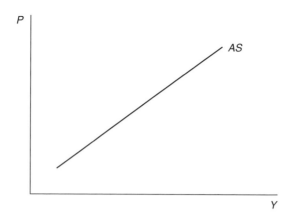

IS–LM–BP: The Mundell-Fleming Model

As seen in the main text of the chapter, the *IS–LM* model may easily be augmented by a relationship that specifies the combinations of *r* and *Y* that ensure overall balance of payments equilibrium (*BP*). The *BP* schedule slopes upwards from left to right, because it is assumed that the current account deteriorates as income increases, and that an increase in the rate of interest is needed to induce an offsetting capital inflow. The slope of BP therefore depends on the value of the marginal propensity to import and the interest rate elasticity of capital (that is, the degree of capital mobility).

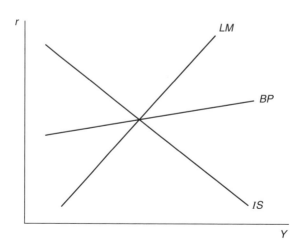

The *IS–LM* model, augmented by the *BP* schedule, provides a useful basis for analysing the open economy.

3 Trade Functions and Capital Movements

Introduction

Following on from the analysis in the previous chapter we now examine in more detail the import and export functions introduced there. We also say a little more about the way in which capital movements may be treated in an open-economy model.

The Import Function

Up to now we have assumed that the import function has the form:

$$M = mY$$

where M represents imports and m is the marginal propensity to import.

This clearly implies a rather simple and unsophisticated relationship which begs a series of questions. These fall essentially into two categories. The first includes questions about the nature of the relationship between imports and income. The second includes questions about other determinants of import demand.

Looking initially at the nature of the relationship between imports and income, the above function suggests that imports will be zero if income is zero. However, it may be claimed either that there will be a positive level of imports even with zero income or that income will have to be significantly in excess of zero before any imports will occur. In any event, there will be a constant term in the import function. In the former case, the sign of this constant will be positive, and in the latter case negative. A change in the constant term, whatever its sign, will alter the equilibrium level of income and the balance of trade, though the balance of trade will alter by less than the autonomous change in imports.

More realistically, then, the import function may be presented as:

$$M = z + mY$$

This function, however, still makes certain implicit assumptions. First, it is assumed that the marginal propensity to import (m) is constant and the import function, therefore, is linear. In fact, it is quite likely that the value of m will vary as the level of income varies. For example, as a country develops it may become more diversified in the range of goods it produces. The substitution of domestic for foreign production will cause both the marginal and average propensity to import (M/Y) to fall. Furthermore, the way in which imports change as income changes may depend on the types of goods imported. Where, for example, a country is unable to produce much of its own staple foodstuff there will be a minimum level below which imports will not fall. At the same time, an increase in income may not result in much increase in the demand for imported food. This may, instead, be much more responsive to changes in the size of population.

Second, the way in which the import function has been drawn in Chapter 2 implies reversibility. The same level of imports will always be associated with the same level of income. In fact, there may be impaired reversibility, and a 'ratchet effect' may exist. Imports may indeed rise as income rises, but then fail to fall back to their original level as income falls back to its original level. As Figure 3.1 illustrates, this ratchet effect may be reinterpreted as a shift upwards in the import function.

Third, imports may not simply be related to the *level* of income, but also to the *rate of change* of income. Where income expands rapidly it may be more difficult to meet this increasing demand from domestic

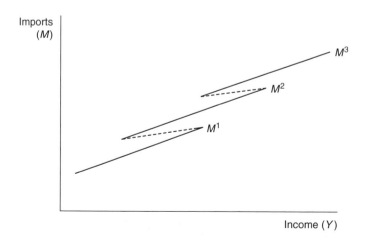

Figure 3.1

supply since bottlenecks occur, and there may be greater incentive to buy goods from abroad. A steadier increase in demand may result in a smaller increase in imports.

All the above points, although challenging the basic simplicity of our original import function, still accept that income is the prime determinant of imports. But is this the case?

First, it needs to be recognised that, from national income accounting, income is equivalent to output and to expenditure. But which of these concepts is more relevant when discussing imports? Much depends again on the nature of imports. If these are intermediate goods, then the output concept is appropriate. For final goods, however, expenditure is more relevant. A change in the composition of expenditure could take place which, while not initially affecting the level of output and income, does affect the demand for imports. If consumption has a higher import content than government expenditure, a switch in expenditure away from the government and towards private consumption will raise imports (and eventually reduce the equilibrium value of income). Even this analysis is at too high a level of aggregation. Different types of government and consumer expenditure will have different import contents.

Second, it is unrealistic to assume that import demand will be unaffected by relative prices. In fact, demand theory clearly predicts that import demand will tend to rise as the price of imports falls, relative to that of home-produced goods. Of course, this assumes that imports can be substituted for home-produced goods. The degree of substitutability will affect the price elasticity of demand. Where home-produced goods and imports are not substitutable the price elasticity of demand for imports will be correspondingly low. It also needs to be remembered that the relative price of imports may change, not only because producers alter the prices they charge, but also because tariffs or exchange rates change. At the same time, however, the imposition or removal of tariffs, or alterations in the exchange rate, need not necessarily lead to changes in the relative price of imports if producers are prepared to alter their prices in order to compensate for such changes.

Third, while price clearly has an important bearing on import demand, it is only one element in the overall terms of sale. Other elements include waiting time (or perhaps more accurately, anticipated waiting time), the availability (and price) of trade credit, sales effort, after-sales service, and quality. Changes in these non-price elements may have an important impact on the demand for imports. Indeed, some observers feel that non-price competition in international markets is more important than conventional price competition.

To some extent the relative terms of sale will be affected by the pressure of demand within a country; that is, the level of aggregate demand relative to domestic aggregate supply. With high demand, pressure prices may rise, queues lengthen and imports increase. Again we see that it is not just the level of aggregate demand that is significant in attempting to explain import demand.

Before leaving the import function we need to note that, while the factors discussed above may shape the *demand* for imports, the *actual* level of imports may not be the same as this. Quantitative restrictions on imports and time lags in supply may keep actual imports below the level demanded.[1]

The Export Function

In the open-economy model built in the previous chapter it was assumed that exports could be treated as being given; that is:

$$X = \overline{X}$$

Although, at first sight, this seems to be a grossly oversimplifying assumption there is a certain internal logic to it. For if we recognise that one country's exports are other countries' imports and assume that imports are a function of income, and further assume that one country has no influence over income in other countries, then it does indeed follow that a country has no control over the demand for its exports.

More realistically, while there may certainly be exogenous influences at work, there can be little doubt that countries do exert some influence over the demand for their exports, as well as over the extent to which the demand is met.

Again bearing in mind that the exports of one country represent the imports of others, it seems reasonable to assume that the same factors that determine imports will also determine exports. The price of exports expressed in terms of foreign currency, the terms of sale, as described earlier, and the quality of goods will all exert an influence over the demand for exports.

However, actual exports depend not only on the demand for them but also on their supply. This will, in part, depend on the price expressed in terms of the relevant home currency, but it may also depend on the internal pressure of demand in the exporting country; although the precise nature of this relationship is rather ambiguous. On one side, a high level of domestic demand may serve to direct resources away from the export sector towards the home market, while also causing prices to rise and queues to lengthen which discriminates against exports. On the other side, buoyant domestic demand may be necessary to encourage exports, and, to the extent that firms enjoy decreasing costs, rising domestic demand may increase price competitiveness.

This suggests that much will depend on the nature of the cost curves which exporting firms face, and the nature of the price-setting mechanism, which will, in turn, be influenced by the market structure in which firms operate. For firms in imperfect markets, a fall in demand need not lead to a fall in price even where short-run marginal costs rise as output rises.[2]

The above discussion suggests ways in which our earlier treatment of the current account of the balance of payments may be made somewhat more realistic. Indeed, by interpreting income to be nominal income it is possible to include the effects of domestically generated inflation on the trade balance. This will now move into deficit as either real income or the price level rises. Changes in the other determinants listed above will tend to shift the balance of payments (*BP*) schedule either upwards or downwards, depending on whether there is a deterioration or an improvement in the current account.

Before moving on to examine the capital account and capital movements, it may be noted that not all components of the current account will respond to the sorts of influences listed so far. In as much as the current account also includes interest payments on previous borrowing, the state of the current account will depend on the volume of such borrowing and on the level of interest rates. The larger the borrowing in the past and the higher the interest rate, the less strong will be the current account. As a result of this element, the current account which is normally seen as a *flow* account, may be seen as being influenced by *stocks* as well – principally the stock of debt. The distinction between stocks and flows is perhaps more relevant when discussing the capital account.

The Capital Account: Flow or Stock Theory?

The model presented in Chapter 2 suggests that a differential between the rate of interest on offer in one country and the rest of the world results in a permanent capital flow. Domestic interest-rate policy can, in these circumstances, be used to nullify the effects of current account disequilibria on the balance of payments overall. The key question is whether such a flow model provides an accurate description of the way in which capital movements actually occur. There are strong reasons for arguing that it does not. After all, much analysis of domestic investment suggests that a change in interest rates works by altering the desired capital stock which, given the resulting discrepancy between the actual and desired stock, then sets off a process of capital stock adjustment, i.e. investment or disinvestment.[3]

Similarly, analysis of the demand for money and portfolio models show how, starting from a situation of portfolio balance, an alteration

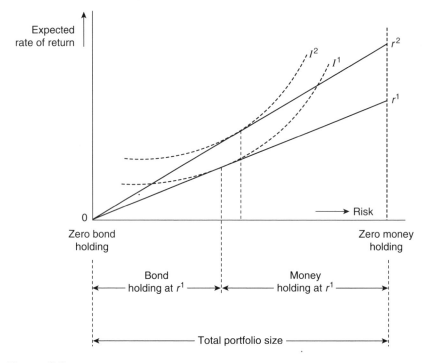

Figure 3.2

in interest rates will disturb this situation of equilibrium and encourage wealth holders to reorganise their portfolios. However, once the reorganisation and a new equilibrium have been achieved no further changes will occur.[4]

It may be useful to dwell on such models for a little longer. The models essentially assume that while people are looking for a high return on their assets, they also want to avoid risk. Risk-averters will have to be offered higher and higher expected returns if they are to be enticed to take on more and more risk. In models of the demand for money these factors have been used to explain why people hold a combination of money (assumed to have zero return but zero risk) and bonds (assumed to have a relatively high return but also a relatively high risk in terms of the variability of the return). Such a model is illustrated by Figure 3.2. An increase in the rate of interest from r^1 to r^2 may there be seen to encourage the wealth-holder to alter the balance of the portfolio away from money and towards bonds, though this represents the outcome of conflicting pressures with the substitution effect encouraging a movement into higher yielding assets but the income effect saying that, with a higher yield on existing bond holdings, the wealth-holder can afford

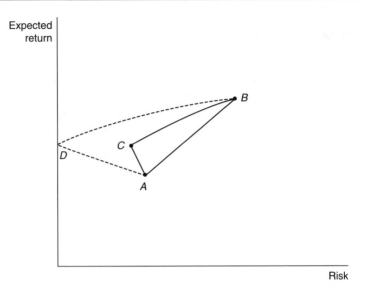

Figure 3.3

to go for reduced risk and more security. Whichever of these effects dominates, the impact of the change in the interest rate is set within the context of a stock adjustment model.

Given their preferences between return and risk, as shown by the configuration of indifference curves, wealth-holders are in essence searching for an efficient portfolio of assets. If it is possible to get a larger return with no extra risk, or to reduce risk with no fall in return, the portfolio is inefficient and wealth-holders will alter the distribution of their wealth holding between assets. The above analysis suggests that an efficient portfolio will be a diversified one.

Let us examine the rationale of portfolio diversification in more detail, but for the time being still retain the assumption that there are only two assets. In Figure 3.3 point *A* shows the combination of return and risk associated with holding *all* wealth in asset *A*, while point *B* shows the combination associated with holding *only* asset *B*. But what happens if *both* assets are held? If the outcomes associated with the assets are perfectly positively correlated then a portfolio incorporating both of them will give a linear combination of the expected return and risk of each asset, as shown by the line *AB*. But not all assets will fare in the same way. The outcomes of holding assets *A* and *B* may be independent of one another or may even be negatively correlated. If this is the case, the collective risk of a diversified portfolio will be smaller than the average risk of each individual asset. The 'opportunities frontier', or

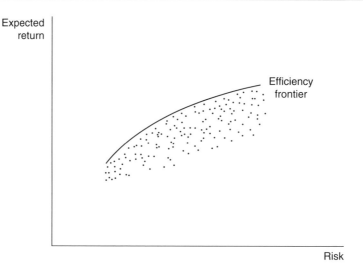

Figure 3.4

the combinations of risk and return from a diversified portfolio, may take the shape *ACB*, with *CB* being the efficient portion of the frontier and *AC* the inefficient portion. If outcomes are *perfectly* negatively correlated, it would be possible to reduce the risk to zero and the frontier would become *ADB* with *DB* being the efficient portion.

Figure 3.4 illustrates the case where there are many assets. There will now be a set of return/risk combinations available, with these being bounded by an efficiency frontier. The boundary will be convex from above if the outcomes associated with different assets are imperfectly correlated.

To discover a position of portfolio balance, we need only combine this efficiency frontier with the wealth-holder's indifference curves between risk and return, as is done in Figure 3.5. Changes in either preferences or the efficiency frontier will disturb the initial equilibrium and alter the way in which the portfolio is distributed between different assets.

Although the above analysis has conventionally been presented to illustrate portfolio selection in the context of domestic capital markets, there is relatively little difficulty in applying it in an international context. Wealth-holders will still be concerned about return and risk. The only difference is that there will now be additional factors influencing these concepts. In particular, lending in an international environment implies the need for country risk analysis and an assessment of creditworthiness. Will the borrower be able and willing to repay? Here it is possible that an increase in interest rates in one country may be seen as so increasing the risk of default that expected

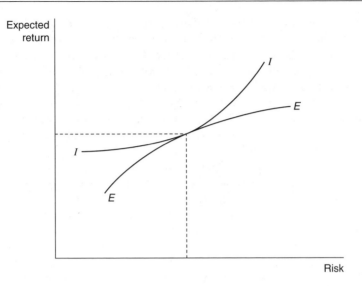

Figure 3.5

returns fall and capital flows out not in. Furthermore, there is an additional risk associated with swapping between currencies when exchange rates are flexible and unpredictable. Although, to an extent, such risk may be eliminated by forward transactions to buy and sell currencies, the reduction in risk can only be bought at a price and this will reduce the expected return. On top of this, wealth-holders may simply not regard assets in different countries as close substitutes for one another and may therefore not respond greatly to changes in the interest rates on offer in different countries.

The discussion in this section reveals considerable shortcomings in the flow model of capital movements presented in Chapter 2. It transpires that a country cannot assume that raising its interest rate will bring about a permanent capital inflow. Where risks, from whatever source, are seen as being high, these may have a dominant effect – even though the theory of portfolio selection suggests that inclusion of a relatively high risk asset may reduce the overall risk of a portfolio if the risk of this asset is inversely related with the risks of other assets in the portfolio. Moreover, even if an increase in the interest rate does generate a capital inflow, this effect is likely to be temporary and to occur merely for as long as it takes for people to adjust their portfolios. In order to generate a permanent inflow, the stock theory suggests that it will be necessary to increase interest rates persistently.

The implication of this is that the *BP* schedule introduced in the previous chapter will become steeper over time with a rising interest rate being required to offset a given current account deficit. How steep the *BP* schedule is over different time periods will depend on how quickly stock disequilibrium is corrected. Starting off from a situation where there is excess demand for a country's assets because of a rise in the interest rate, quick adjustment will lead to a relatively large but temporary inflow whereas slow adjustment will lead to a smaller but more drawn out inflow. The size of the related flow will diminish exponentially as in each period a given proportion of a diminishing short-fall between desired and actual holdings is eliminated.

Where the time-lag in adjusting portfolios is fairly long, it may be legitimate from a policy point of view to regard the related capital movements as if they are quasi flows. In this case the normal state of affairs would be one of disequilibrium with the system always moving towards, though not necessarily reaching, equilibrium.

There is, however, another way in which the flow model may still prove to be of some use within the context of a stock adjustment framework. Where the stock of wealth increases over time, and where the marginal additions to wealth are distributed across assets in the same proportions as these assets bear to the total portfolio, anything that encourages a wealth holder to increase current holdings of a particular asset will imply that the demand for that asset will grow more rapidly than it would otherwise have done. This is the so-called portfolio growth effect. In this way a change in interest rates may have a permanent effect on capital flows.

It needs to be remembered in this analysis that while the effect of changing interest rates on the capital account may be temporary, the effect on the current account, in terms of the related servicing obligations, may last for much longer. A short-term strengthening of the capital account may therefore be bought at the expense of a longer term deterioration in the current account.

Even if we accept the flow model as described earlier, there are reasons to believe that a permanent capital inflow will not be associated with an increase in interest rates. This is because the capital inflow will itself tend to close the interest-rate differential and thereby erode the incentive for further capital inflows. In a perfect capital market the interest-rate differential will indeed disappear and capital flows cease. With an imperfect market the capital inflow may stop before the interest differential is eliminated.

The strong reservations concerning the flow model of capital movements that have been itemised in this chapter so far need to be firmly borne in mind in the subsequent analysis of stabilisation policy in the context of an open economy and in the analysis of currency crisis. At best, the model appears to be only relevant in the context of short-run stabilisation policy. Of course, the relevant question from a policy point of view is how long is the short run? But these are not the only reservations.

Disaggregating Capital Flows

Up to now we have lumped all capital movements together. We have then assumed that they will be positively associated with return (and relative rates of interest) and negatively associated with risk (either default risk or exchange rate risk). In practice, capital movements can take various forms. They may be in the form of bank lending, bonds, portfolio investment or foreign direct investment. It is unwise to assume that the determinants of these different forms will be the same. For example, while an increase in the rate of interest may attract additional short-term capital (or hot money) such as bank loans, fears of any associated recession and corporate difficulties may discourage FDI and portfolio investment. Even short-term lenders may be worried that a sharp increase in interest rates will lead to domestic financial distress, and reduce the risk-adjusted rate of return. Moreover, it is unclear whether an actual currency devaluation will always reduce the perceived probability of future devaluation. The connection between devaluation and exchange rate risk may therefore be more complex than it at first glance appears. Foreign direct investment may be more influenced by differences in wages and policies pertaining to the repatriation of profits.

In short, while useful, the explanation of capital movements incorporated in the *IS–LM–BP* model has strict limitations. It is little more than a first step and there remains a considerable distance to be travelled before we have a satisfactory model (or models) of capital movements. The theoretical deficiencies need to be taken into account where policy is being designed. As we shall see in Chapter 10, disagreement over the theory of capital movements has resulted in lively debate over what is appropriate policy in the midst of a currency and financial crisis. Should interest rates be increased? Can devaluation be relied on to strengthen the capital account? In the following chapters, however, we stick with the simple theory that links capital movements positively to the domestic interest rate, assuming world interest rates are given.

4 Balance of Payments Theory

Introduction

The purpose of this chapter is to build on the model of the open economy constructed and refined in previous chapters. Contained in the model described there is the core of a general theory of the balance of payments or of the exchange rate.

In an environment of fixed exchange rates, underlying forces which serve to shift the *IS* schedule, the *LM* schedule or the *BP* schedule will be reflected by balance of payments disequilibria. Where exchange rates are flexible, on the other hand, the same forces will instead be reflected by changes in the exchange rate.

More specifically, the model developed in Chapter 2 shows how disturbances emanating from either the real side of the economy, affecting consumption, investment, government expenditure and foreign trade, or from the monetary side, affecting the supply of and demand for money, may influence a country's balance of payments or its exchange rate.

The purpose of this chapter is to extend the insights that the basic model provides into the determination of the balance of payments under the assumption of fixed (or pegged) exchange rates. The next chapter then goes on to examine the theory of exchange-rate determination in an environment of floating (or flexible) rates.

A Basic Model of the Balance of Payments

The basic model for analysing the balance of payments from which we start is illustrated in Figure 4.1. Point *A* in this figure illustrates a situation of overall balance of payments equilibrium in the sense that any disequilibria in the current and capital accounts cancel each other out. It needs to be noted, however, that this is a rather narrow definition

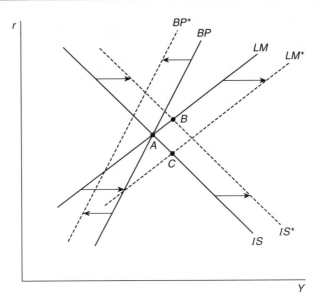

Figure 4.1

of payments equilibrium. First, it implies that governments are indifferent to the composition of the balance of payments, being quite content, for example, to run a large current account deficit for as long as this is matched by an equivalent capital account surplus. Second, it implies that governments are largely unconcerned about the level of employment and unemployment since this does not feature in the figure. In practice, if point *A* coincides with mass unemployment then it may be unrealistic to interpret such a point as representing a situation of policy equilibrium.

Having recognised that Figure 4.1 rests on a number of restrictive assumptions, it does clearly show how a balance of payments deficit will result from anything which causes the *IS* or *LM* schedules to shift to the right, giving us points *B* and *C*, respectively, in Figure 4.1, or from anything that causes the *BP* schedule to shift upwards and to the left. Similarly, a balance of payments surplus will result from factors causing *IS* and *LM* to shift to the left, or *BP* to shift downwards and to the right, as illustrated by points *X*, *Y* and *Z*, respectively, in Figure 4.2.

The remainder of this chapter is structured around analysing shifts in each of these schedules. However, before proceeding, we may note that, for the most part, unemployment and inflation are ignored in the analysis. Those interested may refer back to the section on 'Prices in the Open-economy Model' in Chapter 2, where there was some attempt

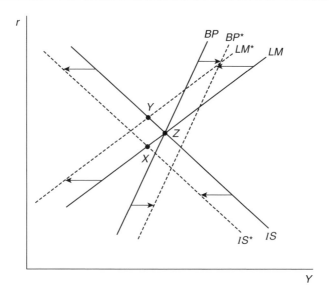

Figure 4.2

to include such considerations formally into the analysis by making use of the *IS–LM–BP* model augmented by a full employment (FE) line.[1]

Shifts in *IS*: The Absorption Approach

Examination of the basic model shows how an increase in domestic expenditure, shifting *IS* rightwards, will tend to weaken the balance of payments. The overall move into deficit represents the outcome of two opposing forces. First, the increase in expenditure induces an increase in imports and a deterioration in the current account (assuming that a movement into deficit or towards a larger deficit may legitimately be regarded as a deterioration).[2] Second, the increase in income also induces an increase in the demand for money. With a given money supply, the rate of interest rises and this generates a capital inflow and an improvement in the capital account.

Let us concentrate on the current account. The effect of changes in domestic expenditure on the current account are conventionally analysed within the context of the absorption approach to the balance of payments. This may be conveniently described by using the income–expenditure equation for an open economy introduced in Chapter 2, i.e.:

$$Y = C + I + G + X - M \tag{1}$$

This equation may be reorganised as follows:

$$M + Y = C + I + G + X \tag{2}$$

The left-hand side (LHS) shows the total resources available to an economy as a result of domestic production and importing. The right-hand side (RHS) shows total expenditure, both from domestic and foreign sources. The equation may, however, be further reformulated to be:

$$X - M = Y - (C + I + G) \tag{3}$$

In this case, the LHS provides a statement of the balance of payments, while the RHS shows how this depends on the difference between domestic output (Y) and domestic expenditure or absorption ($C + I + G$).

Starting off from a situation of payments equilibrium, an increase in domestic absorption relative to domestic output results in a payments deficit. More generally:

$$\Delta BP = \Delta Y - \Delta A \tag{4}$$

where ΔBP is the change in the balance of payments, ΔY is the change in domestic output and ΔA is the change in domestic absorption ($C + I + G$).

Part of the problem with this approach to analysing the balance of payments is that Y and A are not independent of one another. If Y changes, this may induce a change in A, such that:

$$\Delta A = c\Delta Y \tag{5}$$

where c is the marginal propensity to spend. Of course, absorption may also change for reasons unconnected with changes in Y, so that the above expression may be more realistically presented as:

$$\Delta A = c\Delta Y + \Delta Z \tag{6}$$

where ΔZ relates to changes in these other influences. Combining equations (4) and (6) gives us:

$$\Delta BP = \Delta Y - (c\Delta Y + \Delta Z) \tag{7}$$

and:

$$\Delta BP = \Delta Y - c\Delta Y - \Delta Z \tag{8}$$

According to this expression the current account balance of payments will change if there are changes in domestic output and income (though the effects of such changes will be partially offset by induced changes in domestic expenditure), changes in the marginal propensity to spend from domestic income, or changes in autonomous expenditure. Changes in expenditure could in turn, for example, result from changes in investment associated with changing expectations about the future, or from changes in government expenditure associated with changing political objectives.

The absorption approach to the current account of the balance of payments may be presented in a slightly different way by placing the emphasis on saving rather than on consumption. Thus, in place of equation 3 above, we have:

$$X - M = (S - I) + (T - G) \tag{3*}$$

This tells us that current account disequilibria will be associated with private sector imbalances between saving and investment or fiscal imbalances. Current account deficits will be associated with deficient saving (excess consumption) or with fiscal deficits. This reformulation of the absorption approach is useful because it makes plain the possibility that a decrease in the fiscal deficit need not necessarily lead to an improvement in the current account, since the strengthening fiscal situation may be offset by a fall in saving relative to investment. To explain changes in $X - M$ it is necessary to examine simultaneously what is happening to both $S - I$ and $T - G$. In the context of the *IS–LM–BP* model, *IS* will shift to the right as a consequence of either a fall in saving relative to investment in the private sector, or a fall in taxation relative to government expenditure. These changes may, of course, be the consequence of increasing private sector investment and government expenditure rather than declining saving or tax revenue.

Since investment is, by its very nature, forward-looking, and saving represents deferred consumption, this approach to the balance of payments is fundamentally inter-temporal. Current account deficits allow countries to smooth consumption. If we can explain investment and saving, this approach suggests that we have also gone a long way towards explaining the balance of payments.

There is also the point that $(T - G)$ and $(S - I)$ may be connected analytically. The suggestion is that if G increases relative to T, people who are forward-looking will anticipate the fact that taxes will eventually have to be increased to cover fiscal deficits and repay public debt. In these circumstances, and expecting higher future taxes, they increase contemporary saving. The argument is that fiscal relaxation will induce the private sector to alter behaviour in a way that offsets the effects of the fiscal relaxation on the current account of the balance of payments. But are people really that far-sighted? Is this taking rational expectations too far? Most of the available evidence seems to suggest that it is. Even reasonably rational people do not sit at home saying to themselves 'Ah yes, the government is spending more, we had better increase our saving now so as to ensure that we can pay the higher taxes that will inevitably follow.'

Shifts in *LM*: The Monetary Approach

The monetary sector is largely ignored in the absorption approach to the balance of payments, although it may be included on the basic assumption that money supply policy is used to stabilise interest rates. However, the monetary sector forms the centre pin of the monetary approach, which explains variations in the overall balance of payments exclusively in terms of domestic monetary disequilibria. It incorporates both the current and the capital accounts. Here it is rightward shifts in *LM* resulting essentially from increases in the supply of domestic credit which cause payments deficits. Not only does the monetary expansion cause nominal income and therefore the level of imports to rise, it also causes a fall in the rate of interest and therefore a capital outflow.

The monetary approach holds that there is a perfect correlation between the balance of payments and imbalances between the domestic demand and supply of money. If the demand exceeds supply, then this will be reflected in a payments surplus as the excess demand is met by an accumulation of reserves and a related expansion in money supply. If supply exceeds demand, then this will be reflected in a payments deficit as the excess supply spreads abroad through an increase in the demand for foreign exchange and a decumulation in reserves.

The transmission mechanism through which domestic monetary disequilibria are translated into balance of payments disequilibria depends on the responses of households and firms to having either deficient or excess money balances. In the case of excess balances, for example, the key question is, 'on what are these spent?' Essentially there are four alternatives: domestic real assets (home produced goods and services), foreign real assets (imports), domestic financial assets, or foreign financial assets.

If excess balances are spent on domestic real assets, goods prices will tend to rise. The demand for home-produced goods will thus fall and that for goods produced abroad will rise. The current account will therefore weaken. If spent initially on imports, the demand for them will rise directly. If spent on domestic financial assets, domestic asset prices will rise and the interest rate fall. The fall in the interest rate will cause both a capital outflow and an increase in domestic expenditure which will weaken the current account. If spent on foreign financial assets, there will be a direct capital outflow. Whatever way is chosen to dispose of excess money balances it appears that the balance of payments weakens, with excess supply in the domestic money market being converted into excess demand in both goods and asset markets.

Although the description provided so far gives a reasonable flavour of the monetary approach, we should perhaps be rather more precise about its principal features, about the underlying monetary model, and about the principal assumptions upon which it rests.

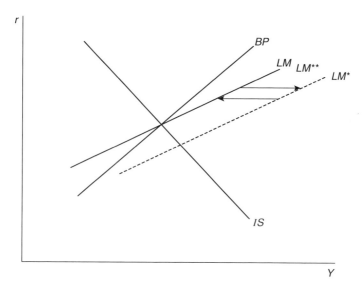

Figure 4.3

The principal features of the monetary approach are as follows. First, imbalances in the balance of payments are seen as reflecting a *stock* imbalance between the demand and supply of money. As such, the monetary approach contrasts with the absorption approach which emphasises the relevance of expenditure *flows*.

Second, the balance of payments alters in order to compensate for, and to eliminate, this domestic monetary stock imbalance. Payments disequilibria are therefore short-term and self-correcting phenomena within the context of the monetary approach. Once the stock disequilibrium causing the payments imbalance has been removed, changes in reserves, which reflect the nature of the payments imbalance, cease. Again, in this regard the monetary approach differs from the flow-based absorption approach. Diagrammatically a rightward shift in *LM* connected with an increase in domestic credit leads to a fall in the reserve-related component of the money supply and a leftward shift in *LM* back to its original position (see Figure 4.3).

Third, and again in contrast with the absorption approach, the monetary approach moves attention away from the current account and towards the balance of payments as a whole, incorporating the capital account.

Fourth, the policy implications of the monetary approach are either to do nothing and allow the self-correcting mechanisms outlined above to operate, or to eliminate the underlying domestic monetary disequilibrium. Of course, the process of self-correction may take some time. The final feature of the monetary approach is that the analysis is essentially long run. Short-run problems are ignored.

The key features of the monetary approach listed above emerge fairly clearly from the underlying monetary model. This may be summarised by the following group of equations:

$$M^d = kPY \tag{9}$$

$$P = \bar{E}P\star \tag{10}$$

$$M^s = D + R \tag{11}$$

$$M^d = M^s \tag{12}$$

$$R = M^d - D \tag{13}$$

and

$$\Delta R = \Delta M^d - \Delta D \tag{14}$$

and

$$\Delta R = \Delta B \tag{15}$$

where M^d is the demand for money, k is the demand for money coefficient, $P\star$ is the world price level, $\bar{E}$ is the fixed price of foreign currency per unit of domestic currency, D is domestic credit, R is the quantity of international reserves and B is the balance of payments.

The assumptions underlying this model are, first, that there are fixed nominal exchange rates (Equation (10)). Second, that the economy is at its natural rate of unemployment (reflected by Y in Equation (9)). Third, that the demand for money is a stable function of nominal income, with the main motive for holding money being its role as a medium of exchange (Equation (9)). Fourth, that, certainly in the long run, changing the money supply has no effect on real variables in the economy. Fifth, that an individual country's price level and interest rate converge towards world levels because there is a high elasticity of substitution between goods and assets in different countries (Equation (10)). And sixth, that changes in the money supply connected with changes in reserves are not sterilised, or offset, by the domestic monetary authorities. In effect, in the monetary model the authorities cannot control the supply of money but only its composition. If they increase the supply of domestic credit this will be offset by a fall in reserves.

On the basis of the monetary model $P\star$ and E are given, and together determine the domestic price level (P). Y is at the level consistent with the natural rate of employment given an implicit production function. The demand for money can therefore be calculated. The difference between the demand for money and the supply of domestic credit (D) equals the level of reserves. If the demand for money rises by more than the supply of domestic credit, the excess demand will be met by an inflow of money (in the form of reserves) from abroad. This inflow continues, however, only for as long as the excess demand for money persists. It is through changes in reserves that equilibrium in the domestic monetary sector is maintained. One of the apparent attractions of the monetary approach is its simplicity. What we appear to have is a unicausal explanation of the balance of payments. However, appearances can be deceptive. A number of questions need to be asked of the monetary model.

First, is the demand for money adequately described? If changes in the supply of domestic credit are offset by changes in the efficiency with which money is used, as proxied by the velocity of circulation, then there may be little or no impact on the balance of payments. Moreover, if money is demanded as a medium of exchange, why should an increase in the demand for money be associated with a fall in the level of spending, as a leftward shift in a vertical *LM* schedule would seem to imply?

Second, by what mechanism does the demand for money and supply of domestic credit change? The domestic price level is given by the world price level and the fixed exchange rate. The level of income is outside the control of the monetary authorities and the demand coefficient (k) is assumed to be unaffected by changes in the rate of interest. Meanwhile, the supply of domestic credit is treated as exogenous with no analysis of what induces it to change. In practice, domestic credit expansion may reflect a government's budget deficit. Monetary expansion will therefore be endogenous.

Third, is the focus on the long run not misplaced? The focus of balance of payments policy is almost always on the short run. The monetary approach tends, therefore, to skate over the interesting and relevant question of the short-run adjustment path towards equilibrium.

Fourth, is it not unrealistic to assume that policy-makers will be indifferent about the composition of the balance of payments? All the evidence is that considerable stress is placed on the importance of the current account as a means of servicing and eventually repaying loans.

Fifth, is it reasonable to assume that there will be no sterilisation of the effects of reserve changes? After all, the authorities have the means for such sterilisation through open-market policy and are likely to have the incentive directly one drops the assumption of permanent full employment.[3]

Finally, do domestic prices actually adjust to world levels, or, in other words, does purchasing power parity hold? More will be said about this in the next chapter, but for the moment we can note that there is considerable evidence to suggest that it does not, at least in the short run.

Let us then move on to examine the remaining element in our analysis of the balance of payments, namely shifts in the *BP* schedule.

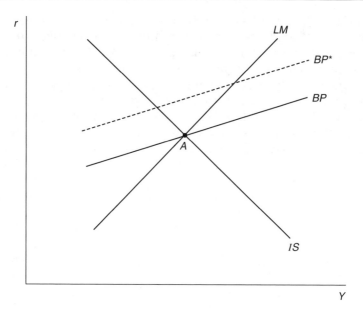

Figure 4.4

Shifts in *BP*: The Structural Approach

A shift in the *BP* schedule will occur where, for any specific level of income, a different rate of interest is now required in order to ensure balance of payments equilibrium, or, where for any specific rate of interest, a different level of income is now required. In Figure 4.4 an upward shift in the *BP* schedule means that the combination of income and interest rate shown by point *A* now co-exists with a payments deficit.

But what lies behind such shifts in *BP*? Basically the location of *BP* will be affected by anything that influences the balance of payments *except* the level of national income and the rate of interest. For example, changes in competitiveness, resulting from the various aspects of the terms of sale described in Chapter 3 (apart from the cost of trade credit which will be affected by changes in the rate of interest) will be significant, as will be factors which alter the credit-worthiness of countries as borrowers and the willingness of capital markets to lend at certain interest rates.

More specifically, factors which alter the relative price of imports or exports will shift *BP*, such as productivity changes and changes in efficiency which affect unit costs, or the introduction or elimination of import tariffs or export subsidies. Or, as we shall see in Chapter 8, the location of *BP* will also be affected by changes in the exchange rate, although in this chapter we are assuming fixed exchange rates.

It is within the context of shifts in the *BP* schedule that it is possible to accommodate a structural explanation of the balance of payments. The structural approach accentuates the importance of the types of goods produced and the efficiency with which they are produced. In a dynamic setting, countries which produce and export goods which have a relatively low income elasticity of demand, and, at the same time, do not produce but import goods which have a relatively high income elasticity of demand, will tend to encounter a secular deterioration in their balance of payments as their income terms of trade decline.

At the same time, a low level of product diversification combined with low price elasticities of demand and supply may, in certain circumstances, also cause considerable balance of payments instability about the trend. Another element of the structural explanation is that it focuses on the importance of changes in output as opposed to changes in expenditure. It represents a supply-side approach to the balance of payments and in this regard may be seen as contrasting with the emphasis placed on demand which is a feature of both the absorption and monetary approaches.

Synthesising the Approaches: Towards a General Theory

Although the absorption, monetary and structural approaches to the balance of payments have frequently been presented by their advocates as offering competing and mutually exclusive explanations, their discussion within the context of the *IS–LM–BP* model reveals that, in fact, they complement one another. Although they lay emphasis on different aspects of the model, they are not inconsistent.

A general theory of the balance of payments recognises that payments disequilibria may result from shifts in *IS*, shifts in *LM*, shifts in *BP*, or a combination of shifts in all three schedules. Indeed, more broadly, a general theory allows for the fact that shifts in the schedules may be interrelated. For example, to the extent that expansionary fiscal policy is financed by an increase in domestic credit creation, *LM* as well as *IS* will shift to the right. The size of the relative shifts, as well as the shapes of the schedules, will determine the extent to which the current and capital accounts alter. Figures 4.5 and 4.6 illustrate two possibilities. In Figure 4.5 the rightward shift in *IS*, reflecting an increase in some element of expenditure, is unaccompanied by any shift in *LM*. The deterioration in the overall balance of payments reflects the outcome of the rise in income, which causes a deterioration in the current account, and the rise in the rate of interest which causes an

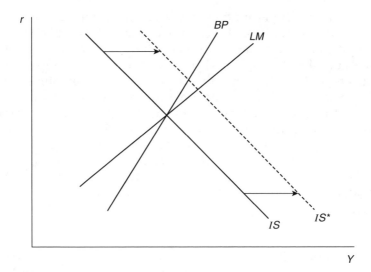

Figure 4.5

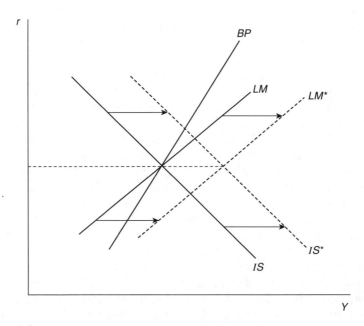

Figure 4.6

improvement (capital inflow) in the capital account. Had *LM* been steeper than *BP*, the capital account effect would have dominated and the overall balance of payments would have moved into surplus.

In Figure 4.6 the rightward shift in *IS* is now accompanied by a rightward shift in *LM*, reflecting an increase in domestic credit creation, which is sufficiently large that the rate of interest remains constant. In this case the deterioration in the balance of payments is more marked, since the increase in income, and therefore the current account deficit, is larger and there is no capital inflow.

Moving from the specific to the general, a moment's thought reveals that by making different assumptions about what causes *IS*, *LM* and *BP* to shift, and about the shapes of the schedules, it is possible to accommodate all the theories of the balance of payments outlined in this chapter.

Another way of integrating the theories is merely to recognise that payments disequilibria reflect an imbalance between aggregate demand and aggregate supply. Payments deficits reflect excess aggregate demand which may result either from an increase in aggregate demand or from a fall in aggregate supply.

We have seen that the same basic model allows us to present each of the three approaches as special cases of a more general theory. We have also seen that in the case of Figure 4.6 the theories may be interdependent. Let us now see if we can take further this idea of interdependency between the theories.

First, the absorption approach does not deny that excess credit creation will cause excess aggregate demand and payments deficits. Even the nature of the transmission mechanism is not in dispute although the elasticity of substitution between money and other assets may be. Nor, as we have seen, is the absorption approach purely a current-account model. It can tell us something about the rate of interest and therefore about the capital account.

Second, while emphasising the significance of credit creation, the monetary approach does not explain why credit is created. Again, the absorption and structural approaches may be used to look behind credit creation at the forces which cause credit to grow. Furthermore, to the extent that the absorption and structural approaches allow us to analyse the processes by which income and output change, they also allow us to talk about forces which influence the demand for money, and this is, of course, central to the monetary approach.

Third, policies directed towards changing the level and composition of domestic expenditure and which fall within the purview of the absorption approach, as well as policies directed towards changing the rate of interest – which may themselves alter the level and composition of expenditure – and fall within the purview of the monetary approach, may have important repercussions on the structure of the economy and thereby on its balance of payments.

What we end up with is a balance of payments theory that is general in a number of ways. But what happens if exchange rates are flexible, is the analysis sufficiently general to allow us to use it to explain variations in exchange rates? It is to this question that we turn in the next chapter.

5 Theories of Exchange-rate Determination

Introduction

The general theory of the balance of payments constructed in the previous chapter may, with little difficulty, be modified to become a general theory of exchange-rate determination. With flexible exchange rates, a position of equilibrium as represented by a point of intersection between *IS* and *LM*, which lies off the *BP* schedule, will result in a change in the exchange rate. Where equilibrium occurs below *BP*, giving a payments deficit, the exchange rate will depreciate. Where it occurs above *BP* giving a payments surplus the exchange rate will appreciate.

Taking the case of a deficit, the size of the required exchange-rate depreciation depends on how responsive imports and exports are to the relative price changes to which depreciation gives rise and on whether depreciation has any impact on the capital account. However, depreciation will not only shift the *BP* schedule downwards, allowing payments equilibrium to be achieved at a lower rate of interest for any given level of income or at a higher level of income for any given rate of interest, but, by changing the level of expenditure, it will also shift the location of *IS*. For example, to the extent that depreciation has an expansionary effect on expenditure *IS* will shift to the right.

The various forces that may cause the exchange rate to change are illustrated in Figures 5.1, 5.2, and 5.3. Starting from an initial point of payments equilibrium, as shown in Figure 5.1, *IS* shifts rightwards causing a balance of payments deficit, a depreciation in the exchange rate, and, in this case, a further rightward shift in *IS*.

In Figure 5.2 it is *LM* which shifts to the right and brings about a depreciation in the exchange rate. In this case the depreciation is larger than in the case of the rightward shift in *IS* since, whereas a rightward shift in *IS* causes the rate of interest to rise, a rightward shift in *LM* causes the rate of interest to fall. In the latter case both the current and capital accounts deteriorate, whereas in the former case the

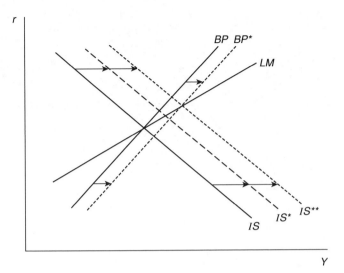

Figure 5.1

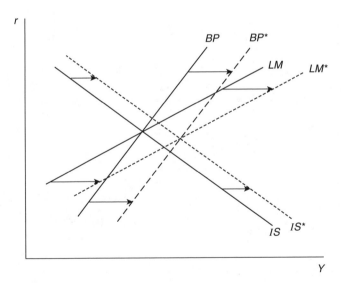

Figure 5.2

deterioration in the current account is partially offset by a strengthening capital account.

Figure 5.3 illustrates the case where structural factors cause the balance of payments to weaken, such that a combination of income and interest rate which previously gave payments equilibrium now combine

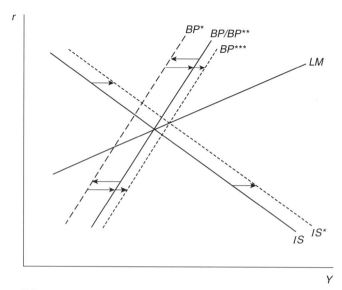

Figure 5.3

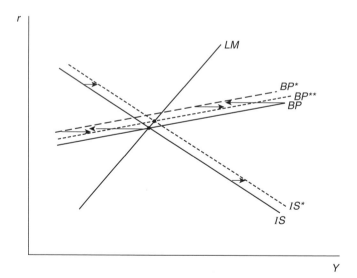

Figure 5.4

to give a deficit. Again, according to the model, the exchange rate will depreciate until the deficit is eliminated, though to the extent that the depreciation causes *IS* to shift to the right the *BP* schedule will not have to shift down to its previous location. Where *BP* is steeper than

LM, as in Figure 5.3, *BP* will shift below its old location since the effect of the rightward shift in *IS* on the current account dominates that on the capital account. However, in the case of Figure 5.4 where *BP* is less steep than *LM*, revealing a relatively high mobility of capital, the strength of the effect of an increase in the rate of interest on the capital account induced by the rightward shift in *IS* means that *BP* only needs to shift part of the way back to its old location.

What we discover is that the same forces that cause variations in the balance of payments and reserves (the quantity variables) under fixed exchange rates, cause variations in the exchange rate (the price variable) under flexible exchange rates.

Against this background the remainder of this chapter investigates further the factors that cause exchange rates to vary.[1]

Structural and Absorption Factors: Shifts in *BP* and *IS*

The structural explanation of exchange-rate movements focuses on the changing pattern of demand for and supply of goods in different countries, resulting from, for example, changing tastes, different or varying income elasticities of demand, changing costs of production and technological progress, and resource discoveries. This approach identifies 'real' factors and current-account disequilibria as being the principal source of exchange-rate changes. However, if the approach is reinterpreted as looking at the differing patterns of saving and investment across countries, then it clearly has a corollary in the capital account through which excess saving in some countries is transmitted to other countries with excess investment.

The absorption approach also focuses on the real economy and real variables. Here excess domestic absorption relative to domestic output results in exchange depreciation and excess output relative to absorption results in appreciation. Again the emphasis is on the flow of goods and services and therefore on the current account as the main source of exchange-rate changes. The capital account can be incorporated into such an approach since disequilibrium in the real sector of the economy will have implications for the financial sector and for interest rates, and changes in these will affect capital flows. For example, whereas an increase in government expenditure which is financed by borrowing will increase the interest rate and will induce a capital inflow, an increase financed by extra credit creation will have no equivalent effect.[2]

However, while the capital account can be integrated into the absorption approach, capital movements are viewed as being only a secondary influence on the exchange rate. The current account remains the centre of attention.

What predictions about the behaviour of exchange rates follow on from such explanations of their determination? First, the impact of shifts in currency demand or supply schedules on the exchange rate will depend on a range of foreign trade elasticities. If these are low, a shift in one of the schedules may clearly be associated with a significant movement in the exchange rate. Alternatively, if elasticities are relatively high smaller changes in exchange rates will be needed to restore balance of payments equilibrium. Moreover, if elasticities are lower in the short run than they are in the long run, an exchange rate may initially 'overshoot' on its path towards its new long-run equilibrium. Such overshooting may make rates appear rather volatile. Second, the structural and absorption approaches to exchange-rate determination do not predict extreme volatility, largely because the factors that are viewed as causing the underlying changes in the demand for and supply of goods and services themselves only change slowly. Furthermore, analysis of changes in demand and supply side determinants, and of foreign trade elasticities, would allow both the direction and size of exchange-rate changes to be anticipated.

Yet a key aspect of exchange-rate movements since the move over to generalised floating in 1973 has been their volatility and unpredictability. Approaches based exclusively on the real sectors of economies and on the current account may therefore leave something to be desired.

The Monetary Approach: Shifts in *LM*

Mirroring the monetary approach to the balance of payments there has also evolved a monetary explanation of exchange-rate changes. This approach incorporates a number of features.

First, an exchange rate is seen as the relative price of two monies. From this observation it follows that exchange-rate changes can be explained by changes in the relative demand for and supply of monies. For example, taking the sterling/dollar exchange rate, if the supply of sterling is increased relative to the demand for it at the same time as monetary sector equilibrium is maintained in the United States, then the price of sterling in terms of dollars will fall; that is, sterling will depreciate against the dollar.

Second, exchange-rate changes are seen as arising from *stock* disequilibria in the monetary sector, even though these stock disequilibria may be temporarily translated into an excess *flow* demand or *flow* supply of goods and services.

Third, the effects of excess domestic money supply growth on domestic prices is brought in via the concept of purchasing power parity (PPP).[3]

The various elements of the monetary approach may be illustrated by the following set of equations, where letters with the superscript* refer to values in (say) the US and letters without superscripts refer to values in (say) the UK. The demand for money coefficient k is assumed to be the same in both countries. Then,

$$M = kPY \tag{16}$$

$$M^* = kP^* Y^* \tag{17}$$

$$P^* = E\ P \quad \text{and} \quad E = \frac{P^*}{P} \tag{18}$$

$$\text{therefore } E = \frac{M^*/kY^*}{M/kY} \tag{19}$$

$$= \frac{M^*kY}{MkY^*} \tag{20}$$

It follows that starting from a given rate, an increase in the UK money supply will result in a sterling depreciation which completely offsets the effect that the induced increase in the UK price level has on both the UK and US balance of payments. There is no import leakage with floating rates and no change in reserves.

As with monetary explanations of many economic phenomena perhaps the principal appeal of this approach is its apparent simplicity. It seems to offer an unambiguous and unicausal explanation of exchange-rate changes. But again, appearances can be deceptive. As with the monetary approach to the balance of payments it rests on a number of restrictive assumptions about the exogeneity of the money supply, the stability of the demand for money and the invariance of output. Furthermore, the PPP doctrine has a number of deficiencies.

Purchasing Power Parity (PPP)

Since PPP is such an important element in seeking to explain exchange-rate movements, we ought to say rather more about it.

Basically it comes in two versions. 'Absolute' PPP suggests that price *levels* expressed in a common currency will be equalised throughout the world. 'Relative' PPP, on the other hand, argues merely that nominal exchange rates will alter in such a way as to maintain equilibrium real exchange rates in the light of differential inflation.

Even in its softer relative version, PPP rests on a number of restrictive assumptions. First, it is assumed that there is a high degree of substitutability between goods in different countries, so that if prices rise in one part of the world purchasers will immediately switch into relatively cheaper sources of supply and away from relatively expensive sources.

Second, it is assumed that there are no barriers to trade which impede buying from the cheapest source.

Third, it is implicitly assumed that all goods are internationally traded. Although arbitrage may well tend to equalise the prices of substitutable traded goods, this will not be the case with non-traded goods. Price levels overall may therefore not move in step because of different trends in non-traded goods prices. As a result, higher prices overall may not necessarily lead to exchange-rate depreciation. Where the rate of productivity growth is faster in the traded goods than in the non-traded goods sector, it is quite possible that a rising price level will go hand in hand with an appreciating exchange rate. PPP is thus more likely to hold for neutral monetary disturbances which affect all prices alike than for relative price changes associated with real structural change.[4]

Fourth, PPP suggests that it is an increase in the money supply which causes the exchange rate to depreciate and the price level to rise. But in practice it may be the rise in the price level which causes the exchange rate to depreciate.

Fifth, PPP may be more a feature of long-run equilibrium than a theory of exchange-rate determination. Certainly there is plenty of evidence to suggest that it does not hold in the short run.

Sixth, in the simple PPP theorem interest rates and wealth effects are largely put to one side, although in the real world these may be important. An increase in the domestic money supply resulting in a depreciation in the exchange rate, a strengthening in the current account and the accumulation of domestically owned claims on foreigners will raise interest payments from abroad. The new equilibrium trade balance will have to reflect this and the new equilibrium real exchange rate may be different from the old one.

Seventh, to ignore changes in other factors emanating from both the demand side and the supply side of the economy, which will alter the real equilibrium exchange rate, and to concentrate instead on differential inflation rates as the prime cause of movements in the nominal rate may be regarded as a somewhat exclusive explanation of the exchange rate.

Although the monetary approach emphasises the key role of the stock of money it is still consistent with a largely current-account explanation of exchange-rate changes, with an excess supply of money being reflected in an excess demand for goods. However, money may be demanded as an asset as well as a medium of exchange. Focusing on the asset demand for money shifts attention towards the capital account as the source of exchange-rate changes.

The Asset Market Approach

The asset market approach to exchange-rate determination suggests that it is the interaction between the stocks of monies as assets and the preferences of asset-holders that dominates the determination of exchange rates.

The principal factors influencing the demand for different monies as assets are, first, relative interest rates and, second, expected movements in exchange rates. Demand for any particular currency will strengthen as the interest-rate differential in its favour widens and as the size of any expected appreciation increases.

Given these determinants, and that in equilibrium the world's stock of monies has to be willingly held, what condition will ensure such asset stock equilibrium? Assuming that holders regard assets in different countries as perfect substitutes the condition is that:

$$ER^e - ER^a = i^* - i$$

where ER^e is the expected exchange rate, ER^a is the actual exchange rate, i^* is the foreign interest rate and i is the home interest rate. In words, the expected exchange-rate change equals the interest-rate differential. If the interest rate in one country is below that on offer abroad, holders of the currency will need to feel that the value of the currency will rise sufficiently to compensate them for the interest-rate disadvantage to which they are exposed. The system will always tend towards this condition even if it does not hold initially, although lack of substitutability between assets and transactions costs may mean that an inequality between expected exchange-rate changes and interest-rate differentials persists. If the anticipated appreciation does not compensate for the interest-rate disadvantage, the currency will normally be sold and the actual exchange rate (ER^a) will tend to depreciate until the difference between this rate and the expected future rate (ER^e), i.e. the expected appreciation, is big enough.

In the context of the asset market approach, changing the stock of different assets affects interest-rate differentials and thereby expected exchange-rate changes. But what is the relationship between expected future movements in exchange rates and current movements in the spot rate? If the rate is expected to appreciate in the future this will increase the current demand for the currency and the spot rate will therefore rise. It will continue to rise for as long as appreciation is expected. The spot rate will rise by the full extent of the expected appreciation.

Expectations and Exchange Rates

Expectations are then a central part of the asset market approach. But how are they formed? This is a question of some general interest not only with respect to the analysis of exchange rates.[5] There are a number of possibilities. First, it may simply be expected that the current rate will persist. Second, past changes in the exchange rate may lead to the expectation that future changes in the same direction will occur either at the same rate or at a faster or slower rate.

Third, dealers may have a notion of what is the 'normal' rate and will expect the rate to move towards it. They would then expect any movement away from the normal rate to be reversed.

The first two methods by which expectations are formed rely exclusively on examining the past performance of the exchange rate. But is this rational? An alternative assumption is that the market will use all the information that is available to it at the time that the expectation is formed. This will include historical information but will also include current and anticipated future developments. Since 'news' is continually becoming available expectations will be continually modified in the light of fresh information. Moreover, if news is unpredictable and volatile so will be exchange rates. To argue that exchange rates are determined by expectations and that exchange-rate volatility reflects the volatility of expectations may be accurate but gets us no further in providing an explanation upon which predictions can be based.

Overshooting

One attempt to provide a more formal explanation of exchange-rate volatility, and of the fact that PPP does not appear to hold in the short run, suggests that different prices adjust to disequilibria at different speeds. More specifically it is suggested that while asset prices adjust instantaneously goods prices adjust only slowly.

Having made this key assumption, let us further assume that an economy is in equilibrium in terms of the asset stock equilibrium condition discussed earlier. Now assume that there is an unforeseen increase in the domestic money supply. This results in an immediate fall in the domestic rate of interest (since asset prices rise instantaneously) and a *gradual* increase in the price level (since goods prices rise only slowly). However, since a rise in the price level will be expected, so will be the exchange depreciation required to restore purchasing power parity in the long run. The combination of low interest rate and expected exchange-rate depreciation will lead to an immediate capital outflow and an immediate depreciation. In order to restore asset stock equilibrium in circumstances where the domestic interest rate is below the world level an expected exchange-rate appreciation is necessary. But since the new long-run nominal equilibrium exchange rate is lower than it was before the money supply was increased, it follows that such an expectation will only be formed if the exchange rate initially falls below, or overshoots, its new long-run equilibrium.

As goods prices gradually rise and nominal income rises the nominal demand for money will rise, as will the nominal interest rate. The negative interest-rate differential will close and the required expected exchange-rate appreciation will therefore be less. Eventually, and with no further shocks to the system, the new set of equilibrium values will be reached with the ultimate fall in the nominal exchange rate just offsetting the increase in prices. For a time during the adjustment process the interest rate, prices and the exchange rate will all be rising – a combination of phenomena inconsistent with many other models of exchange-rate determination including PPP. In this model of exchange-rate overshooting PPP holds only in the long run.

The analysis of overshooting may be more formally presented by making use of the model introduced in the section on 'IS–LM and the Open Economy' in Chapter 2. Starting from point A in Figure 5.5 let us assume that there is an unforeseen increase in the money supply with the result that LM shifts to the right to LM*. Although this creates excess demand in the goods market, prices do not immediately rise. However, asset prices do rise and the rate of interest falls. With this fall in the interest rate and the devaluation which is expected in order to offset the anticipated eventual increase in the price level, the exchange rate immediately depreciates and BP shifts to BP*. As goods prices do begin to rise and the demand for money increases so LM shifts back towards its old location. The rate of interest rises and the exchange rate appreciates. At the end of the adjustment process the real exchange rate is restored to its original level with the nominal devaluation being just sufficient to offset the increase in the price level, as indeed PPP predicts. During the process the nominal rate depreciates by more than this amount, as shown by point B in Figure 5.5. In other words, the exchange rate overshoots, and PPP does not hold in the short run.

How does the analysis differ if the initial shock comes from a change in fiscal rather than monetary policy? Let us first of all assume that the LM schedule is vertical – an essentially monetarist assumption. Now a

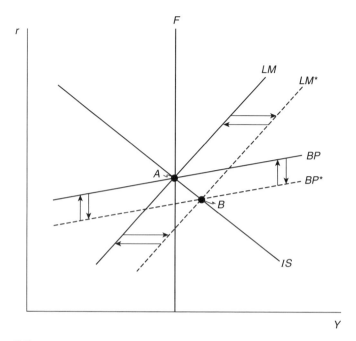

Figure 5.5

rightward shift in *IS*, associated with fiscal expansion, causes a rise in the rate of interest but no excess demand for goods and therefore no increase in prices, delayed or otherwise. The rise in the rate of interest causes a capital inflow and an appreciation in the exchange rate. Indeed, it is through this appreciation that the demand for exports and import substitutes is crowded out thus making room for the extra government expenditure. Since sticky goods prices are not an effective constraint on the adjustment process, the movement in the exchange rate up to its new and higher equilibrium real value occurs immediately and there is no overshooting. Nor does PPP hold since, with no further change in fiscal policy, the equilibrium real exchange rate permanently alters.

Of course, other scenarios are possible if different assumptions are made about the shape of LM.[6]

A conclusion with regard to exchange rates is that, while monetary policy has tended to become more stable, short-run exchange rates have remained quite volatile. The theory of exchange-rate overshooting based on unstable monetary policy does not therefore seem to fit the facts. How can exchange-rate risk be handled?

Forward Markets

The asset market approach to exchange-rate determination has some interesting implications for the relationship between the spot market and the forward market. Forward markets in foreign exchange enable traders and investors to sell the risk associated with exchange-rate variations. They can therefore fix the parameters of any deal by covering forward and securing a 'closed' rather than an 'open' position. However, they will get a less good rate of exchange in the forward market than they would do in the current spot market; there will be a forward discount. Eliminating their risk is not costless.

Arbitrage will tend to ensure that the forward discount on a currency's exchange rate equals the interest-rate differential between the two countries involved, a state of affairs called closed or covered interest-rate parity. Again, looking at it on the basis of the asset market approach, if interest rates are higher in the USA than in the UK, UK investors will be tempted to switch sterling into dollars and to make loans in the USA rather than in the UK, entering into future contracts to sell a specified amount of dollars in exchange for sterling at the forward exchange rate which will involve a lower sterling price for dollars than the current spot rate. Making loans in the USA will be preferred for as long as the forward discount on dollars does not offset the interest-rate advantage in the USA. But the impact of the transactions will be to lower the US interest rate, raise the UK interest rate and cause the price of dollars on the forward market to depreciate, until interest rate parity is achieved.

The interesting thing is that the condition for asset stock equilibrium states that the expected change in the exchange rate equals the interest-rate differential. It follows, therefore, that the forward discount (or premium) on a currency equals the expected spot market depreciation (or appreciation), or, what comes to the same thing, the forward rate is equal to the expected future spot rate. Expectations may, of course, not be fulfilled and the spot rate in three months' time may not actually equal the value predicted on the basis of the forward rate, since extra news will become available in the intervening time which will affect the spot rate. In circumstances where investors do not regard assets in different countries as perfect substitutes for one another, i.e. where there is imperfect capital mobility, or where there are significant transactions costs, neither interest rate parity nor the asset stock equilibrium condition will hold.

Of course, if one group of transactors is selling risk in the forward foreign exchange market another group must be taking it on. These are the 'speculators' who set out to make profits through variations in the spot price of currencies. If they sell a currency forward, their hope is that they will be able to buy it in three months' time (or whatever the length of the forward contract is) more cheaply. Speculation involves holding an open or uncovered position. As more traders wish to sell a currency forward so the forward rate will drop. The forward discount is the incentive needed to persuade speculators to take on the risk of buying the currency forward. Where the forward discount required to clear the forward market exceeds the interest-rate differential speculators are in effect being offered a 'risk premium'.[7]

Synthesising the Approaches: Some Tentative Conclusions

So what does determine exchange rates? Although the asset market approach undoubtedly provides certain insights by drawing attention to the importance of the capital account, stock adjustments and expectations, it has a number of limitations. First, assets in different countries are surely unlikely to be regarded as perfect substitutes. Expected exchange-rate changes will not correspond exactly to interest-rate differentials, covered interest parity will not hold and currencies will carry risk premia (portfolio balance models of the exchange rate have been developed which attempt to deal with this weakness). Second, asset prices may not adjust instantaneously, instead they themselves may be sticky. Third, goods prices may adjust more rapidly than is assumed by the theory, or there may be asymmetries in the speed of adjustment with prices moving more quickly upwards than downwards. Fourth, if goods prices do not respond to financial stock disequilibria it may be that real output does. It may therefore be real income that changes rather than prices. Recognising the possibility that output may change brings into consideration a whole range of 'real' factors affecting the level of capacity utilisation and aggregate supply as potential determinants of exchange rates – the real economy has perhaps been too readily ignored in recent exchange-rate models.[8] Again leading on from this, and fifth, it seems unwise to ignore either the current or the capital account – not least because the two are interrelated. For example, an increase in investment which influences domestic absorption and the current account will increase the volume of assets in an economy and may therefore affect the capital account via the asset market mechanism. Or again an increase in government expenditure – another component of domestic absorption – unmatched by increased taxation leads to an increase in assets and liabilities. The implications for overall expenditure depend on the responses of those acquiring the extra assets and liabilities. These may not be symmetrical.

What one is left with is a feeling that monetary models of the exchange rate beg as many questions as they answer. Indeed, they may be seen as failing to answer the really fundamental questions or as providing at best only an approximate answer. What is needed is an explanation which accommodates all the various real and financial variables which seem likely to exert some influence over the exchange rate. In the absence of such a model it is unwise to base exchange-rate policy exclusively on any one of the existing models, which both in terms of their theoretical underpinning and empirical support seem to be lacking.

The basics of such a synthesising model might be as follows. Exchange-rate changes are caused by something disturbing what is an initial state of macroequilibrium. The disturbance may emanate from the demand side or the supply side of the economy, or from outside the economy, and it may reflect financial or real changes; that is, it may occur as a result of a change in any factor that helped to determine the initial equilibrium. The response to disequilibrium may be reflected by changes not only in the exchange rate but in other macroeconomic variables as well, but these are likely to interact with the exchange rate. Short-run changes in the variables affected may differ from long-run changes if, as seems likely, they adjust at different speeds. Adjustment speeds and indeed the scope for adjustment in particular macroeconomic variables may differ both within and between countries – for example, there may be more real wage resistance in some countries than in others. Furthermore, the level of capacity utilisation will be important, full employment cannot simply be assumed. The extent to which different variables change will depend on a range of supply factors as well as demand factors such as price and income elasticities and elasticities of substitution between money, goods and assets. In what ways, for example, will people choose to dispose of excess cash balances, and what will influence their choice?

One helpful way of disentangling the various influences on the exchange rate is to differentiate between their importance over different time periods. In the shortest of short runs output and prices may be relatively fixed and the exchange rate will be dominated by changing expectations, by speculative runs and by uncertainty. Extending the period slightly may allow asset market factors to become more important as the changing composition of portfolios becomes important. Moving into the medium term the exchange rate may be influenced by, and may in turn influence, real output, expenditure, prices, and the current account. Meanwhile, viewed from a long-term perspective, the maintenance of PPP may have considerable relevance – though the long-run stationary state may never be attained, with the long run in fact comprising a series of short-run situations which may approach but never reach long-run equilibrium.

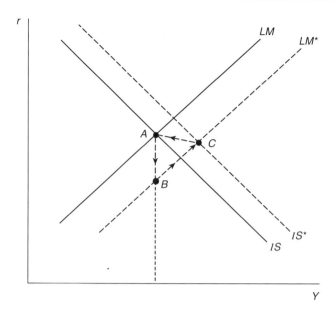

Figure 5.6

This process of adjustment is illustrated in Figure 5.6. Here, an initial state of equilibrium (point *A*) is disturbed by an increase in the money supply. With rigidities in real output and goods prices, the exchange rate initially overshoots to a level represented by point *B*. In the medium term, the depreciation in the exchange rate induces an increase in expenditure and a rightward shift in *IS* to point *C*. In the long run, prices and wages rise such that *IS* and *LM* return to their original locations. We are therefore back to point *A*. In the long run, nothing real has happened. Prices have risen and the nominal exchange rate has depreciated to compensate for this.

6 Theories of Currency Crisis

Introduction

A feature of the 1990s and 2000s has been the incidence of currency and financial crises in the world economy. Compared to a gradual deterioration in the balance of payments associated with a weakening current account, currency crises – as the word 'crisis' implies – are rather more sudden and dramatic. They usually involve rapid reversals of capital, and have therefore shifted attention away from the current account and towards the capital account as the source of balance of payments problems. To try to explain them, a number of approaches have been developed, with additional attempts being offered to explain crises that were explained inadequately by previous approaches. There have essentially been three generations of currency crisis model. This chapter sets out to explain them briefly and to examine other aspects of crisis. In Chapter 14, we apply these ideas to help explain some of the economic crises the world has experienced in the 1990s and 2000s.

Currency Crisis Models

The First-generation Model

The first-generation currency crisis model basically tells a fairly familiar story. It begins with a country running a fiscal deficit which is financed by monetary expansion. This results in inflation, which in turn causes the real exchange rate to appreciate. As a consequence, the country loses competitiveness and its current account balance of payments weakens as exports decline and imports increase. Disequilibrium in the current account can be handled in various ways, as we have seen in previous chapters.

The first-generation currency crisis model assumes that the government concerned is keen to retain a pegged nominal exchange rate. This means that the current account deficit has to be financed in some way, or corrected by pursuing alternative adjustment policies.

However, there may be both economic and political limits on how quickly alternative adjustment policies work. It may be difficult to reduce aggregate domestic demand if there are rigidities in the tax system and in government expenditure. It is also likely that expenditure-reducing policies will be politically unpopular. At the same time, and with a deteriorating current account, a country may not appear to be particularly creditworthy to international capital markets. The running down of international reserves may seem to be the most feasible and attractive option. The problem here is that reserves are finite. Running them down is therefore not a long-term solution, and the realisation that this is the case sows the seeds of the crisis.

As reserves fall, capital markets begin to perceive that the current account deficit is unsustainable. Confidence is lost and devaluation anticipated. In such circumstances it becomes less attractive to hold the currency. Foreign investors sell it and reserves fall further, leading to an even greater loss of confidence. There is an internal dynamic at work where declining confidence feeds on itself. For as long as creditors believe that reserves are adequate to allow the country to meet its external obligations, a crisis may be avoided. But once the threshold is reached where reserves are less than short-term external debt obligations, creditors will become concerned about getting out their money. Confidence will implode and there will be a 'rush for the exits'. The crisis will have arrived.

The basic mechanics of the crisis may be shown using the open economy models presented in Chapter 2. Incorporating a government sector alongside a private sector, the current account may be expressed as:

$$X - M = (S - I) + (T - G)$$

where X is exports, M is imports, S is domestic saving, I is investment, T is tax revenue and G is government expenditure.

From this expression it may be seen that if G increases relative to T, and there is no change in $(S - I)$, then $(X - M)$ will fall. If $S - I = 0$, then with $G > T$, it follows that $M > X$. With a pegged exchange rate, international reserves will decline in order to finance net imports. Fiscal deficits and their impact on reserves lie at the heart of the first generation currency crisis model.

Figure 6.1 provides an illustration of what is going on, using the IS–LM–BP model. Fiscal excesses shift IS to the right from IS^1 to IS^2. We now assume that the related fiscal deficits are financed by monetary expansion rather than by borrowing: that is, they are monetised

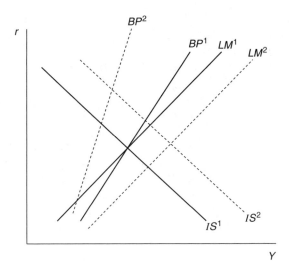

Figure 6.1

rather than bond-financed. This means that *LM* shifts to the right from LM^1 to LM^2. We further assume that there is a pegged exchange rate. Given the configuration of *IS*, *LM* and *BP* in Figure 6.1, it may be seen that the new point of intersection between IS^2 and LM^2 lies well below *BP*. In other words, there is an overall balance of payments deficit. Any capital inflows that there may be, fail to offset the current account deficit, with the result that the country's holdings of international reserves fall. With no change in the underlying situation, and no change in policy, the decline in reserves may initially be modest. But, as reserves continue to fall and are eventually perceived to be inadequate, confidence will be lost. Capital outflows will make the overall balance of payments deficit larger. Diagrammatically, the *BP* schedule in Figure 6.1 will become steeper, as shown by BP^2. It is also likely to shift upwards. Reserves will fall more rapidly and the crisis will have arrived.

Having arrived, how can the crisis be overcome? The conventional answer draws on the conventional theory relating to capital movements that we discussed in Chapter 2. Of course, the long-term answer is to eliminate the underlying cause of the problem, which is the fiscal deficit. However, in the short run, the challenge is to reverse the outflow of foreign capital and stop the depletion of reserves. This implies that the domestic interest rate needs to be increased and the domestic currency's value needs to depreciate. There will be an incentive for the authorities to allow the currency to overshoot the long-run equilibrium exchange rate and to go for a more pronounced devaluation, in an attempt to create expectations that in the short run its value will bounce back. Relatively high interest rates and an expected exchange rate appreciation seem the circumstances most likely to attract foreign capital, according to conventional theory – although the precise blend between them will be something over which governments may have some discretion.

Emphasising devaluation may have the advantage of inducing a price effect favouring internationally traded goods and an improvement in the current account, whereas higher interest rates may be more contractionary and rely on reducing imports by lowering expenditure. But there are other considerations, to which we turn later in the chapter after we have discussed the third-generation currency crisis model. For now, we can simply underline that the first-generation model emphasises domestic economic mismanagement in the form of fiscal deficits, monetary expansion and pegged exchange rates as the ultimate sources of currency crisis.

The Second-generation Model

The second-generation currency crisis model tells a rather different story. It starts off by pointing out that governments opt for a pegged exchange rate because they see its advantages as outweighing its disadvantages. The principal advantage of a pegged exchange rate is as a counter-inflationary device and a way of encouraging trade with the country to whose currency the peg is installed (and with other countries pegged to the same currency). The principal disadvantage is that any economic adjustment that is required will have to be achieved using other policy instruments. Having made the choice, an element of inertia creeps in. Governments may become increasingly reluctant to abandon a peg that they were uncertain about establishing in the first place. They may be concerned that abandoning it will affect their counter-inflationary reputation adversely, and that devaluation will have politically undesirable effects on income distribution. Moreover, abandoning the peg may be seen as a sign of weakness and economic mismanagement.

Let us assume, and it may be a heroic assumption, that when the currency peg is initially selected, the chosen exchange rate is the equilibrium one, in the sense that there is no overall balance of payments deficit or surplus at times when the government is achieving its domestic policy objectives of economic growth and quasi-full employment. There is therefore consistency between internal and external targets at the particular chosen pegged exchange rate. In these circumstances there seems little reason why a currency crisis should occur, according to the second-generation model.

But what if fundamental equilibrium is replaced, for some reason, by fundamental disequilibrium, where there is an inconsistency between internal and external targets at the pegged exchange rate?[1] For example, imagine that the current account of the balance of payments weakens. Since the value of the currency is pegged, devaluation is ruled out, and the government will be forced to reduce the demand for imports by contractionary fiscal and monetary policies. Contractionary monetary policy will also push up interest rates in a way that it is believed will attract capital and help finance the current account deficit, at least for as long as the commitment to the peg remains credible. In these circumstances, governments have to make a choice. Is it their priority to avoid balance of payments deficits, or is it to avoid recession and unemployment? If they initially prioritise the external target, will this remain their choice? After all, the subjugation of domestic policy objectives is likely to carry a high and probably increasing political cost. Capital markets may sense the inevitability of currency devaluation well before the government is prepared to abandon the peg. They may come to believe that the political costs of abandoning the peg and devaluing the currency will be seen by the government as significantly less than the political costs of recession and unemployment. Here is the essence of the second-generation model.

If markets begin to believe that devaluation is probable, or even inevitable, they will begin to sell the currency in advance of it. They do not want to be holding a currency that falls in value. The very act of selling it will, however, put downward pressure on the currency's value in foreign exchange markets. How will the government respond? It needs to try to alter the expectations of capital markets and convince them of its commitment to the durability of the currency peg. Actions may speak louder than words. The only option may be to raise interest rates in an attempt to provide an incentive for capital markets to buy the domestic currency and to demonstrate a commitment to defending the peg. But there is an in-built problem here. Speculators were selling the currency as they believed that domestic interest rates were unsustainably high because of their impact on the domestic economy. The government's response was to raise the rates still higher, thereby giving the speculators an even greater incentive to anticipate devaluation. Theory suggests that two basic things affect capital movements; relative interest rates and expected changes in exchange rates. In a second-generation crisis, an increase in interest rates, which may normally be anticipated to exert a positive effect on capital inflows, in practice raises still further the probability of a decline in the value of the currency. The policy of increasing the rate of interest is therefore unlikely to avert a crisis and, in an apparently rather perverse way, may make it more likely.

The role of speculators is central to the second-generation model. But it is easy to misinterpret. Speculators do not cause second-generation crises. Rather, it is the inconsistency between internal and external targets at the pegged exchange rate – that is, the problem of fundamental disequilibrium – that is the root cause of the crisis. And yet, given this fundamental disequilibrium, the actions of speculators determine whether it will result in a crisis. The 'end-game' can be different according to how speculators respond. A key element of the second-generation model is therefore the existence of multiple equilibria. If capital markets believe that maintaining the peg is a government's absolute priority, such that the probability of devaluation is almost zero, why should they sell the currency? In these circumstances, a currency crisis can be avoided, even though the related recession and unemployment may be interpreted as an economic and political crisis. However, if they doubt the strength of the government's commitment to the peg (as compared with other policy objectives) their response will be to sell the currency, and their actions may then provoke a crisis and the very devaluation they anticipated. In the second-generation model, therefore, much comes down to the perceived commitment of governments to maintaining a currency peg. Does their exchange rate policy have credibility? In large measure this depends on its perceived costs in terms of domestic economic performance.

The Third-generation Model

The third-generation currency crisis model shares some elements with the first- and second-generation models, but it has generally been seen as sufficiently different to warrant its separate status. It is a model that focuses on the part played by capital movements, and is very much a capital account crisis model. Fundamental to the model is an understanding of the factors that influence capital mobility, although, quite conventionally, it points to the importance of differences in interest rates (that is, return) and to risk, both in the form of default risk and exchange rate risk.

Capital will tend to flow into a country where interest rates are relatively high and where there is a very low perceived risk of either default or exchange rate depreciation. In extreme circumstances there may indeed be a flood of inflowing capital. There will be a boom. However, this boom may be fragile and vulnerable. The circumstances leading to capital inflows can change rapidly. Interest rates elsewhere in the world may increase, so that the interest rate differential narrows or disappears. Or a corporate or financial failure may change the market's perception of default risk; especially if the government does not mount a rescue operation in response to it. Moreover, the actions of some foreign investors may be influenced by those of others, accentuating swings in capital flows.

With a narrowing in the interest rate differential and an increased perception of default risk, capital inflows may turn around and become capital outflows. Again the seeds of a crisis are sown. How will things evolve? It is quite likely that, during the boom period, the country experiencing the capital inflow will also have been running a current account deficit. This may not have appeared to be any cause for concern while strong capital inflows were sufficient not only to finance the deficit but also to allow the country to accumulate international reserves. The assumption here, if you recall, is that the government is maintaining a pegged exchange rate, so the capital inflows will not have resulted in an appreciation in the nominal exchange rate. With capital now flowing out, how is the current account deficit to be financed? The likely choice is to run down reserves. The net outflow of capital will, of course, lead directly to a fall in reserve holdings. We are now in the familiar territory of the first-generation model since, while the decline in reserves may not initially cause anxiety, if they continue to fall a perception will be created that they have become inadequate. At this stage, foreign investors who would not initially have sought to withdraw their funds may decide to exit, and investor panic may follow. Governments will be forced to respond, probably in fairly conventional ways by raising domestic interest rates and by eliminating the expectation of devaluation by actually devaluing.

In the case of the third-generation model, fiscal deficits and current account deficits may exist but they are not of central importance. The model therefore differs from the first-generation model. In common with the second-generation model, the actions of capital markets may help determine the final outcome, but unlike the second-generation model there is no significant inconsistency between internal and external policy objectives. Rather, it is a narrowing in interest rate differentials, or a changed perception of default risk, that converts the boom of capital inflows into the bust of capital outflows, and it is this reversal that is at the heart of the crisis.

Figure 6.2 provides an illustration of what happens during a third-generation currency crisis using the $IS–LM–BP$ model. During the boom period, capital inflows finance an increase in investment – often speculative in nature – and the IS schedule shifts from IS^1 to IS^2. At the same time, the government does not want the capital inflows to drive up the price of the currency, so it intervenes to buy the incoming foreign exchange and supplies the domestic currency that is being demanded. As a result, LM shifts from LM^1 to LM^2, but the intersection between IS^2 and LM^2 lies above BP^1. There is an overall balance of payments surplus with capital inflows more than offsetting any current account deficit. A shock, for example in the form of a corporate default, now increases perceived default risk such that the BP schedule shifts and becomes

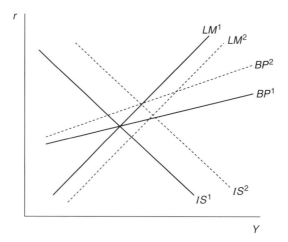

Figure 6.2

much steeper (BP^2 rather than BP^1). There is therefore an overall balance of payments deficit because capital that had previously been flowing in begins to flow out. As the decline in reserves further erodes confidence, *BP* continues to shift and to become steeper, and the fall in reserves becomes unsustainable. In short, the crisis has arrived.

Can Crises be Anticipated?

As we noted in the Introduction to this chapter, theories of currency crisis have evolved in response to the failure of inherited theory to explain new crises. This implies that crises are difficult to predict accurately. At the same time, experience and the econometric investigation of crises has enabled progress to be made in identifying the circumstances in which crises are more, or less, likely. There can be a probabilistic approach to crises.

Crises are improbable where all the so-called economic fundamentals are strong. They tend not to come 'out of a clear blue sky'. At the other extreme, where the fundamentals are weak and there is both poor economic policy and poor economic performance, a crisis becomes much more likely; though even here the timing of the crisis may not be easy to predict. It is perhaps hardly surprising that a country with a large and growing fiscal deficit, rapid monetary expansion and debt accumulation, fast inflation and currency overvaluation is more likely to encounter problems than one where the opposite set of circumstances exists.

Trickiest to assess is the probability of a crisis where, even though fundamentals are not strong, neither are they dire. Occupying this middle ground, countries will be in a 'zone of vulnerability'. They may avoid a crisis. But, if a shock occurs, it may be enough to spark a crisis. Crises in general tend to happen when two things combine. First, the country is economically vulnerable. Second, occupancy of the zone of vulnerability coincides with a 'trigger'. Triggers may take various forms. They may involve corporate or financial default, or a crisis in another country, probably a geographically proximate one, or there may be a political shock.

Much of the difficulty in forecasting crises accurately comes not from identifying which countries are vulnerable – though inadequate or imperfect statistics may mean that this is not an easy task – but rather from foreseeing the shocks that might trigger a crisis. Semantically, shocks would not be shocks if they could be foreseen. There is an analogy with avalanches. Experienced mountaineers can assess the risk of an avalanche. Science and experience teach them what to look for. But even so it remains difficult to predict exactly when an avalanche will occur, particularly since it is difficult to predict the trigger that will release it. But what variables help us to anticipate currency crises?

Empirical investigation into currency and financial crises has helped to identify some of the lead indicators. First, financial liberalisation, particularly when the sequencing of it is inappropriate, is a factor. Domestic financial liberalisation, unaccompanied by prudential regulation and adequate supervision, can weaken the domestic financial system. Similarly, capital account liberalisation can facilitate a rapid inflow of capital, perhaps attracted by a rising domestic interest rate, which is then used to finance speculative domestic investment. Maturity and foreign exchange mismatches can in these circumstances contribute to vulnerability. Domestic banks may have borrowed short-term and in foreign currency but lent long-term and in domestic currency. This makes them fragile.

Second, and as all the theories of currency crisis suggest, the probability of crisis rises alongside the degree of currency overvaluation. An overvalued currency will be associated with current account balance of payments deficits and deindustrialisation. It will discriminate against exports and the domestic production of tradables, and in favour of imports. It will foster expectations of future devaluation. The practical difficulty here is in measuring the degree of currency overvaluation. In principle, it can be measured by the amount by which the value of a currency exceeds its equilibrium value. The problem is in determining the equilibrium real exchange rate. Attempts to calculate equilibrium exchange rates have been notoriously imprecise, and the notion that exchange rates are at their equilibrium when the resulting balance of payments is sustainable hardly helps, because the sustainability of the balance of payments is itself difficult to measure.[2] Even so, if, starting from a situation where the balance of payments was in approximate equilibrium, there has been a pronounced rise in the real exchange rate, without there being any justification for it in terms of economic fundamentals such as the long-run terms of trade, there can be a reasonable claim that the currency is overvalued, and this makes a crisis more likely.

Third, and also as predicted by currency crisis theory, the running-down of international reserves appears to be a precursor of crises. However, difficulties exist here as well. As the theory shows, reserve decumulation need not always result in a crisis. The question is whether reserves have become inadequate. But measuring the adequacy of reserves is not straightforward.[3] Crises are perhaps more likely when reserves continue to fall, and fall increasingly rapidly. But the rapid implosion of reserves is what is being used to identify crises. Measured in this way, it is hardly surprising that crises are associated with a pronounced loss of reserves, since this is what defines the crisis.

Finally, in an attempt to capture the idea of reserve inadequacy, particularly in the context of capital account crises, econometric studies have investigated the connection between crises and short-term external debt denominated in foreign exchange, relative to reserve holdings. The evidence is broadly consistent with the theory. Where debt increases relative to reserves, or reserves fall relative to debt, the probability of crisis appears to increase.

In short, guided by advances in our theoretical understanding, statistical investigation has allowed us to become more confident about the key variables affecting the probability of currency crises. However, our ability to identify increasing vulnerability to crisis does not necessarily mean that we can predict crises accurately. Prediction will always be hampered by the problems encountered in anticipating triggers. Moreover, it remains likely that crises will be avoided in some cases where vulnerability appears to be relatively high, and will occur in other cases where vulnerability appears to be relatively low. From a policy point of view, this implies that while our increasing understanding of crises may enable us to avoid some of them by taking pre-emptive action, it may also be sensible to put in place policies to deal with those crises that cannot be prevented.

Crises and Contagion

As noted in the previous section, a crisis in one country may act as the trigger for a crisis in another. A concern in a world where economies are interconnected via trade and finance is that crises will not be contained in the countries in which they originate.

There are various mechanisms through which contagion may occur.
Figure 2.8 in Chapter 2 showed how contagion may result from trade,
although that figure illustrates the transmission of a positive shock. In
the case of a crisis, aggregate demand will fall in the crisis country. As
a consequence, national income falls. Since imports depend on income
($M = mY$) imports will also fall. This will be one way in which the crisis country deals with the crisis and reduces its current account deficit.
However, the crisis country's imports will be other countries' exports.
Their ($X - M$) schedules will shift down, causing both their current
account to weaken and their national income to fall. The weakening in
the current account may then make these countries more prone to crisis themselves. The above course of events is illustrated in Figure 6.3,
where Country A is the country in which the crisis originates and
Country B is the one that is 'infected' by the crisis through its trade
with Country A. The potency of the contagion will depend on the size
of the fall in national income in Country A, the value of A's marginal

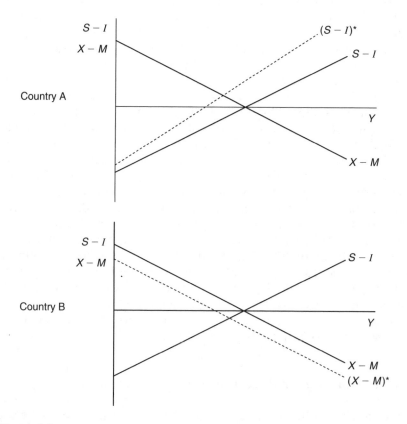

Figure 6.3

propensity to import, and the pattern of its trade; what proportion of Country A's imports comes from Country B?

In addition to the trade route described above, contagion may occur in other ways. Devaluation in the initial crisis country, which is designed to strengthen its competitiveness *vis à vis* other countries will, if successful, clearly weaken the competitiveness of these other countries. This will be another reason why the $(X - M)$ schedule in infected countries shown in Figure 6.3 will shift down, creating current account deficits and economic recession. But contagion may also occur via the capital account, which is not shown in Figure 6.3. As we have seen, the response to the crisis in the initiating country is likely to be to raise domestic interest rates. If this policy is effective in attracting foreign capital, the capital will, by definition, be leaving other economies. The capital inflow to the original crisis country will be a capital outflow from elsewhere. The countries experiencing the capital outflow may now encounter their own capital account crises. On top of this, the original crisis may make foreign investors in general more risk averse. They may perceive that the risks of foreign lending are higher – particularly perhaps in the geographical region affected by the original crisis. There will be a scramble for additional liquidity and this may again lead to foreign investors withdrawing funds from non-crisis countries; withdrawals that then make crises in these countries more likely. In short, a crisis in one country may have an adverse effect on the whole market mood or psychology and, where one foreign investor is strongly influenced by the actions of others, a bandwagon effect may occur, that serves to transmit the crisis from one country to others. But which others? What determines whether a country is protected against economic contagion? The above analysis suggests that it will be countries that are integrated most closely with the original crisis country through trade and finance that will be the worst affected. For countries where trade is more insulated from the crisis, or where financial assets are perceived as being much less at risk, and where the country is still regarded as being highly creditworthy, there will be economic immunisation. Indeed, for these countries, one effect of the crisis may be to generate stronger capital inflows as foreign investors search for a safe haven. If the degree of trade and financial integration is greater for countries that are geographically proximate, it follows that contagion may be more pronounced regionally than globally.

Policies During a Crisis and the Aftermath of Crises

Discussion in earlier sections of this chapter has suggested that the conventional response to a currency crisis is to raise domestic interest rates and to devalue the exchange rate. The principal justification for this combination of policies is to try to strengthen the capital account of the balance of payments, and either staunch capital outflows or attract capital inflows. But the policies may also strengthen the current account through both expenditure switching and expenditure reducing effects. Will such a policy response always be the appropriate one?

In the case of second-generation crises, policy needs to eliminate the fundamental disequilibrium that has caused them. Prior to the crisis, interest rates have been too high to allow domestic targets of economic growth and low unemployment to be achieved. Essentially, the problem has been one of currency overvaluation. In these circumstances, while devaluation is strategically important, governments are likely to combine the devaluation not with an increase in interest rates but rather with a decrease. As far as capital flows are concerned, the elimination of currency overvaluation (and with this the expectation of devaluation), as well as the belief that after the crisis domestic interest rates are at a more appropriate level to encourage economic growth may well provide a stronger incentive for foreign capital to flow in rather than out. In any event, if the devaluation is associated with the selection of a more flexible exchange rate regime, capital flows may not be deemed as important as they were before the crisis. The impossible triad, which says that countries cannot simultaneously have pegged exchange rates, independent monetary policy and free capital mobility, has been broken by abandoning the commitment to a specific currency value.

Even in the context of third-generation currency crises, there has been lively debate among economists about an appropriate blend of policy.[4] Conventional policy has not been without its detractors. On what grounds may a policy of monetary and fiscal retrenchment in combination with devaluation be criticized? First, and as far as fiscal policy is concerned, a crisis is likely to result in a decline in private sector investment and possibly even an increase in saving. This means that $(S - I)$ may increase, implying that $(T - G)$ may not need to increase by as much as if $(S - I)$ had remained unaffected. There is a danger of fiscal overkill. Second, with regard to monetary policy, the danger is that a sharp rise in the domestic interest rate may cause corporate and financial failure. Borrowers may be unable to honour their obligations if interest rates rise. Moreover, is it certain that higher domestic interest rates will attract foreign capital? A sharp and dramatic increase in the rate of interest may be seen as a panic measure and an indication of economic malaise. This will hardly restore confidence. It is also important to distinguish between the types of international capital. Although high interest rates may attract short-term bank lending, they may not attract portfolio investment, or foreign direct investment, since high domestic interest rates may be seen as leading to economic recession. Why would foreigners want to invest in a country heading for recession?

Third, even devaluation can carry potential dangers. Where domestic financial institutions and corporations have borrowed in foreign exchange and lent or invested in domestic currency, devaluation will weaken their balance sheets. In domestic currency terms, liabilities will increase relative to assets. Even assets may be less valuable if recession is likely and default risk rises. This is the so-called 'balance sheet effect' of devaluation, and, if significant, it implies that devaluation could result in severe problems for the domestic financial and corporate sectors and lead to economic recession.

So what is the right answer to the policy conundrum? The consensus would probably be that it is unwise to run counter to the conventional wisdom and go for fiscal and monetary expansion and no devaluation. However, the detractors from conventional wisdom are right to post warnings. These suggest that conventional policy responses have to be measured and balanced, and have to make allowance for the potentially negative effects of contractionary fiscal policy, rising interest rates and exchange rate devaluation. The consensus may also offer a more temperate assessment of the use of capital controls, not only to moderate capital inflows during a boom, but also to reduce capital outflows during a bust. Controls may offer a way of allowing domestic interest rates to better reflect the perceived needs of the domestic economy rather than to focus exclusively on trying to influence capital movements. Here, the impossible triad is broken in a way that permits monetary policy to pursue domestic objectives independently, at least to some degree. At the same time, there are problems with capital controls which suggest that they are not a long-term solution. Applying a tourniquet to staunch the flow of blood may allow the patient to arrive at the hospital alive, where appropriate longer-term treatment may be given, but it is not a cure in itself. Capital controls may help a country to get through a crisis, but they will not correct underlying economic problems.

The aftermath of crises will be affected by whether the fundamental problems that crises reflect are corrected. Have fiscal deficits been reduced? Has the domestic savings rate increased? Has the inflation rate declined? Has exchange rate policy been modified to allow more flexibility? Many of these things may take time to resolve. In the short term, the aftermath of the crisis will reflect whether policy-makers opted for an appropriate blend of policy as a response to the crisis. With fiscal overkill, excessively high interest rates, and significant balance sheet effects associated with devaluation, it may involve significant recession. This in turn will imply current account balance of payments surpluses. With more tempered macroeconomic policies, and with a strong trade response to devaluation resulting from relatively high foreign trade price elasticities, economic recession may be avoided or at least short-lived.

Currency crises in the form in which they occurred in the 1990s and 2000s are a phenomenon we are still seeking to understand with a view to reducing their future incidence and increasing our ability to deal with them when they do occur. It would be unwise to assume that a run of a few years without a crisis implies that international macroeconomics has answered satisfactorily all the questions to which crises give rise.

Part II

Policy

7 Balance of Payments Policy

Introduction

In Part I of this book we examined a range of theories that seek to explain why balance of payments disequilibria occur. We also sought to better understand what it is that determines exchange rates, and why currency and financial crises happen. In this part of the book we focus on policy. Chapter 8 discusses the choices of stabilisation policy in an open economy, concentrating in particular on the use of monetary and fiscal policy. Chapter 9 focuses on exchange-rate policy and the choice of exchange-rate regime. Finally, Chapter 10 examines the policy problems associated with capital volatility and how best to try to overcome them.

The coverage of these forthcoming chapters leaves to one side a series of other policy issues relating to the balance of payments. Should countries attempt to eliminate current account balance of payments deficits, or should they instead opt to finance them? Does commercial policy offer a feasible approach to correcting current account deficits? Is structural adjustment based on increasing aggregate domestic supply a superior approach to one based on managing aggregate domestic demand? And on the basis of what criteria do governments choose between alternative balance of payments strategies, and how much discretion do they have in their choice? This chapter touches briefly on these questions.

To Adjust or to Finance?

Faced with a current account balance of payments deficit, countries in effect have two options. One is to finance it by international borrowing or by running down foreign exchange reserves; while the other is to eliminate it by pursuing adjustment policies that increase exports or reduce imports. Since it is unlikely that a country will be able to finance its deficits in perpetuity, there is a trade-off between financing and the speed or timing of adjustment. The contemporary financing of current account deficits therefore represents postponed adjustment. However, assuming that the current account does not change for other reasons, contemporary financing implies that a larger amount of adjustment will be required in the future in order to release resources to repay creditors the finance that has been borrowed.

The theory behind the optimum combination of external financing and adjustment is relatively straightforward. Countries will tend to choose a financing-intensive strategy where the deficit is temporary and self-correcting, where the cost of financing is low relative to the cost of contemporary adjustment (both in economic and political terms), and where there is a high social discount rate. In the latter case, the costs of future adjustment will be heavily discounted. From a political point of view, governments will be under considerable pressure to finance current account deficits since this allows them to maintain contemporary living standards at a higher level than if they opted for contemporary adjustment. Governments may be expected to try to defer the costs of adjustment to some time in the future – preferably as far as possible in the future, or at least until after the next election.

A number of problems crop up when we move from the theory just described to the practice. First, it is extremely difficult to judge at the time whether a deficit is temporary or likely to be more lasting. For example, does a fall in the price of a country's major export represent a permanent deterioration in its terms of trade, or merely a short-term blip? Second, the costs of financing and adjustment cannot easily be measured. Indeed, it is probably not possible to measure them objectively at all. On the financing side, the nominal rate of interest on loans may be relatively straightforward, but what about the real rate, and what will happen to the value of the currency in which the debt is denominated? Furthermore, creditors may seek to impose conditions relating to economic policy that erode national sovereignty. To what extent is this a cost? On the adjustment side, reducing a current account deficit in the short term will involve a cost in terms of sacrificed domestic consumption; but what will the political costs of this be to the government? Third, it is notoriously difficult to calculate social discount rates. To what extent will a society prefer consumption now compared to consumption in the future?

The list of problems does not end here. There may be binding constraints on a government's freedom to choose its balance of payments strategy. Many countries may have impaired access to international capital markets, or low levels of reserves. The external financing constraint they encounter then dictates the speed at which the deficit needs to be eliminated. Or creditors, in the form of aid donors or the IMF and World Bank, may only provide financial assistance if a specific programme of economic adjustment is put in place. Again, governments effectively may have little discretion. In this sense, financing is not a substitute for, but rather a complement to, adjustment. Governments may also face constraints in terms of the amount of contemporary adjustment that is politically feasible. Why would they put in place a balance of payments strategy that maximises the probability of their own political demise? For these reasons, nobody should claim that designing balance of payments policy is easy. But it gets more complicated. If a government favours external financing, from which source should the finance come, given the available options? For example, is it better for a sovereign government to borrow short-term from international banks, or to issue long-term bonds? If the government intends there to be a measure of economic adjustment to reduce the deficit, which adjustment policies, or combination of them, should be selected? Easy answers to these questions do not exist. Balance of payments policy is therefore a matter of judgement.

What Does Adjustment Involve?

In almost all cases it is likely that the selected balance of payments strategy will involve some degree of economic adjustment. What does this have to achieve? One simple way of answering this question is to point out that it needs to remedy the underlying causes of the deficit, as described in Chapter 4. This may entail reducing domestic absorption, eliminating excess domestic monetary growth or correcting structural shortcomings. Policy instruments may then be judged in terms of their efficiency in delivering these outcomes.

Alternatively, and traditionally, balance of payments policies have been classified as having expenditure-switching or expenditure-changing effects. Expenditure-switching policies set out to encourage people to switch the pattern of their expenditure in such a way that exports go up and imports go down. There are different policy instruments through which the switch may be brought about. Some, such as devaluation or commercial policy, attempt to bring it about by changing the structure of relative prices; for example, by raising domestic currency import prices or reducing foreign currency export prices. These policies set out to induce people to reorganise their expenditure. Other switching policies may be more direct in their approach. These include quantitative restrictions on imports through quotas or import licensing, or foreign exchange controls. They do not rely on the effectiveness of changing incentives via the structure of relative prices.

A danger with expenditure-switching policies is that, by increasing the demand for domestically produced goods and services, they may lead to accelerating inflation that reduces the incentive to switch expenditure. For this reason it has conventionally been suggested that expenditure-switching policies will be more effective when there is spare productive capacity, or where they are accompanied by policies designed to create spare productive capacity.

Expenditure-changing policies – expenditure-reducing in the case of current account balance of payments deficits – are the logical policy consequence of both the absorption and monetary approaches to the balance of payments. In the case of the absorption approach, the objective of the policy is to reduce domestic expenditure comprising consumption, investment and government expenditure. However, given that these components are likely to have different import intensities – with, for example, the import intensity of private sector consumption generally being higher than that of government expenditure – the composition of the total expenditure reduction will be important. In the case of the monetary approach, expenditure reduction will instead focus on reducing monetary demand by means of contractionary monetary policy.

Balance of payments policy may, in principle, not be limited to manipulating domestic expenditure. After all, the balance of payments reflects the difference between domestic output and domestic expenditure. It follows, therefore, that policy may instead involve seeking to increase domestic output. There is a supply-side approach to the balance of payments as well as a demand-side approach. Indeed, a moment's thought tells us that this is an attractive alternative. The proposition is that the balance of payments is strengthened via economic growth. There is adjustment with growth. Additional exports are created not by a country's nationals giving up some of their former consumption, but by producing more goods and services. There is still an opportunity cost to reduce the current account deficit but it is now in terms of sacrificing the chance of higher levels of consumption. Politically this is an alluring proposition. It may be feasible, as well as being alluring, where the economy has spare productive potential that may be utilised relatively easily. But if the economy is already on its production possibility frontier it becomes trickier, since the frontier now needs to shift outwards.

Since the chapters that follow have a good deal to say about monetary and fiscal policy, as well as exchange-rate policy, this chapter moves on to briefly discuss expenditure-switching policies that do not involve altering the exchange rate, and about structural adjustment policies that set out to increase domestic output. The treatment will be perfunctory, since the focus of this book is on international macroeconomics and not on trade and economic liberalisation.

Commercial Policy and the Balance of Payments

A country's own nationals as well as foreigners may be persuaded to switch the pattern of their expenditure by altering the relative prices of internationally traded goods or by imposing direct restrictions of some sort on imports. Tariffs will tend to raise the price of imports, subsidies can be used to reduce the price of exports, and quantitative restrictions such as quotas will limit *directly* the quantity of imports (rather than working via the intermediation of prices); although a restricted import supply will then affect the domestic currency price of imports.

In one sense, import tariffs and export subsidies may be used to *simulate fiscally* the effects of devaluation, which also tends to increase domestic currency import prices and reduce foreign currency export prices (see Chapter 9). However, whereas devaluation will affect all such import prices and export prices irrespective of the price elasticity of demand for the goods and services concerned, tariffs and subsidies may, in principle, be targeted specifically on those imports and exports that have a relatively high price elasticity. In these circumstances, commercial policy appears to be more subtle and discriminatory, and able to have a greater impact on the current account. But if tariffs are put on imports for which demand is price inelastic, their impact on the balance of payments will be more muted. The imports will still be demanded, but at a higher price, and this will have consequences for the domestic price level and inflation, undermining competitiveness. Of course, by the same token, in these circumstances, the tariff will be an effective mechanism for generating tax revenue. Many developing countries have been attracted to the use of tariffs primarily as a source of tax revenue that is difficult to raise in other ways.

Again in principle, and with an 'all-knowing' government, the fiscal simulation of devaluation could be an initially appealing balance of payments strategy. But what do we mean by 'all-knowing'? The government will need to know the values of the price elasticities of demand for individual imports and exports. It will need to know which imports are important from the point of view of maximising future domestic economic growth and development. Some imports will be significant inputs for exporters. Pushing up the price of these imported inputs may therefore reduce the future competitiveness of exports as the higher price of imports is passed on to final consumers, and this will do little for the balance of payments. Given this interpretation of 'all-knowing', it is highly improbable that any government will know all, or even perhaps enough.

There are other issues associated with commercial policy from the point of view of the balance of payments – apart from the welfare issues that we do not investigate here. A complex system of tariffs, subsidies and quotas that seeks to use different rates of tariff and subsidy according to different demand and supply elasticities, is likely to be highly bureaucratic. It will be administratively expensive to operate and open to rent-seeking activity and corruption, which in turn have adverse macroeconomic consequences. Price changes associated with tariffs, and the additional profitability of exporting that will be associated with subsidies, may fail to induce the behavioural responses that they would if they had been the result of an outright devaluation, since they may be regarded as temporary and reversible. If tariffs fail to raise tax revenue because they effectively reduce the demand for imports, while subsidies increase government expenditure, commercial policy will have a net adverse effect on the fiscal balance, and this may in turn weaken the current account of the balance of payments.

Additionally, import controls will only suppress rather than cure current account balance of payments problems by frustrating the demand to import. By allowing an overvalued exchange rate to be maintained, they discriminate against exports. Finally, of course, most governments will be members of the World Trade Organization, and perhaps signatories to regional trade agreements, and this will constrain their ability to use commercial policy as a way of affecting their balance of payments. For this reason, this section has been brief. Readers interested in trade policy will need to consult an international economics textbook that deals more fully with the topic.

Structural Adjustment and the Supply Side

In principle, structural adjustment makes a great deal of sense. Where countries encounter balance of payments problems, because they concentrate on exporting goods that have a low income elasticity of demand or produce exports less efficiently than their competitors, it is wise to diversify and become more efficient. In terms of the familiar current account equation:

$$X - M = Y - (C + I + G)$$

how much better it is to increase Y than to depress $(C + I + G)$. It almost seems to be a 'no-brainer' that governments should opt for structural adjustment. The problems emerge when a supply-side strategy is examined in more detail. First, there is a problem of timing. Increasing Y is not something that can be achieved quickly unless there is spare productive capacity that can be easily used. This means that structural adjustment needs to be complemented by short-to-medium term external finance in order to cover the current account deficits that will take time to eliminate. Second, it is generally accepted that investment plays a key role in encouraging economic growth. So, for future period Y to increase, current period I may also have to increase. But, for firms to invest, consumption may have to be buoyant, and complementary government expenditures on infrastructure may be needed.[1] This implies that $(C + I + G)$ needs to increase. But at current output levels this will make the current account deficit bigger. Even if increasing consumption was not needed to encourage investment, and even if a government could protect its capital expenditure by cutting current expenditure, there are still problems. Will a government that is anxious to maintain power want to cut consumption as well as its expenditure on subsidies, welfare payments and the wages of public sector employees? Probably not.

Big as these problems are, there is a bigger one, at which we have so far only hinted. The question is, which policies will bring about a faster rate of economic growth and lead to expanding domestic output? Will trade liberalisation help? Is liberalisation of the financial sector important? Does industrial structure need to be changed to introduce more private ownership and greater competition? What is the most appropriate relationship between the market and the state? These are fundamental questions when it comes to discussing structural adjustment, but they remain difficult to answer. There is considerable debate among economists (and others) about them, and the available evidence leaves sufficient ambiguity to make resolving them difficult. We shall not pursue the issues further here. The basic point for us is that, as attractive as the notion of structural adjustment is, it does not provide clear guidance on the design of balance of payments policy. Indeed, in many ways it raises more questions than it answers. Even 'market fundamentalists' or strong believers in 'neoliberalism' would probably be reluctant to argue that the related policies they favour offer a quick and easy solution to balance of payments problems. In the remainder of this book we focus more narrowly on policy instruments designed to bring about short-term macroeconomic stabilisation (monetary and fiscal policy), and exchange-rate policy. Indeed, the next two chapters move on to examine precisely these issues. However, before ending this chapter there are two other issues to examine briefly. What determines the choice of balance of payments policy; and are there differences between a national and a global perspective?

Choosing a Balance of Payments Policy: The Political Economy Dimension

It will be governments that choose balance of payments policy; and governments are concerned about politics as well as economics. In general terms, they will want a policy that is both effective and efficient. In other words, if their aim is to reduce a current account deficit they will need a policy that will deliver this outcome. However, they will also have other policy objectives, such as avoiding high levels of unemployment and maintaining satisfactory rates of economic growth. A government will therefore favour a policy that, in addition to being effective in terms of the balance of payments, inflicts minimum damage on these other policy objectives. There may be a presumption that a policy will be more efficient if it tackles the root cause of the problem. If, for example, the current account deficit has been caused by excessive government expenditure relative to tax revenue, it is unlikely to be efficiently resolved by (say) exchange rate devaluation. The devaluation may provide temporary help, but over time the balance of payments problems will tend to re-emerge.

Governments will also be concerned about the distributional consequences of policies, who gains and who loses, and about the timing of the effects of a policy. They will not want to impose costs on groups on whose support they depend in order to maintain power. And, generally speaking, they will prefer a combination of short-term benefits and long-term costs over one that involves short-term costs and only long-term benefits.

It is the politics of balance of payments policy that may lead to disagreements between governments and international financial institutions (IFIs). There may be little difference of opinion on the need for improved balance of payments performance or on the range of alternative policies, but the political neutrality of IFIs may lead them to favour a different strategy from the one favoured by incumbent governments. Much of the debate about balance of payments policy will therefore not reflect technical disagreements – although some of it will – but more likely political economy issues. This will be the case in spite of the fact that the political economy issues may be hidden beneath a cosmetic layer of technical disagreement.

Policy at National and Global Levels

Up to now, this chapter has discussed balance of payments policy from a national perspective, and indeed most of what follows in this part of the book does the same. But there is an important global dimension to balance of payments policy. This has at least three elements to it.

First, policies adopted in one country will have *spillover effects* for other countries. There will be externalities. If one country succeeds in switching expenditure towards the goods and services it produces, it will be switching it away from goods and services produced by other countries. Similarly, if a country pursues contractionary policies to reduce expenditure, its demand for imports will fall, and these goods will be other countries' exports. While a national government may reasonably consider the implications of its policies on its own nationals and its own policy objectives, a justification for international agencies – and in particular the IMF – is to try to internalise these externalities in the decision-making about balance of payments policy.

A second element to the global dimension is that, in giving advice to individual countries, IFIs may encounter *a fallacy of composition*. What may work for one country in isolation may not work for a group of countries. For example, a combination of exchange rate devaluation and the compression of aggregate demand in one country may increase its exports and reduce its imports. But what if other countries are also seeking to reduce the international value of their currencies and to depress domestic demand? The first country will then find that the additional competitiveness associated with its devaluation will be neutralised. It will also find that its exports are affected adversely by the reduced levels of aggregate demand in the countries in which it is trying to sell them.

A final global element is associated with the observation that the global balance of payments is a *zero sum game*. Although errors in reporting may not show it empirically, in principle, current account deficits in one part of the world will be matched by equivalent surpluses elsewhere. This means that balance of payments policy in one country may be frustrated by policies being pursued in others. It will, for example, be much more difficult for a country to reduce its deficit if other countries are not prepared to see their current accounts weaken. Measures to make exports more attractive will be ineffective if the countries importing these goods and services pursue policies to reduce their demand for imports. It is this global dimension that may lead to international tensions. Much depends on whether the balance of payments objectives of countries are compatible. It will be feasible for one country to run a deficit if others are prepared to run the accommodating surpluses. But if not, balance of payments policy may become internationally competitive. Where countries resort to protectionism and demand deflation, global economic performance will be adversely affected. There may be circumstances in which balance of payments policy needs to be co-ordinated internationally, and we shall discuss this in more detail in Chapter 11.

8 Stabilisation Policy in an Open Economy

Introduction

The question to be tackled in this chapter relates to how macro-economic policies may be organised to achieve their principal object-ives. An approved way of approaching this question is, first, to describe the targets that the policy-making authorities are setting out to achieve; second, to describe the policy instruments through which attempts are made to realise these targets; and third, to analyse how the instruments may be combined in the most efficient fashion.

What emerges is that very much depends on the macroeconomic environment in which policy is being formulated. Different answers are derived according to the degree of exchange-rate flexibility and capital mobility. We attempt in this chapter to work our way through the approach outlined above and to reach conclusions on the basis of different sets of assumptions.

The chapter focuses on the use of monetary and fiscal policy with Chapter 9 turning attention to exchange rate policy.

Targets

One way of summarising targets is to say that the authorities hope to achieve both internal and external balance within the economy. This, of course, immediately begs the question of what is meant by internal and external balance. Candidates for internal balance include full employ-ment, price stability, economic growth, a specific distribution of income and an acceptable physical environment.

A list of this nature, however, generates a series of questions. What do we mean by the terms used, and is it always reasonable to assume that economic welfare is negatively related to unemployment and inflation and positively relatively to economic growth and (say) the degree of income equality? There are notorious difficulties associated with defining unemployment, inflation, economic growth, income distribution, and the quality of the environment. It is also possible to make out an argument that on occasions unemployment and inflation may be good things and economic growth and income equality bad things.[1]

Problems do not come to an end even if agreement can be reached on definitions and on what is good and what is bad. For now we need to recognise that there may be trade-offs between different internal targets. Coming closer to realising one may involve moving further away from realising another. We need to allow for such incompatibilities and to formulate a list of priorities, attaching different weights to different policy objectives.

The problems are no fewer when we turn to external balance. Starting with a definition that there is external balance when there is equilibrium in the foreign exchange market, this implies that the authorities are indifferent as to the composition of the balance of payments. It implies more specifically that they do not have any target for the current account. Moreover, if instead it is assumed that they do set out to achieve equilibrium in the current account, this may at first sight seem to neglect the fact that a current-account deficit may imply a net inflow of goods and services which, in the short run at least, raises the domestic standard of living. The problem with deficits lies in financing them rather than in the deficits themselves. Current account deficits only become a problem when they are unsustainable.

Combining internal and external objectives into a single welfare function leads to yet further problems because it is quite likely that to get closer to internal balance implies moving further away from external balance and vice versa.

Having pointed to some of the problems involved with discussing targets we shall ignore most of them in what follows and will make the simplifying assumption that governments possess fixed policy targets of full employment and overall balance of payments equilibrium. However, we need to bear in mind the simplifying nature of this assumption.[2]

Instruments

Given that we have now defined the government's policy targets, the next question is whether there is a mechanism that will automatically bring them about or whether the government will need to undertake some positive policy action. Much depends here on the underlying macroeconomic model that is assumed to operate. Under classical macro-economic analysis both full employment and payments equilibrium are assured through Say's Law and the gold standard mechanism respect-ively.[3] Under a Keynesian model, on the other hand, it is quite possible, and indeed likely, that macroeconomic equilibrium, defined as a point where both planned investment in the economy is equal to planned saving and the demand for money is equal to the supply of money, will coincide with unemployment and payments imbalance.

In a new classical framework the economy will tend to equilibrate at the 'natural' rate of unemployment and output, while new Keynesians envisage a role for stabilisation policy at least in the short run. In the context of the balance of payments, and for an economy with good access to international capital markets, a current account deficit is sus-tainable and is not a problem. It simply reflects a national preference for current consumption and an intertemporal redistribution of con-sumption towards the present and away from the future. Future saving will then correct the current account deficit and generate the resources necessary to repay the external debt that has been accumulated. In this context current account deficits enhance national welfare, allowing countries to choose when they consume and when they save. Of course not all countries have equivalent access to international capital. For those that are liquidity-constrained current account deficits will be unsustainable and policy action will be needed. But what policy instru-ments are available to the authorities in trying to reach their targets?

Again, and as was the case with targets, there are problems in dis-cussing instruments. First, there is the problem of classification. For example, is the rate of interest a policy instrument or is it the supply of money? Second, there is the problem of the level of aggregation to be used. Is fiscal policy one instrument or should it be broken down into the level of government expenditure, the structure of government expenditure, the level of taxation, the structure of taxation and so on. Third, there is the problem of whether the government can actually control its policy instruments and whether the instruments are effec-tive. There may be a range of technical, political, legal and institutional problems in actually implementing policy. Such instances occur where policies to control the money supply are frustrated by induced changes in the velocity of circulation, or where changes in monetary and fiscal policy only have their impact after a long and variable lag. Finally, instruments may be interrelated and not independent. A certain fiscal stance is, for example, likely to have monetary repercussions.

As will be seen later, the analysis of stabilisation policy tends to ignore, or at least understate, these problems, and therefore gives an artificial impression of the ease with which policy may be implemented. In the real world life is rather more complicated than the model suggests.

Matching Targets and Instruments

In trying to provide some ground rules for the formation of stabilisation policy, the 'Tinbergen rule' has established that in order to achieve a certain number of targets simultaneously governments need an equivalent number of effective and independent instruments.[4] In a slightly weaker form the rule states that there should be at least as many instruments as targets, although in these circumstances there is no unique policy solution.

A Model of the Assignment Problem

In addition to having enough instruments, it is also argued that each instrument should be directed towards the target upon which it has relatively greatest impact. In other words, policies have to be used efficiently. This idea Mundell called 'the principle of effective market classification'.[5]

With this principle in mind, the design of stabilisation policy may be discussed in the context of Figure 8.1. According to this figure there are two targets, full employment (or internal balance, *IB*) and balance of payments equilibrium (or external balance, *EB*) and two instruments,

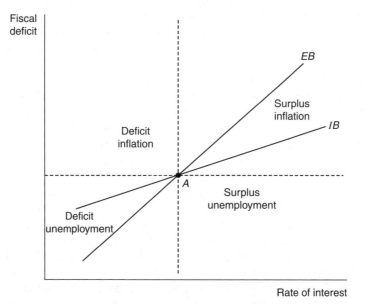

Figure 8.1

monetary policy, as reflected by the rate of interest, and fiscal policy, as reflected by the size of the fiscal deficit. *IB* shows the combinations of interest rate and fiscal deficit that give full employment. It slopes upwards to the right since an increase in the rate of interest has a deflationary effect on the economy unless it is matched by an increase in the fiscal deficit. Above *IB* inflation occurs because, for any given interest rate the fiscal deficit is larger than that required to give full employment, or, for any given deficit, the rate of interest is lower. Below *IB* there is unemployment.

EB shows the combinations of interest-rate and fiscal deficit that give balance of payments equilibrium. It too slopes upwards to the right since an increasing fiscal deficit, which causes the current account to deteriorate, has to be matched by an increase in the rate of interest in order to generate an offsetting capital inflow. Above *EB*, for any given rate of interest the fiscal deficit is too large to give payments equilibrium and there is a payments deficit. Similarly, for any given fiscal deficit the rate of interest is too low. Below *EB* there will be a payments surplus. Because of the additional impact that monetary policy has on the balance of payments *EB* is assumed to be steeper than *IB*.

Point *A*, where *IB* and *EB* intersect, dictates the stance of fiscal policy and monetary policy required to hit simultaneously the twin targets of full employment and payments equilibrium.

A number of features of this figure are noteworthy. First, along either the horizontal or vertical lines through *A* it is necessary to alter only one policy instrument. If we are on the horizontal line fiscal policy is appropriate but monetary policy is inappropriate. If we are on the vertical line then it is fiscal policy that is inappropriate and has to be changed.

Second, in other areas of the figure both instruments are inappropriate and will need to be changed. In the top left-hand quarter both fiscal and monetary policy need to be contractionary. In the bottom right-hand quarter they both need to be expansionary. In the top right-hand quarter fiscal policy needs to be contractionary but monetary policy expansionary. While in the bottom left-hand quarter fiscal policy has to be expansionary and monetary policy contractionary.

Third, as shown by Figure 8.2, starting from a position other than point *A*, the sequential use of fiscal policy to achieve full employment and monetary policy to achieve payments equilibrium will move the economy towards point *A*. Using fiscal policy for external balance and monetary policy for internal balance will, however, move the economy away from point *A*. The principle of effective market classification seems to imply that fiscal policy is best directed at hitting the internal target and monetary policy at hitting the external one. The model implies that compliance with this principle ensures that full internal and external balance can relatively easily be attained.

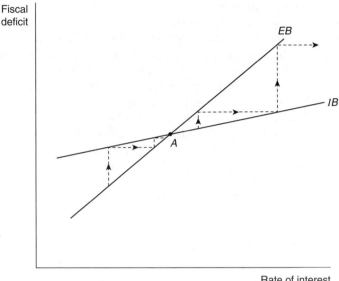

Figure 8.2

Criticisms of the Model

The above analysis, for all its apparent ease and simplicity, rests on a number of restrictive assumptions. These need to be spelt out.

First, the model is based on capital *flows*. Once an interest-rate differential has been opened up it is assumed that capital will continue to move into the country where the interest rate has risen. With a stock adjustment model, on the other hand, the capital movement will be temporary. Indeed, in the long run an increase in interest rates may cause the balance of payments to deteriorate as higher ongoing debt service payments weaken the current account and as worries about creditworthiness reduce the inflow of new capital.

Second, it is assumed that an increase in interest rates in one country will not generate a competitive reaction abroad and will therefore create a differential. In the real world, changes in interest rate policy in one country may induce changes elsewhere.

Third, it is assumed that *EB* slopes upwards to the right. If fiscal expansion in fact leads to an increase in the demand for money and an increase in the rate of interest, then the stance of monetary policy required depends on the relative strengths of the effects of fiscal policy on the current and capital accounts. If the current account weakens by less than the capital account strengthens, expansionary fiscal policy will have to be matched by expansionary monetary policy and *EB* will slope downwards from left to right.

Fourth, the impact of fiscal policy is assumed to be perfectly proxied by the size of the fiscal deficit. Balanced budget analysis shows that the size of the budget is also important, as is the composition of the budget as between government expenditure on goods and transfers and as between direct and indirect taxation.[6]

Fifth, the model allows current-account deficits to be permanently financed. In the real world, the elimination of the deficit on the current account will almost certainly be required eventually.

Sixth, as noted earlier, the model is based on fixed targets. No allowance is made for a more broadly based welfare function with flexible targets and trade-offs between targets. In the real world, governments may respond asymmetrically to different states of disequilibrium, not perhaps being equally concerned about unemployment and inflation, or payments surpluses and deficits.

Seventh, the model assumes an elementary explanation of inflation and unemployment in terms of the level of aggregate demand relative to aggregate supply. Inflation reflects excess demand, unemployment deficient demand.[7]

Eighth, the model assumes that policy may be used to fine tune the economy. Policy is seen as flexible and fluid. In the real world, it may be much more inflexible than the model suggests. Policy may be constrained in various ways ignored by the model.

Finally, the prescriptions that emerge from the model rest heavily on the assumption that exchange rates are fixed. In such an environment an attempt to raise output by monetary expansion will be self-defeating as the falling interest rate causes a capital outflow and a fall in the domestic money supply. Meanwhile, expansionary fiscal policy will induce an increase in the rate of interest and a capital inflow which will endorse the fiscal expansion. With flexible exchange rates, on the other hand, monetary expansion will result in exchange-rate depreciation, an improvement in the current account and further expansion, whereas fiscal expansion may cause the exchange rate to appreciate, which has a contractionary effect on aggregate demand. In these circumstances monetary policy seems to be better suited than fiscal policy to achieving internal balance, and the prescription emerging from the fixed exchange-rate model is reversed.

Policy Analysis Within the *IS–LM–BP* Model: With Fixed Exchange Rates

The analysis undertaken above may be reinterpreted in terms of the *IS–LM–BP* model constructed in Chapter 2. The object of the policy

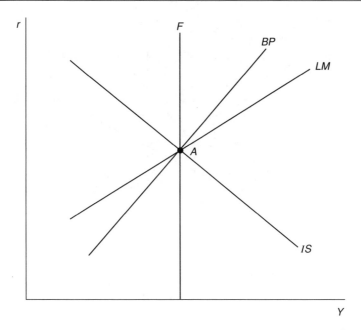

Figure 8.3

exercise is to achieve a situation as represented by point A in Figure 8.3, where the economy is in macroeconomic equilibrium at a point which coincides with both full employment and payments equilibrium.

But what if the economy is not in this happy state of affairs? Say it is at point A in Figure 8.4 where there is unemployment (Y^e is to the left of Y^f) and a payments deficit (r^e is below r^b). The question is, 'how should policy be modified?'

Where the prior policy objective is to obtain payments equilibrium, restrictive monetary policy, which in any case will tend to be caused by the reduction in the money supply associated with the payments deficit, will be more efficient than restrictive fiscal policy in terms of minimising lost output; compare the respective reductions in Y involved with a leftward shift in LM to LM^1 and a leftward shift in IS to IS^1. Where, on the other hand, the prior objective is full employment, then expansionary fiscal policy is preferable to expansionary monetary policy on the grounds that it minimises the related payments deficit; compare the rightward shift in IS to IS^2, with the rightward shift in LM to LM^2.[8]

In fact, as noted above, policy-makers will want to achieve both targets simultaneously. This desire may be fulfilled by using the appropriate blend of fiscal and monetary policy. In the circumstances described previously the appropriate blend is fiscal expansion, directed at removing

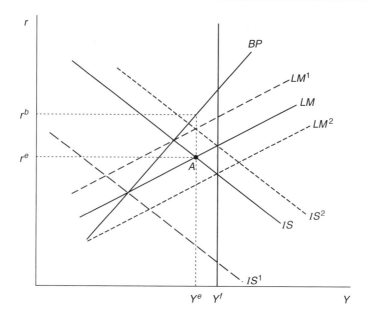

Figure 8.4

unemployment, and monetary contraction, directed at correcting the balance of payments deficit. Figure 8.5 illustrates this assignment of policies.

Let us examine a different starting point. The economy is experiencing inflation and a payments surplus. This is illustrated in Figure 8.6. Here the appropriate policy mix, assuming fixed exchange rates, is monetary expansion (LM to LM^1) and fiscal contraction (IS to IS^1). In fact there will be pressures which automatically push in these directions. The payments surplus will increase the domestic money supply, although against this inflation will increase the nominal demand for money. Meanwhile, inflation will also erode real balances thus causing increased saving and reduced expenditure. Finally, inflation will also cause the real exchange rate to appreciate, if there is no change in the nominal rate, and this appreciation will tend to shift IS to the left.

The two economic situations discussed above require a balancing of either fiscal expansion with monetary contraction or monetary expansion with fiscal contraction. As established earlier, situations do exist where instruments are called upon to work in the same direction. In the case of unemployment and a payments surplus, illustrated in Figure 8.7, the appropriate policy mix involves both fiscal and monetary expansion. With inflation and a payments deficit, uniformly contractionary policy is required.

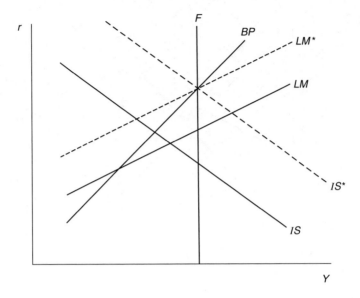

Figure 8.5

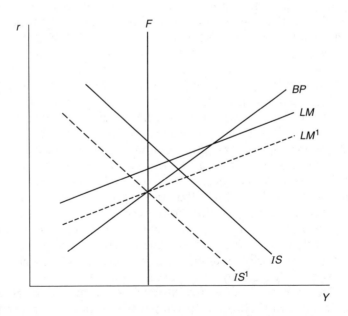

Figure 8.6

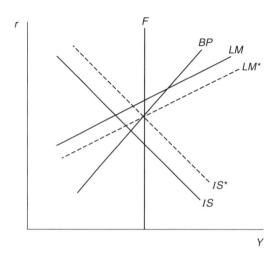

Figure 8.7

Furthermore, there may be cases where only one instrument needs to be used. These will occur where either *IS* or *LM* intersect the point where *BP* and *F* cross. If *IS* goes through such a point then only LM has to be shifted, whereas if *LM* goes through it only *IS* has to shift.

Neat as this presentation of the policy mix is, it is subject to a number of weaknesses and limitations. Many of these relate to the problems associated with the *IS–LM* model itself and need not detain us here.[9] Another weakness relates to the way in which the *BP* schedule has been drawn, again this need not detain us since we have discussed the issue in Chapter 2. What we can comment on is the assumption of the model that only *IS* and *LM* may be shifted; that is, the only policy instruments are fiscal and monetary policy. Full employment output is taken as given. There is therefore no analysis of aggregate supply and no presumption that the authorities may be able to shift the location of *F*.[10] Perhaps even more central to our analysis, we have assumed up to now that *BP* cannot be shifted. We have done this by assuming fixed exchange rates. However, even with fixed exchange rates, the authorities may still be able to shift *BP* by other policies which work on the current or capital accounts. Any policies that raise competitiveness or frustrate imports through controls will increase exports relative to imports, while policies designed to enhance creditworthiness will tend to increase capital inflows at given interest rates. Where the authorities can use such policies they now possess more than two instruments with which to achieve their two basic targets. Either they can decide to abandon one of their other instruments in order to restore the two instrument case, or they can select from a wider range of policy mixes.

The most conventional way of shifting *BP*, however, is to alter the exchange rate, and it is to an examination of how the repercussions of fiscal and monetary policy change when exchange rates are fully flexible that we turn in the next section.

Policy Analysis Within the *IS–LM–BP* Model: With Flexible Exchange Rates

Having seen how the *IS–LM–BP* model may be used to analyse stabilisation policy in the context of fixed exchange rates, let us now move on to examine how things change if we have flexible rates. On the basis of our earlier discussions we should be able to show how the original prescriptions, confirmed in the previous section, break down with flexible exchange rates.

To make the analysis easier let us assume, first, that domestic prices are constant so that movements in the nominal exchange rate imply similar movements in the real rate. Second, that expectations do not have a role in explaining exchange-rate movements. Third, that adjustment is instantaneous, meaning that holdings of international reserves are constant and that the domestic money supply only changes because of changes in domestic credit creation. Fourth, that there is no attempt by the authorities to manage the exchange rate. And fifth, that capital is mobile and that capital movements are in the nature of flows.

Against the background of these assumptions let us see how fiscal policy might operate.

Fiscal Policy

Let us start with Figure 8.8 and assume that the economy is initially located at point *A*. Fiscal expansion causes IS^1 to shift to the right to IS^2. As a result the rate of interest increases, there is a capital inflow and the exchange rate appreciates; that is, *BP* shifts upwards to BP^2. However, the exchange-rate appreciation, because of its adverse affect on the trade balance, causes *IS* to shift back to IS^3. At the final equilibrium, point *B*, both the level of income and the rate of interest have risen. The precise impact of the rightward shift in *IS* may be seen to depend on the shape of *LM* and the sensitivity of capital flows to interest rates, since these factors influence the extent to which the balance of payments (BoP) moves into surplus and the extent therefore of the exchange-rate appreciation.

Remember that with fixed exchange rates and capital mobility, the capital inflow would have resulted not in an exchange-rate appreciation

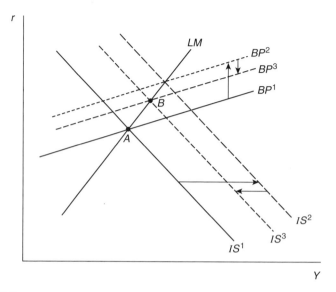

Figure 8.8

but rather an increase in the money supply and a rightward shift in
LM. In this case the increase in income would have been greater and
the increase in the interest rate less.

The conclusion seems to emerge that with capital mobility the effect
of fiscal policy on output and employment is less where exchange
rates are flexible than where they are fixed, since an appreciation in
the exchange rate is induced which has a dampening influence on
demand.

But let us pursue this question further by assuming that BP is
steeper, i.e. there is a lower degree of capital mobility, and that LM is
flatter, such that LM is less steep than BP. This state of affairs is illustrated in Figure 8.9.

From the initial situation of equilibrium, point A, fiscal expansion
shifts IS^1 to the right to IS^2. The rate of interest rises, although not as
much as before because LM is less steep, and the BoP moves into deficit
instead of into surplus. As a result, the exchange rate depreciates and
BP shifts downwards. The depreciation causes a further rightward shift
in IS to IS^3.

In this case fiscal policy seems to be a potent weapon for raising output and employment with the effect of the fiscal expansion on the
current account dominating its effect on the capital account.

As a general rule it would appear that the steeper LM, and the larger the
increase in the rate of interest associated with a given fiscal expansion;

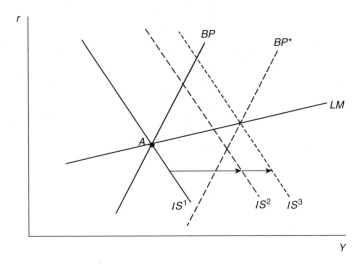

Figure 8.9

and the flatter *BP*, and the more interest elastic are capital flows, the more muted are the effects of fiscal policy. Whereas the flatter *LM*, and the smaller the increase in the rate of interest; and the steeper *BP* and the less interest-rate elastic are capital flows, the more powerful is the effect of fiscal policy on income and employment. The general rule may be further illustrated by looking at the two extreme cases of zero and perfect capital mobility.

In the case of *zero capital mobility*, illustrated in Figure 8.10, fiscal policy again has a potent effect on income and employment, since a rightward shift in *IS* leads to exchange-rate depreciation – there is no effect, by assumption, on the capital account – and a further right-ward shift in *IS*.

In the case of *perfect capital mobility*, the rightward shift in *IS* and the resulting rise in interest rates generates a capital inflow which is suffi-ciently great as to cause the exchange rate to appreciate just enough to reduce expenditure on exports and import substitutes by the same amount as the increase in government expenditure, thereby shifting *IS* back to its original location. The effects of fiscal expansion are com-pletely crowded out by the exchange-rate appreciation and there is no effect whatsoever on income or employment, see Figure 8.11. We can note in passing that with fixed exchange rates the capital inflow would not have resulted in exchange-rate appreciation but in an increase in the money supply. In these circumstances fiscal expansion is very powerful.

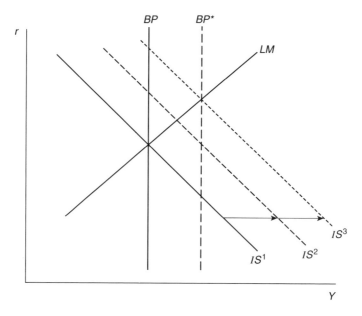

Figure 8.10

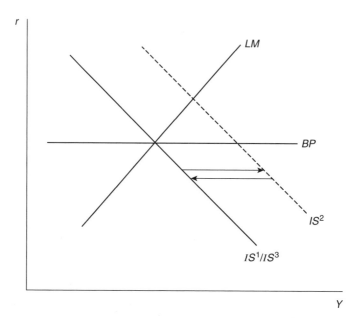

Figure 8.11

Monetary Policy

The effects of monetary policy are illustrated in Figure 8.12. Here, starting from point *A*, a rightward shift in *LM* leads to a fall in the rate of interest, a capital outflow, a rise in income, a BoP deficit and exchange-rate depreciation with *BP* shifting down to *BP*[1], which in turn shifts *IS* to the right. At the new point of equilibrium, *B*, income has risen and the rate of interest has fallen.

Had the exchange rate been fixed, the fall in the interest rate would have caused a capital outflow and an offsetting leftward shift in *LM* negating the impact of the original monetary expansion. The conclusion emerges that monetary policy has a powerful impact on income and employment under flexible exchange rates if capital is mobile, in contrast to the situation with fixed rates.

But do things change if *BP* is steeper than *LM*? In fact, as Figure 8.13 illustrates, in the case of monetary policy the relative slopes of *BP* and *LM* seem to matter little, and the same general conclusion emerges. Let us however look briefly at the special cases of zero and perfect capital mobility.

With *zero capital mobility*, as illustrated by Figure 8.14, we again find that monetary expansion has a powerful influence on output and employment, since the exchange-rate depreciation induced by the fall

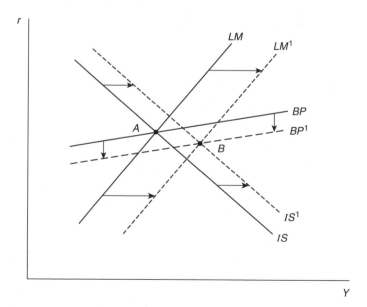

Figure 8.12

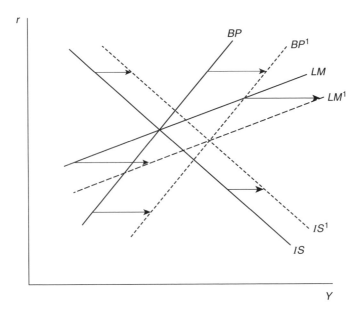

Figure 8.13

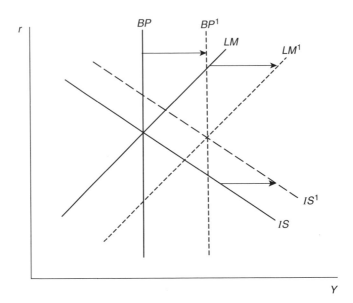

Figure 8.14

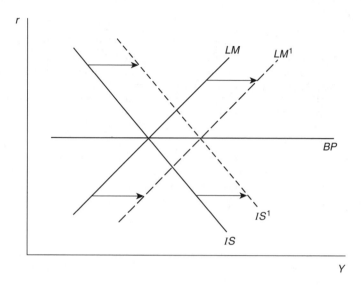

Figure 8.15

in the interest rate and the payments deficit associated with the rise in income shift IS to the right.

With *perfect capital mobility* shown in Figure 8.15 exchange-rate depreciation is, in addition, required to offset the capital outflow associated with the fall in the interest rate. This outcome contrasts sharply with the case of fixed exchange rates where the capital outflow causes a fall in the money supply and a leftward shift in *LM* which offsets the original monetary expansion.

It may be useful at this stage to summarise the conclusions we have reached about the effectiveness of fiscal and monetary policy as stabilisation tools under different exchange-rate regimes and assumptions concerning the degree of capital mobility. This is done in Table 8.1.

As with all economic models, however, we need to remember that the conclusions that emerge are likely to be only as strong as the assumptions upon which the models are based. In the case of the analysis undertaken above the restrictive assumptions should certainly not be forgotten.

If, for example, different assumptions are made about the determination of capital movements, allowing for stock adjustment, wealth effects, risk, and other influences; the role of expectations in causing movements in exchange rates; the effects of exchange-rate changes on the domestic economy; and inflation, it is possible to generate rather different conclusions from those reached above. Certainly, it is quite feasible that the long-run effects will be different from the short-run

Table 8.1

	Fixed exchange-rate capital mobile	Fixed exchange-rate capital immobile	Flexible exchange-rate capital mobile	Flexible exchange-rate capital immobile
Fiscal Policy	Effective (Monetary effect endorses fiscal effect)	Effective (But less so than in the case of capital mobility since there is no endorsing monetary flow)	Relatively ineffective (Completely ineffective with perfect capital mobility)	Very effective (Exchange-rate change endorses fiscal change)
Monetary policy	Relatively ineffective (Completely ineffective with perfect capital mobility)	Effective (Since there are no offsetting monetary flows)	Very effective (Exchange-rate change endorses monetary flows)	Effective (Exchange-rate change endorses monetary changes but exchange-rate change muted by lack of capital mobility)

effects. The conundrum is that as the assumptions become more realistic, assuming that we know what is more realistic, so it becomes progressively more difficult to reach clear-cut conclusions. If, indeed, diminishing returns to increasing sophistication rapidly set in there may be something to be said for sticking to the fairly basic analysis outlined above. Ideally one would wish to find robust conclusions that hold irrespective of the assumptions made, but at the present state of the art it is by no means clear if these exist.

Macroeconomic Interdependence: The Transmission of Policy Changes

Before leaving the analysis of stabilisation policy it is worth asking the question as to how changes in policy in one country are likely to affect other countries.

The conventional view is that, with fixed exchange rates, disturbances in one country spread abroad; disturbances are exported abroad and, indeed, imported from abroad. An increase in domestic aggregate demand leads to an increase in domestic imports and therefore foreign exports via both an income and a price effect. Also the accompanying current-account deficit implies an outflow of money which further reduces the domestic impact of the increase in demand and increases the extent to which the impact is felt abroad.

With flexible exchange rates it is the price variable (that is, the exchange rate), that changes and not the quantity variable (that is, the balance of payments). An increase in domestic aggregate demand results in a depreciation in the exchange rate. There are no money flows since the balance of payments is kept in equilibrium, and the domestic economy takes the full force of the domestic disturbance. Of course, by similar reasoning the domestic economy is protected or insulated from disturbances emanating abroad.

However, the foregoing analysis concentrates on the current account. What happens if instead we focus on the capital account and assume a relatively high degree of capital mobility? Much now depends on whether the disturbance originates from a change in fiscal or monetary policy because of the different effects they have on the rate of interest.

With fixed exchange rates fiscal expansion leads to an increase in the interest rate, a capital inflow and an increase in the domestic money supply. The effect on the domestic economy is enhanced and there is a contractionary effect abroad. Monetary expansion, on the other hand, leads to a fall in the interest rate, a capital outflow and a fall in the domestic money supply. The expansionary effect is felt abroad and not in the domestic economy.

Moving to flexible exchange rates we find that fiscal expansion with its associated rise in interest rates leads, via the induced capital inflow, to an exchange-rate appreciation. The stimulus is therefore felt abroad because of the relative depreciation in the value of foreign currencies. Monetary expansion, again in contrast, results in a fall in the interest rate, a capital outflow, and exchange-rate depreciation, which in turn generates a stimulus for the domestic economy and contraction abroad.

The above analysis suggests that the key question in trying to sort out the distribution of the effects of changes in the stance of domestic fiscal and monetary policy, as between the domestic economy and the rest of the world, relates to the relative significance of the current and capital account effects. Underlying these effects is the nature of trade functions and capital movements discussed in Chapter 3.

Appendix

In the main text of the chapter we have examined an approach to the analysis of stabilisation policy based on the *IS–LM–BP* model. In this appendix we examine another approach to the analysis of the appropriate policy mix that is frequently used.

The Swan Approach to Internal–External Balance[11]

This is illustrated in Figure 8A.1.

EB represents the combinations of cost ratio (the ratio of foreign prices to domestic prices) and real demand giving external balance. It slopes upwards to the right since an increase in internal demand leads to a deterioration in the balance of payments, unless the cost ratio improves adequately. *IB* likewise represents the combinations of cost ratio and real demand which generate full employment. *IB* slopes downwards to the right since as the cost ratio gets worse, and the value of exports therefore declines, domestic demand will have to compensate for this if full employment is to be maintained.

EB and *IB* divide the diagram into a number of regions. To the right of *EB* there will be a payments deficit since with a given cost ratio, domestic demand has expanded, whilst to the left of *EB* there will be a payments surplus. To the right of *IB* there will be inflation since again with a given cost ratio there is greater domestic demand, whilst to the left there will be unemployment.

The appropriate policy mix will not be determined by the region in which the economy is located but by the economy's location *within* a region. Drawing in the horizontal and vertical lines through the point of intersection between *IB* and *EB*, it may be seen that whereas, for example, both point *M* and point *N* indicate a deficit and unemployment, at *M* the appropriate policy is an improvement in the cost ratio and an increase in real demand, while at point *N* it is an improvement

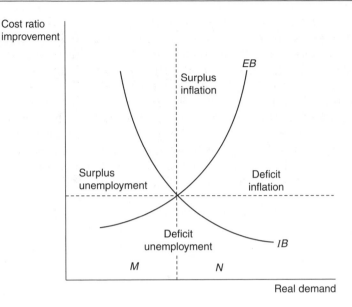

Figure 8.A1

in the cost ratio and a decrease in real demand. Swan thus demonstrates that signals in the form of surpluses, deficits, inflation and unemployment may give a misleading guide to policy-makers.

This approach provides us with a broad treatment of internal–external balance, since the analysis is no longer restricted to monetary and fiscal policy. Although there remain basically two instruments in the form of demand management and cost ratio adjustment, these general instruments incorporate a whole range of subinstruments. Demand management, for example, may be conducted through both fiscal and monetary policy, whilst the cost ratio may be influenced *inter alia* by exchange-rate alteration, incomes policy, and competition policy. In this respect the policy choice available to policy-makers is more accurately stated.

Qualifications to the Swan treatment of the problem of internal–external balance include the fact that retaliatory action is again assumed away. In addition, it is implicitly assumed that there is sufficient information available upon which to construct the curves. Instead uncertainty regarding the demand for exports, the elasticity of substitution between exportables and importables, the propensity to import, and the dynamic properties of the *IB* and *EB* relationships means that the implied precision may be unsupportable. The greater the uncertainty about these factors, the less precise may we be. Indeed, as with both the Mundell and the *IS–LM–BP* approach, one might ponder on the implications of *EB* sloping downwards to the right, as an increase in real demand, with money supply fixed, results in an increase in the rate of interest and a capital inflow which more than offsets the deterioration in the trade balance. Depending on the relative slopes of the internal and external balance curves, this may clearly affect the location of policy regions and the changes in cost ratio and real demand that are required. Indeed, the Swan approach does not deal adequately with the capital account and focuses normally on the current account. This means that it is not well-suited to analysing policy where the capital account is significant, as indeed it is for emerging economies, and advanced economies. The above qualifications impose limitations upon policy-makers' ability to identify the correct policies. A final limitation is that the model does not allow for simultaneous inflation and unemployment.

9 Exchange Rate Management and Policy

Introduction

The previous chapter focused on the use of fiscal and monetary policy in an open economy, making different assumptions about the degree of capital mobility and the flexibility of exchange rates. In this chapter, the focus is on the effects of currency depreciation. This could take the form of either a fall in the value of a currency within a free foreign exchange market, or an administered devaluation within an adjustable peg regime. For our purposes, the details of the regime within which the decline in the currency's value occurs does not matter too much; we concentrate on the impact of the currency's decline on the balance of payments and on macroeconomic performance. However, within the chapter there is some discussion of regime choice. Given that more attention is generally paid to balance of payments deficits than to balance of payments surpluses, the chapter concentrates on the effects of currency depreciation. But, to a large degree, the analysis could also be applied to the effects of currency appreciation in reducing balance of payments surpluses. As the chapter proceeds, the analysis of the effects of a changing exchange rate will be linked to the theory of the balance of payments developed earlier in the book (Chapter 4). An appendix provides further analysis of the effects of exchange-rate devaluation within the context of the foreign exchange market.

Devaluation, Foreign Trade Elasticities and the Current Account

By changing the relative prices of home and foreign goods, exchange-rate devaluation represents an attempt to encourage people (both nationals and foreigners) to switch the pattern of their expenditure in favour of goods (and services) bought from the country whose currency is devalued. Devaluation aims to make the country whose currency has been devalued more competitive and thereby strengthen its current account. Two questions lead on from this basic statement. First, how is competitiveness affected; how do relative prices change as a result of devaluation? And second, how do quantities respond to these price changes?

With regard to the first question, and holding other things constant, devaluation raises the domestic currency price of imports and either reduces the foreign currency price of exports or raises their domestic currency price depending on the currency in which the price is denominated.

But will other things remain constant? Might they change in ways that prevent the relative price effects of devaluation materialising? What are these other things?

First, devaluation increases the domestic currency price of imports. If the average propensity to import is high and the price elasticity of demand for imports is low, this increase may push up significantly the level of producer and consumer prices. This may then lead to higher wage claims as workers attempt to protect their real wages from the effect of higher prices. Devaluation may therefore not only lead to a higher price level, but also to higher inflation. In principle, the inflation 'pass through' could be sufficient to wipe out completely the additional competitiveness associated with devaluation. In these circumstances, a nominal devaluation has no effect on the real exchange rate.

Second, foreign producers may change their pricing policies in such a way as to offset the effects of devaluation. They may opt to reduce the price of their goods expressed in terms of their own currencies in order to prevent the price of them rising in terms of a currency that has been devalued. The disadvantage is that this will reduce their profits by comparison with the situation prior to the devaluation. But it will enable them to maintain their market share and may be a profit-maximising strategy where the foreign demand for their goods is price-elastic. At the extreme, what would be the point of maintaining the price of their exports in terms of their own currency and allowing the foreign currency price to rise by the full extent of the foreign country's devaluation, if this resulted in them selling no exports in the foreign market? The answer is, of course, that there would be no point.

Third, devaluation may be part of a package of policies. Not uncommonly, it may coincide with trade liberalisation, such as tariff reduction. But while devaluation will raise the domestic currency price of imports, reducing tariffs will lower their domestic currency price. In principle, therefore, a policy of tariff-cutting could eliminate the impact of devaluation on import prices. On the export side, the idea of devaluation is to increase the profitability of exporting, either by raising the demand for exports (where prices are denominated in the currency of the devaluing country), or by raising the domestic currency price of exports where they have their prices quoted in foreign currencies. But the effect on profitability could be eroded if any subsidies that were previously provided are simultaneously withdrawn.

Finally, the decision to devalue in one country may induce other countries to retaliate in some way, either by themselves devaluing or by modifying their commercial policy – for example, by imposing tariffs on imports from the country that has devalued.

The bottom line is that much of the effectiveness of devaluation on the current account of the balance of payments depends first and foremost on it changing relative prices. If it fails to do this, and therefore does not influence competitiveness, it will become a much weaker tool of balance of payments policy. But even if the relative price changes do occur, as empirical evidence suggests they will – even if not to the full extent of the devaluation, it cannot be guaranteed that the current account of the devaluing country will strengthen. This is where the values of key foreign trade price elasticities come into play.

Recall that the object of the exercise is to strengthen the current account balance of payments or, what comes to the same thing – the net foreign exchange position. This can be achieved by reducing the demand for foreign exchange (reflecting a reduced demand for imports) or by increasing the supply of foreign exchange (in association with improved export performance). However, to begin with, let us assume that all the relevant foreign trade price elasticities are zero. We are therefore assuming that exactly the same quantities of goods are traded after the devaluation as before it. What are the implications of this? The devaluing country's domestic currency terms of trade will deteriorate, since import prices will increase, but export prices will not change. However, if we assume that foreign trade price elasticities are zero, the negative terms of trade effect will have no counterbalancing quantity effects.

The demand for foreign exchange will remain the same as it was before the devaluation as the real inflow of imports is maintained, but the supply of foreign exchange will fall as foreigners need to spend less of their own currency to buy an equivalent real amount of the devaluing country's exports. There will therefore be a net fall in foreign exchange earnings. A crucial question then relates to the quantity responses to the price changes induced by devaluation; that is, to the foreign trade elasticities. How big do the quantity responses need to be in order to offset the negative terms of trade effect?

Which elasticities are important? The answer is that it depends on the sort of country being studied. For small open (dependent) economies it is conventionally assumed that the elasticity of import supply and of export demand are infinitely large, export prices are expressed in foreign currencies and therefore do not change in response to the devaluation of the home currency. The significant values are therefore the price elasticity of demand for imports and the price elasticity of supply of exports. After all it will have been the domestic currency price of exports that will have risen as a consequence of devaluation.

For large industrial countries, on the other hand, it is conventionally assumed that it is import supply and export supply that are infinitely elastic; with diversified economies being able easily to switch domestic output into exports and out of home consumption. Here it is the price elasticities of import and export demand that are significant.

But what values do these elasticities have to possess? Remember that the assumed object of the exercise is to reduce the demand for foreign exchange by reducing the demand for imports, and to increase the supply of foreign exchange by selling more exports.

Taking the dependent country case first, the demand for foreign exchange will fall if the price elasticity of demand for imports is greater than zero. Meanwhile, the supply of foreign exchange will rise if the price elasticity of export supply is greater than zero. Overall, devaluation will strengthen the current account if the sum of import demand elasticity and export supply elasticity is greater than zero.

In large industrial countries, where export supply is assumed to be infinitely elastic, the supply of foreign exchange (that is, the revenue from export earnings) will rise if the price elasticity of export demand exceeds one. For each unit sold less foreign exchange is now earned. Just as in the analysis of the effect of price reductions on a firm's total revenue in imperfect competition, total revenue will only rise if elasticity is greater than one. However, the current account may still improve even if the export demand elasticity is less than one. This will be the case if the demand for foreign exchange falls by more than the implied fall in foreign-exchange earnings and this depends on the price elasticity of demand for imports.

Overall, devaluation will strengthen the current account of an industrial country if the sum of export demand and import demand elasticities exceeds one.[1]

Elasticity Pessimism

Having seen in the preceding sections that the effects of devaluation depend in large measure on the values of certain foreign trade elasticities, the next question is whether the elasticities are likely to be above or below the required values. Is there good reason to be optimistic (or pessimistic) about the effects of devaluation on the trade balance?

One implication of low price elasticities needs to be stressed. If elasticities are so low that devaluation becomes an ineffective weapon for strengthening the current account then it logically follows that revaluation will be effective. Not only this, revaluation will also improve the terms of trade and have a counter-inflationary effect. The observed fact that countries do not revalue in an attempt to strengthen their balance of payments, and that over-valuation leads to payments deficits and not surpluses seems to suggest, as does other empirical evidence, that trade elasticities are above the critical values.

However, it is true that there are grounds for expecting the elasticities to be higher in the long run than in the short run. The long-run impact of devaluation on the current account may thus be more marked than the short-run impact. Indeed, as far as the balance of payments is concerned, things may get worse before they get better. After all, the immediate effect of devaluation is to worsen the domestic currency terms of trade. There may be a time lapse before quantities respond to this change in relative prices. Furthermore, if export prices are invoiced in the devaluing country's own currency, the supply of foreign exchange will fall immediately upon devaluation. In contrast, if import prices are invoiced in foreign currency the demand for foreign exchange will not fall immediately. This gives rise to the so called *J*-curve phenomenon illustrated in Figure 9.1. Again there may be differences here between countries, since by invoicing their exports in foreign currency dependent economies escape the downward part of the *J*-curve.

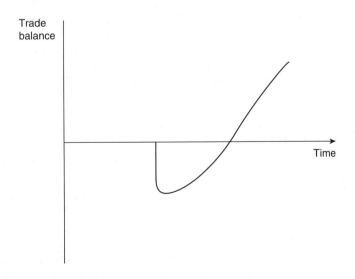

Figure 9.1

Income Elasticities

In the above analysis the importance of price elasticities in discussing the effects of devaluation has been stressed. A rather different view is that it is income elasticities and not price elasticities that are important. While the price changes induced by devaluation may have a temporary effect, it is perhaps more so the underlying income elasticities of demand for imports and exports that determine the balance of payments in the long run. This view of devaluation clearly ties in closely with the structural approach to the balance of payments discussed in Chapter 4. Of course, goods which possess high income elasticities may also possess high price elasticities. If this is the case, the analysis carried out above continues to have relevance even within a framework which emphasises the significance of income elasticities.

Devaluation, Absorption and the Monetary Sector

The conventional view was that devaluation has an expansionary effect on domestic aggregate demand. For both advanced and dependent economies, domestic expenditure switches away from imports, since they are now more expensive, and towards home-produced goods. At the same time, for advanced economies, the foreign demand for exports will rise as (foreign currency) export prices fall. For small, dependent economies it will be the additional profitability of exporting associated with the increase in the domestic currency price of exports that increases claims on domestic resources to help produce extra exports. The danger that, via its expansionary effect on demand, devaluation will cause inflation has been used to justify the simultaneous pursuit of domestic demand contractionary policies alongside it. The idea is to create the spare productive capacity that devaluation then exploits to produce extra import substitutes and exports.

In contrast, a counter view claims that devaluation can have a contractionary effect on domestic demand. In what ways may this happen? First, with the rise in import prices, a higher proportion of domestic currency expenditure might be directed towards buying imports, with less remaining to buy home-produced goods. The strength of this effect depends on the average propensity to import and the price elasticity of demand for imports. With a high propensity to import and a low price elasticity of demand, the effect would be at its most significant.

Second, devaluation has a redistributive effect.

As inflation occurs in an economy which has a progressive tax system, government revenue will rise relative to expenditure since tax-payers are moved into higher tax brackets. Although such 'fiscal drag' may reduce domestic expenditure, the fiscal effects of devaluation in general remain somewhat uncertain since much hinges on the other policies that are simultaneously pursued. Changes in tariffs, quotas and subsidies, all of which frequently go hand in hand with devaluation, affect the fiscal balance. Furthermore, to the extent that devaluation and these other policies influence income and employment there will be additional effects on tax revenue and government expenditure.

The distribution of income may also be altered if devaluation increases profits relative to wages. Certainly our earlier analysis suggests that devaluation will raise profitability in the traded-goods sector. If, as normally assumed, the marginal propensity to save from profits is higher than that from wages then such a redistribution will raise the economy's average propensity to save and reduce its average propensity to consume. How long-standing this effect is depends on how quickly wage earners realise that redistribution has taken place and how well equipped they are to resist it.

Third, for economies which have significant amounts of debt denominated in foreign currency, devaluation may have an additional deflationary effect on domestic expenditure. In such cases devaluation raises the domestic currency cost of servicing any given external obligation, and expenditure is thereby diverted abroad and away from the domestic economy.

Fourth, devaluation will affect the domestic monetary sector. By increasing the domestic price level it will increase the nominal demand for money. With no change in the nominal money supply, the rate of interest will rise, and this will dampen domestic expenditure by reducing investment and consumption. Inflation may also reduce the real value of savings and induce people to cut back on current consumption in order to replenish their stock of savings.

More recently, an additional mechanism has been added by which devaluation may be contractionary. This is the so-called 'balance sheet' effect of devaluation. It occurs when financial institutions or companies in a devaluing country have borrowed heavily in a foreign currency and lent in domestic currency. They then have their liabilities denominated in foreign currency and their assets denominated in domestic currency. They are exposed to an exchange-rate risk against which they opted not to hedge. Why would they not have hedged against the risk? Largely because they perceived that there was little chance of there being a devaluation. Following the devaluation, their liabilities, expressed in terms of the domestic currency that has fallen in value, will have risen. Moreover, to the extent that devaluation reflects poor economic performance, the value of assets may also fall. In short, their balance sheet will have weakened, thus increasing the probability of financial and corporate distress. There will be a recessionary effect on the economy as a whole.

The above discussion of the effects of devaluation on absorption and on monetary variables carries further implications. In the event that the net effects are contractionary, it may be via the negative impact on absorption rather than through the effect of changed relative prices on trade that devaluation exerts its principal influence on the current account of the balance of payments. Moreover, the timing of the various effects of devaluation may differ. For example, the recessionary impact of balance sheet effects may work quite quickly, whereas the expansionary effects working through trade may take some time to come through. This creates an additional challenge for policy-makers. It is not simply a matter of whether devaluation is expansionary or contractionary: it may be contractionary in the short run and expansionary in the long run. But, then, how long is the short run and how long is the long run? It is these uncertainties that make the design of economic policy so difficult. But there are also other difficulties. Even if policy-makers have decided to countenance a fall in the value of the domestic currency, how large should the fall be, and by what means should it be brought about?

The Size, Method and Pace of Exchange Rate Depreciation

In one sense, determining the size of the needed exchange-rate depreciation is easy. It is simply a matter of calculating the size of currency overvaluation and then depreciating to eliminate it. The size of the overvaluation is attained by comparing the contemporary actual exchange rate with the fundamental equilibrium one. But this is where the problems begin, since calculating the long-run equilibrium rate (that is, the rate that would allow domestic and external targets to be achieved simultaneously) is far from easy. There are at least three approaches that could be used. The first is to use purchasing power parity (PPP). Similar goods should have similar prices in different countries when expressed in a common currency. The size of any deviation from PPP may therefore indicate the size of currency misalignment. But the law of one price may not hold in reality. Goods may be differentiated in the minds of consumers, not all goods are traded, the structure of the price index may differ across countries, and there may be barriers to trade of one form or another. PPP may provide guidance, but may fail to offer a precise and accurate calculation of currency misalignment (see Chapter 5).

Second, the official exchange rate may be compared with the black market or parallel rate. Does this enable us to measure the size of currency misalignment? Again, there are problems. The parallel rate will be affected by both the demand for and supply of currencies that come on to the unofficial foreign exchange market. If, for example, the supply is strictly limited, the black market exchange rate will reflect this, and it may be expected that a free foreign exchange market would generate a higher value for the domestic currency in terms of other currencies than exists in the parallel market. The black market may therefore overstate the extent of currency overvaluation and the size of the currency depreciation needed.

Third, a historical point in time may be identified where the exchange rate was at its fundamental equilibrium value. From this point, the size of the appreciation in the real exchange rate can be calculated. Does this tell us by how much the currency's value needs to fall? The problem here is that things change over time, and these things are likely to have affected the equilibrium real exchange rate. Thus it is not simply a matter of restoring the old real exchange rate by allowing depreciation in the nominal rate to offset inflation. A country's income terms of trade may have changed, long-term capital flows may have changed, and the equilibrium real exchange rate will need to be adjusted to allow for them. This is easier said than done.

The difficulties in calculating real equilibrium exchange rates explain, in part, the attraction of free flexibility. It is superficially appealing to let the market decide the appropriate rate and size of the devaluation. But there are problems here as well. Do markets know best? They may be driven by short-term 'cosmetic' factors. Individual operators in the foreign exchange market may be influenced by the actions of others, leading to large swings in the values of currencies. There is broad consensus that there have been periods of pronounced currency misalignment even when countries have opted for flexible exchange rates. Leaving things to the market may lead to overshooting, with the value of a currency falling significantly below its long-run equilibrium rate. A country's monetary authorities may therefore work to orchestrate a more controlled depreciation in the real exchange rate.

One option would be to leave the nominal rate alone and depreciate the real rate by reducing the domestic rate of inflation below that of other competitor countries. This would be acceptable, except for the fact that it will take time. Moreover, it is necessary for the monetary authorities to be able to control inflation, when it was quite possibly their inability to control inflation that led to currency overvaluation in the first place. A large, discrete devaluation may be more effective in the short run, and may transmit a stronger signal of a change in policy direction. The danger is that it may be inflationary. A gradual sliding or crawling depreciation offers the prospect of minimising the inflationary consequences. But whereas a once-and-for-all devaluation may eliminate expectations of further devaluation, a gradual slide may not. This means that monetary policy needs to be designed in a way that offsets the expected exchange-rate depreciation. Interest rates will have to be that much higher than they would have been had the exchange rate already reached its equilibrium rate. Even with relatively high interest rates, the actions of speculators may make it difficult for the monetary authorities to manage the speed of the depreciation. If they sell the currency heavily, an outright devaluation may be forced on the authorities, whatever their intention.

Currency Depreciation and the Capital Account

Up to now, we have concentrated on the effects of currency depreciation on the current account of the balance of payments. What about its implications for the capital account? We have already seen that capital movements will tend to be related to interest rate differentials, expected changes in exchange rates, and the perceived risk of default. Since devaluation changes the exchange rate and raises the interest rate, does it follow that it will have a positive effect on capital flows? Not necessarily. Different types of capital will be more or less sensitive to interest rates. Short-term capital may be attracted. But higher interest rates may cause economic stagnation and recession, and may discourage portfolio and foreign direct investment. Along with the balance sheet effects of devaluation, they may also cause corporate and financial distress. Moreover, a contemporary devaluation may lead investors to expect a further devaluation in the future, and this will not encourage an inflow of capital.

In short, currency depreciation as part of a credible package of policies designed to improve economic performance may strengthen the capital account. On the other hand, if perceived as a panic measure which is taken without there being any attempt to rectify underlying problems associated with fiscal deficits, monetary expansion and inflation, it may merely weaken any residual confidence in a government's commitment to defend the value of the currency. In these circumstances, it may repel foreign capital rather than attract it.

From a balance of payments accounting point of view, and since capital inflows are in a sense used to finance current account deficits, there is a link between the effect of devaluation on both the current and the capital accounts. Where devaluation reduces the current account deficit it will also reduce net capital inflows, assuming that there is no change in the holding of international reserves. If it is unsuccessful in eliminating a current account deficit, this either means that net capital inflows will continue, or, if they do not, that international reserves will fall. In these circumstances, future exchange-rate depreciation is extremely likely until some equilibrating effects are induced.

The Political Economy of Currency Depreciation

Governments generally have the power to influence the exchange rate. Policy relating to the exchange rate will therefore be influenced by politics. A decision has to be made to devalue, or to allow market forces to drive down the value of currency without intervening to prevent or moderate it. Even a passive policy is still a policy. Up to now, this chapter has focused on the economics of exchange-rate policy; but what about the politics?

Exchange-rate devaluation or depreciation may have significant political ramifications. It may lead to inflation, and in some cases, recession. How politically sensitive are these phenomena? If a government has worked hard to reduce politically unpopular inflation it may not want to risk recreating it via devaluation. But if inflation has been less of a problem, the government may be less worried about devaluation.

Then there is the timing of the effects. The recessionary effect, if any, may be short-term, while the trade-related expansionary effects may take some months, or even years, to make their impact. But when is the next election due? If it is scheduled before the expansionary effects are due to work, a government may be reluctant to devalue. In any case, devaluation may be perceived as an indication that the government's economic policy has been unsuccessful. It may be viewed as a badge of failure, and incumbent governments may be reluctant to pin it on. On this basis, new incoming administrations may be less concerned about devaluing because they can blame the previous administration, and even use the devaluation to reinforce their claims that the opposition party they have replaced mismanaged the economy. The timing of elections will therefore affect the probability of devaluation.

Governments may also have joined exchange-rate or monetary unions, and may have agreed to defend the value of the currency. What would be the political costs of disengaging? The size of these costs will clearly influence the decision to devalue. If a government perceives that there are large political benefits from monetary integration, it will tend to be more reticent about pursuing an exchange-rate policy that appears to put these at risk.

Politics is a great deal about distribution; who gets what? So another factor influencing the political decision to devalue will be its distributional consequences. Who gains, and who loses? As we have seen, devaluation tends to lower real wages and raise the profitability of producing traded goods. In a country where urban workers are politically powerful, a government will be worried about the effects of devaluation on their support. Rural workers may be in a better position to mitigate the effects of devaluation on their standard of living because they have a higher degree of self-sufficiency in growing food, and may therefore be less likely to oppose devaluation.

Although we have not emphasised the distinction between the various forms of exchange-rate depreciation, this may also be important politically. A relatively gradual decline in a currency's value within the context of a flexible exchange-rate regime may have significantly different political consequences from a similarly sized decline orchestrated by the government in the form of a discrete devaluation. If the political costs of the latter are higher, an incumbent government may prefer to announce a move to a flexible exchange rate, where market forces can then be accused of forcing the currency to depreciate, than to announce a devaluation that reflects the government's own policy choice.

The political economy of devaluation is even more complex than the above discussion suggests. Just as there are political costs associated with devaluation, there will also be political costs associated with *not* devaluing. In one sense, this is another way of looking at the benefits of devaluation. Not devaluing means that the real exchange rate will remain overvalued. And overvaluation involves political costs. Domestic producers will find it more difficult to compete with foreign producers both in their home markets and those overseas. De-industrialisation and economic stagnation may result, and carry significant adverse political implications for the government. Domestic producers may put pressure on the government to introduce protectionist measures, and this may lead to further political problems, both domestically and internationally. Devaluation may seem to be one way of avoiding these problems – except to the extent that it may also be viewed as a competitively aggressive policy.

If a government rejects currency depreciation as a way of improving the balance of payments, it will have to find alternative policies. The political dilemma is that reducing a current account deficit means making a sacrifice in terms of domestic consumption. Real wages have to fall, by comparison with what they would otherwise be, to strengthen the current account. It is not that there is a painless policy option. The political question is therefore not whether devaluation involves political costs but whether it involves fewer costs than the other policy options.

Where it allows governments to modify other policies that were previously needed to support currency overvaluation, such as a high interest rate, devaluation may contribute to higher economic growth. In these circumstances, the political cost of the sacrifice of consumption will be much less; and it will be against a background of a rising standard of living. The political costs of giving up something that one has not had are generally speaking lower than those of giving up something that one has had. If devaluation facilitates economic growth it may be politically popular.

All in all, the political economy of currency depreciation is very complicated, and there are many issues involved, covering both economics and politics. These pull in different directions; and for every argument there seems to be a counter-argument. The uncertainties involved and the existence of potential costs have two implications. First, devaluation will frequently be postponed. It is not a decision that governments rush to make. But, as we saw in Chapter 6, which dealt with currency crises, postponing devaluation may be unwise. Delayed devaluation will probably involve higher costs than timely devaluation. But the perceived short-term costs and benefits continue to encourage incumbent governments to delay. Second, the uncertainties – and to some extent economic theory – make governments reluctant to rely exclusively on devaluation as a way of strengthening the balance of payments. Devaluation is therefore commonly just one component of balance of payments policy, and it tends to be combined with other policies relating to trade liberalisation or aggregate demand management. Appropriately designed, this may improve matters. Inappropriately designed, however, it will make them worse. But, given the debate about whether devaluation is expansionary or contractionary, the desire to maintain economic growth and the need to reduce domestic consumption below what it would otherwise be, who is to say what design is appropriate? Herein lies the policy problem.

The Choice of Exchange Rate Regime

The analysis in this chapter has explored the decision to depreciate the exchange rate either by orchestrating devaluation or by allowing market forces to push down the currency's value. But another decision relates to the choice of the exchange-rate regime. There is a range of options from which to choose. At the extremes are free floating and immutable fixity. A free-floating regime allows the exchange rate to be market determined; the monetary authorities do not seek to influence its value either by intervening in the forex market or by setting the domestic rate of interest in order to affect the demand for the currency. Immutable fixity, at the other extreme, can ultimately be achieved by giving up the exchange rate altogether through adopting a unified currency with other members of a monetary union, or by adopting another country's currency for internal use. The euro is an example of a unified currency, while dollarisation is an example of adopting another country's currency. However, while these regimes give immutable fixity with regard to other members of the eurozone or with regard to the US dollar, respectively, they do not give fixity in terms of other currencies against which the euro and the dollar are floating. There is a significant difference between a country fixing its exchange rate in the context of a generalised fixed exchange-rate system, where fixing to one means fixing to all, and fixing it relative to another currency when that currency is floating against third currencies. Within an international monetary system where the major currencies are floating, the decision by other countries to peg their exchange rates in some way also involves deciding to which currency or basket of currencies to peg.

Pegging to a foreign currency (or currency basket) while retaining one's own currency may in principle still involve immutable fixity, but in these circumstances the option of changing the peg always exists. Thus currency board arrangements involving firm pegging, and a government's commitment not to intervene to offset the effects of the balance of payments on the domestic money supply, have often turned out to be less than immutable. There is always the option to withdraw from a currency board. And this is rather easier than withdrawing from a unified currency or from dollarisation.

In between the two extremes of free floating and immutable fixity lie various other exchange-rate regimes. These may be closer to floating or closer to immutable fixing. Managed floating allows governments the discretion to influence the exchange rate. Constraints are imposed on the extent or speed of the change in a currency's value in foreign exchange markets. These constraints may take the form of target zones. Within the zone, the currency's value is market determined. At the limits of the zone, however, the authorities intervene to keep the currency's value inside the zone. The authorities may 'go public' about the zone or they may operate it informally. Again, the size of the zone and the vehemence with which the authorities defend its outer limits may vary.

Another blend between fixity and flexibility is the 'adjustable peg'. This sees the pegged value of a currency being defended, but only up to a point. If the pegged exchange rate becomes associated with currency overvaluation the authorities will alter the peg by devaluing. However, they then seek to defend the new exchange rate. The idea is to derive the advantages of pegging without allowing severe currency misalignment to persist.

How do countries decide which regime is best for them? There are a number of elements to the decision, but they may not all point in the same direction. Moreover, they may change over time. What makes sense in one set of circumstances may not make sense in another.

The conventional arguments in favour of selecting a fixed exchange rate include the following. First, it removes exchange-rate uncertainty with respect to the value of the domestic currency in terms of the foreign currency to which it is pegged. This may encourage trade with that country. The larger the amount of potential trade with the country, or indeed the larger the number of countries participating in the pegging arrangement, the larger the benefits. Second, by eliminating the exchange-rate risk, the need to hedge against the risk is also eliminated, and this again encourages trade with the country or countries against whose currency pegging takes place. Third, pegging eliminates the price instability associated with movements in exchange rates, although movements against 'outside' currencies will remain a source of price instability. Finally, pegging may be used as a central component of a counter-inflationary strategy. By pegging the value of the currency to that of a low-inflation country, a government may seek to transmit a signal that it intends to keep inflation equally low. Stabilisation is based on maintaining the currency peg, and the bilateral exchange rate becomes a 'nominal anchor'.

It is important to note, however, that the benefits from fixing the exchange rate only tend to follow if the fixing is credible. For example, if a government's commitment to defending a peg is credible, workers may moderate wage demands, because they believe that any resulting inflation will lead the government to pursue contractionary policies that may create unemployment: better to have a higher level of employment and lower real wages, than to be unemployed. But if workers do not find the commitment to the peg to be credible, they may push for higher wages, believing that any inflation and balance of payments deficits that result will lead the government to abandon the peg and devalue. It is then not just a matter of pegging the exchange rate, but also of finding a way to peg it that carries credibility.

There are a number of conventional arguments against fixed exchange rates even where the regime is credible. First, to the extent that shocks continue to occur, something will have to respond to restore balance of payments equilibrium. If it is not the exchange rate it will have to be fiscal and monetary policy or commercial policy. Although the exchange rate varies less, the rate of interest varies more. There is more uncertainty regarding monetary policy. In a sense, the adoption of fixed exchange rates merely reallocates uncertainty. Domestic investment and economic growth may be adversely affected.

Second, if the pegged rate becomes a disequilibrium rate there will be problems of currency misalignment. In one case it may be that relatively rapid domestic inflation pushes up the real exchange rate and leads to currency overvaluation. With a fixed exchange rate there is no way to adjust the nominal exchange rate to compensate for the inflation and restore the real exchange rate to its former level. But another possibility is that a permanent change in the terms of trade or in capital flows alters the equilibrium real exchange rate. With a pegged nominal rate, one way of adjusting the real rate is ruled out. In these circumstances, economic adjustment will depend on the effectiveness of other policies. If they are not very effective, or are only effective in the long run, there may be a significant cost associated with maintaining a pegged nominal exchange rate.

Third, by pegging against a currency that is floating, variations in the value of the 'anchor' currency will translate into variations in the value of the domestic currency against third currencies: the third currency phenomenon. These movements may be inappropriate. It is for this reason that countries may peg to a basket of currencies in a way that offsets the effects of movements in value of any one particular anchor currency.

Finally, where pegged exchange-rate regimes lack credibility, they will be vulnerable to speculative attack. They will be crisis prone. It is largely for this reason that some people argue that, if a country is contemplating fixing its exchange rate, it needs to opt for a form of fixing that is genuinely immutable, since it will only be in these circumstances that confidence in the durability of the regime will be created. But it remains something of balancing act, since, with firmer fixing, the other costs of pegging the exchange rate become more pronounced.

To say that there are potential problems associated with fixed exchange-rate regimes is not to say that flexible exchange rates are necessarily a good idea. There are also potential problems with floating. Flexible exchange rates may be unstable and volatile in the short run. Market sentiment may be ill-grounded on fundamentals, and expectations about future exchange rates may be highly elastic. Traders may be affected by what others are doing, and this will magnify swings in a currency's value. The volatility in currency values may then discourage foreign trade and investment; it may discriminate against those with an inability to hedge against the risk; it may create additional price instability; and it may make it more difficult to manage a portfolio of international reserves. For these reasons, some countries have exhibited what has been called a 'fear of floating'. They have been reluctant to adopt flexible exchange rates. In fact, it has tended to be the developing and emerging economies that have been most suspicious of flexible exchange rates. Advanced economies such as the USA, Japan and the Eurozone have opted for flexible rates. It is not difficult to see why. Advanced economies are diversified and their balance of payments may, as a consequence, be more stable. They can hedge the risk of exchange rate instability, and they are less vulnerable to speculative attack because they are creditworthy and can borrow.

The exchange rate is therefore more likely to be stable. The effects of exchange-rate instability on the domestic price level may be relatively low where economies are relatively closed (or self-sufficient). Trade and investment do not seem to be affected greatly by instability in their exchange rates, and, in any case, little success has been shown in calculating equilibrium exchange rates.

This having been said, while members of the Eurozone have opted to allow the value of the euro to float against other world currencies, they have also opted to eliminate all exchange-rate variability among themselves by adopting a single currency. This was the outcome of a lengthy process of monetary integration.

Monetary Integration

Monetary integration is an imprecise concept. It may simply involve establishing an exchange-rate union within which countries agree to peg the values of their currencies. It may, in addition to this, involve policy co-ordination, common monetary institutions and common monetary policy. Ultimately, it may involve a single currency. An important question is therefore what determines whether a group of countries is well qualified to engage in monetary integration; and what factors determine an optimum currency area (OCA). In what follows, we initially explore the issues involved in forming an exchange-rate union, and then go on to examine the question of a single currency. There are cases, however, where abandoning the domestic currency and adopting the currency of another country (for example, dollarisation) happens in the absence of major institutional reform.

Optimum Currency Areas

The theory of optimum currency areas has gradually evolved to develop a number of criteria that delineate the boundaries of exchange-rate unions. There is a general guideline, however, and it is this: an optimum currency area will exist between countries that are either unlikely to have to adjust to balance of payments disequilibria among themselves, or are able to finance the disequilibria on a quasi-permanent basis or adjust by means other than altering exchange rates. Indeed, membership of an exchange-rate union will be more attractive in circumstances where changing the exchange rate is a relatively ineffective policy instrument either because it fails to change relative prices or because foreign trade price elasticities are low.

Balance of payments disequilibria are less likely to occur among a group of countries facing similar trade-offs between inflation and unemployment and selecting similar points on such trade-offs, experiencing similar trends in their underlying economic fundamentals such as productivity and economic growth, and which are synchronised in terms of their business cycles. They are also less likely where countries have similar industrial structures and encounter symmetrical external shocks.

Where balance of payments disequilibria do arise among a group of countries, good candidates for inclusion in an exchange-rate union should be able to sustain these disequilibria by means of the countries in surplus providing finance for the countries in deficit. This implies a relatively high degree of financial integration and a willingness to make such transfers. Alternatively, the disequilibria need to be capable of being corrected effectively and efficiently without changing the exchange rate. This will depend in part on the degree of labour market flexibility. Can the structure of wages be altered to regain competitiveness in circumstances where it has been lost? It will also depend on the extent to which the fiscal management of domestic demand has an impact on imports, and on unemployment and economic growth. Where the marginal propensity to import is high, domestic aggregate demand will need to be reduced less in order to achieve a targeted reduction in the current account deficit than if the propensity is high. For this reason, open economies that trade a great deal with each other will be relatively good candidates to join exchange-rate unions. This same characteristic will mean that changes in exchange rates will, in any case, tend to destabilise price levels. The effects of contractionary fiscal policy on unemployment will depend on the shape of the Phillips curve. If this is vertical, reducing inflation will involve no cost in terms of unemployment. Countries with a vertical Phillips curve will be good candidates for joining an exchange-rate union.

The earliest contribution to the theory of optimum currency areas focused on labour mobility as a substitute for exchange-rate changes as a way of correcting balance of payments disequilibria. To illustrate the idea, imagine that there are two regions between which there is a high degree of labour mobility. In one region there is a trade deficit and an excess supply of labour (partly as a consequence of the trade deficit), and in the second region there is a trade surplus and an excess demand for labour. Labour now migrates from the first to the second region in search of work. This both eliminates the labour market disequilibria in both of the regions and corrects the trade disequilibria, since what was formerly home demand in the first region becomes export demand, and what was formerly export demand in the second region now becomes home demand. There are a number of implicit assumptions here: namely that the goods produced in the two regions are equally labour intensive, and that labour in the two regions is broadly substitutable. But if these assumptions hold, the need to alter an exchange rate between the two regions to induce a switch in the pattern of expenditure can be avoided.

Labour mobility and labour market flexibility may be relevant within countries contemplating joining an exchange-rate union as well as between them. Where structural adjustment is required to maintain balance of payments equilibrium, this will be attained more easily with flexible labour markets. Labour mobility will allow workers to move out of declining industries and into expanding ones. Labour market flexibility will allow labour markets to adjust by reducing real wages in declining industries rather than by enduring a large amount of unemployment. Countries with flexible labour markets once more emerge as better candidates for joining an exchange-rate union than those with inflexible labour markets.

There are potentially important endogeneities at work in the context of exchange rate and monetary unions. Labour markets may, for example, be forced to become more flexible where there is a strong and credible commitment to an exchange-rate union. Similarly, trade with partner countries will be encouraged by a strong commitment to pegging. Furthermore, the formation of an exchange-rate union may force the member states to synchronise economic performance and policy. The internal dynamics of exchange-rate unions may therefore combine to create the conditions under which they work best. But there are factors that could work in the opposite direction. Where enhanced trade encourages greater specialisation and additional trade between industries (inter-industry trade) this could increase the probability of the union being affected by asymmetrical shocks, which might result in larger balance of payments disequilibria that threaten the durability of the union.

Single Currencies and Dollarisation

Given their vulnerability to speculative attack, a concern is whether exchange-rate unions can ever generate the degree of credibility required to make them work effectively and to deliver the benefits they promise. To create such credibility, does the ability to alter the exchange rate need to be removed from the list of policy options? This question moves us on to the issue of single currencies.

Single currencies have a number of well-rehearsed benefits. These include: reduced transactions costs, those previously associated with moving between currencies; reduced information costs, since prices in different countries become transparent; the elimination of exchange risk resulting in a higher level of investment and faster economic growth; enhanced trade in financial services; and the reduced need to hold unproductive international reserves to defend individual currency values. In addition to these, the above discussion suggests that the benefits of monetary union will only be gained if commitment to the union is credible, and that commitment will only be credible with a single currency.

Against these benefits are the costs. In essence, these are the same costs as those associated with belonging to an exchange-rate union, except that the loss of monetary sovereignty is even greater with the loss of the national currency. There is an analytical paradox. The argument for a single currency is that retaining a currency peg also retains a devaluation escape route which undermines confidence in the durability of the exchange-rate union: there is a moral hazard problem. However, escape routes are designed to avert disasters. Does the removal of the devaluation escape route increase the risks of disaster? What if balance of payments disequilibria arise within the union; what if surplus countries are not prepared to finance deficit countries in perpetuity; and what if other adjustment policies impose economic costs that prove to be politically unacceptable? Since the political commitment involved in establishing a single currency is higher, the political costs of dismantling it will also be higher. Is this a risk worth taking?

The issues involved with a single or unified currency can be summarised conveniently. There is no nation state that does not possess a unified currency. This clearly implies that there are significant benefits from having one. But also within nations, the concepts of regional disequilibria, regional adjustment and regional transfers have a relatively low profile. There is little political resistance to the idea of richer regions supporting poorer ones. Also within nations, labour mobility may be higher than across nations. The question is whether the kinds of conditions that make single currencies a 'no brainer' within nation states can be replicated across nation states.

Similar issues arise with dollarisation. It removes exchange-rate risk, helps to avoid speculative crises, and removes the need for risk premia on interest rates that discriminate against investment and raise the costs of servicing government debt. It imposes a counter-inflationary discipline, since the possibility of monetising fiscal deficits is eliminated. Moreover, it encourages trade with countries using the dollar. It carries greater credibility than a commitment merely to defend the value of the national currency. The downside of dollarisation also involves familiar arguments. Dollarising countries lose a substantial degree of policy discretion. They lose the seigniorage from printing money (the difference between the costs of producing the domestic currency and its purchasing power) and the central bank may find it more difficult to perform some of its textbook functions, particularly as a lender of last resort. Moreover, balance of payments correction will have to be achieved in ways other than by using the exchange rate, with the problems that this implies.

Again, it is not difficult to see why different countries will make different choices, or even why the choice they make may change over time as circumstances themselves change. But how easy is it to move from one exchange-rate regime to another?

Regime Change

It has been observed a number of times in this chapter that exchange-rate regimes may not be established for ever. Circumstances may change in such a way that what at one time was the best regime for a country to adopt is no longer the best. However, orchestrating a change is itself a risky business, largely because of the response to which it may lead in international capital markets. Abandoning a peg at a time when the currency is overvalued may engender expectations of depreciation that feed on themselves, and the currency may go into free fall. Fear of this happening may dissuade governments from abandoning the peg in the first place, but then delaying the change merely makes the eventual collapse more likely.

A number of basic points can be made. When the move is from a flexible to a fixed rate it is important to try to ensure that the rate to be fixed is an equilibrium one, and that the circumstances are created that will best support a pegged rate. This may involve some degree of macroeconomic convergence between the countries that are moving towards a pegging arrangement. Where the move is in the opposite direction, it may seem best to implement it at a time when the value of the currency is likely to rise, in order to avoid a speculative implosion. However, politically, this may be an unattractive option since it will weaken the country's competitiveness. Undervalued currencies are often politically attractive, because they encourage export-led growth. It is also important that, where a currency peg has been used as a nominal anchor to control inflation, some alternative counter-inflationary policy, such as inflation targeting, is put in place.

This leads to a final and important point. Exchange-rate policy and exchange-rate regimes should not be seen in isolation. They are just one part of an overall macroeconomic strategy and policy mix. It is therefore really a matter of whether governments are making internally consistent choices. Devaluation combined with other appropriate macroeconomic policies may be successful, but combined with inappropriate macroeconomic policies, it will fail. Exchange-rate unions or monetary unions may succeed or fail depending on the other macro-economic policies that are pursued. Flexible exchange rates may be stable and sustainable where they are accompanied by measured fiscal and monetary policy. In the absence of a credible counter-inflationary macroeconomic strategy they will offer little in the way of a long-run solution.

As this chapter has shown, there are no easy answers when it comes to exchange-rate management and policy, but an awareness of the issues and problems may represent progress.

Appendix

The Effects of Exchange-rate Changes

The basic model underlying the analysis in the main body of the chapter may be illustrated very simply in Figure 9A.1. What we have here is a model of the foreign exchange market. The items traded are currencies, and there are both demand and supply curves for these. We assume that there are two currencies; dollars and sterling. The point of intersection between the demand and supply curves gives the equilibrium price of one currency in terms of another, i.e. the exchange rate, as well as the equilibrium quantity traded. Any exchange rate other than this one will, according to this figure, be a disequilibrium rate and there will be excess demand for or excess supply of a particular currency.

Figure 9A.1, however, conceals a good deal and we therefore need to look at it in more detail. As it has been drawn there is a downward sloping demand curve for dollars, with the demand increasing as the sterling price of dollars falls, and an upward sloping supply curve for dollars with the supply of dollars increasing as their sterling price rises. Assuming, as we are, that there are only two currencies, dollars and sterling, an increase in the demand for dollars implies an increase in the supply of sterling, and similarly an increase in the supply of dollars implies an increase in the demand for sterling.

Taking the demand for dollars first, what underpins the demand curve shown in Figure 9A.1? The demand for dollars is a derived demand, reflecting the demand for US goods and services, as well as the need to pay interest on or indeed to pay off debt. US goods will initially be priced in dollars but the demand for US goods emanating from the UK will be a function of their sterling price. As this rises, demand will tend to fall, and as the sterling price falls so the demand for US goods will tend to rise. To find out the demand for dollars we need to translate the demand for US goods at a specific sterling price into its dollar equivalent. This is done by using the sterling/dollar exchange rate. With a given

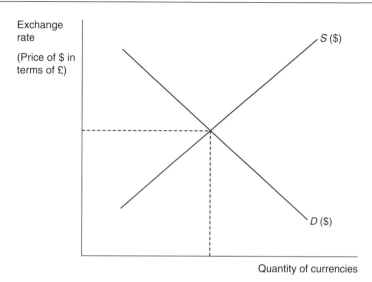

Figure 9A.1

exchange rate and a given dollar price of US goods we can work out the sterling price of these goods. We can then translate the demand for US goods at this sterling price into a demand for dollars. As the exchange rate changes so the sterling price of US goods also changes, though their dollar price remains the same. Furthermore, as the sterling price changes so the demand for US goods changes and so too does the demand for dollars. How the demand for dollars changes in response to changes in the exchange rate depends on the UK's sterling price elasticity of demand for imports from the US.

A sterling devaluation, i.e. a fall in the dollar price of sterling or a rise in the sterling price of dollars, makes the sterling price of goods imported from the US higher and, depending on the demand elasticity for these imports, tends to reduce the demand for dollars, as shown in Figure 9A.1. However, if demand is completely price inelastic, the demand for dollars will be unaltered by a sterling devaluation (i.e. dollar appreciation), and the demand curve will be vertical.

Let us now move over to the supply curve of dollars; what factors underpin this relationship? The supply of dollars depends on the quantity and price of UK exports sold. The UK's supply of exports depends on their sterling price. Through the exchange rate the sterling price of exports may be converted into an associated dollar price. It is upon this dollar price that the US demand for UK goods depends. Again the point of intersection between the demand curve for and supply curve of UK exports expressed as a function of the dollar price gives the equilibrium

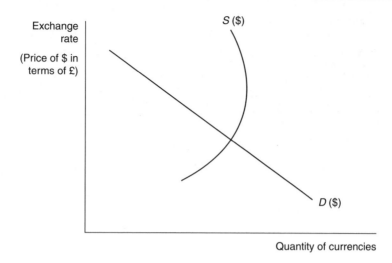

Figure 9A.2

quantity of exports sold and therefore the supply of dollars at a particular exchange rate. As the exchange rate changes so the dollar price
of goods priced in sterling changes. With a sterling depreciation (dollar
appreciation) the dollar price of UK goods falls, and depending on the
price elasticity of demand, the demand for UK exports in the US will
tend to rise. However, for the supply of dollars on to the foreign exchange
market to rise, the price elasticity of demand for UK exports has to be
greater than one, i.e. the demand response in terms of quantity has to
more than offset the fact that each unit of UK exports now earns fewer
dollars. With a price elastic demand curve for UK exports the supply
curve of dollars will indeed be upward sloping as shown in Figure 9A.1.

Up to now the analysis is relatively straightforward. It is essentially
simple demand and supply analysis. However, as noted above a com-
plication can occur if the price elasticity of demand for exports is low.
Let us briefly examine this potential problem.

If the demand for UK exports into the US is price inelastic a sterling
depreciation (dollar appreciation) will mean that fewer dollars are
supplied on to the foreign exchange market. Indeed, at the extreme, if
demand is completely inelastic the fall in the supply of dollars will
perfectly match the fall in the dollar value of sterling. The US will
need only the same quantity of sterling but will need to pay fewer
dollars in order to purchase it. In the case where US demand is price
inelastic the supply curve of dollars will, as a result, bend backwards as
shown in Figure 9A.2.

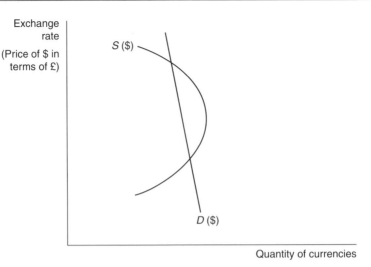

Figure 9A.3

But does the existence of a backward bending supply curve of dollars necessarily mean that sterling depreciation will fail to improve the UK's balance of trade? The short answer is 'no'. In the case illustrated by Figure 9A.2 it may be seen that although the sterling depreciation does indeed reduce the supply of dollars, the demand for dollars falls by even more. However, it is certainly possible to conceive of a case where the demand curve for dollars is inelastic, as in Figure 9A.3. Here, over a certain range of sterling devaluation, the supply of dollars falls by more than the demand for them and the depreciation weakens the UK trade balance.

10   Dealing with International Capital Volatility

Introduction

Previous chapters in this book have examined theories that seek to explain capital movements. We have also seen how balance of payments problems may be associated with capital volatility, and how the instability of capital flows may contribute to currency crises. In this chapter, we extend our coverage of capital flows. The early sections revisit the underlying analysis, say a little about the empirical evidence, and consider whether international capital mobility is a good or bad thing. These are followed by a section that examines in more detail the macroeconomic effects of capital inflows and outflows. The final section considers policy responses to deal with the problems arising from excessive capital mobility.

Revisiting Theory

Our simple model of capital movements, explained in Chapter 3, saw them as being influenced by interest rate differentials, and by both default and exchange-rate risks. Capital will flow to where returns are higher and risks are lower. Moreover, our simple analysis of the balance of payments suggests that countries with deficient domestic savings will run current account deficits and will import capital to finance them; they will be *capital importers*. Meanwhile, countries with excess domestic savings will be *capital exporters*.

These ideas do indeed have the appeal of simplicity, but are they realistic? We saw in Chapter 3 that the analysis tends to present capital movements as flows, suggesting that they will continue in perpetuity. However, further consideration raises some doubts about this. Capital movements may themselves help to eliminate the circumstances that initially caused them to occur. First, by increasing the supply of loans, capital inflows may reduce domestic interest rates; second, they may drive up the value of the currency, leading to a loss of competitiveness and an enhanced risk of devaluation; and third, they may facilitate speculative investment that increases the risk of default.

In addition to this, capital movements may reflect foreign investors seeking to achieve an optimum portfolio of assets. Changed economic and political circumstances may rearrange the optimum portfolio, leading to 'stock' adjustment. While this stock adjustment is happening, it will be reflected by capital movements, but once the new equilibrium has been reached, the capital movements are likely to diminish, unless circumstances change again. This having been said, portfolio growth may mean that they do not stop completely. In addition, but still within the context of portfolio theory, it is quite possible that investors will be attracted to a high-risk asset as a means of reducing the overall risk to their portfolio. The important thing here is the covariance of risks. How closely correlated are they? Diversification to include assets where the risks are negatively correlated offers a way of reducing portfolio risk.

But there is also the underlying problem of calculating risks, whether they are default risks or exchange risks. International investors have devised methods of risk assessment but these are far from foolproof. International credit rating agencies have a notoriously bad record for anticipating economic crises. Moreover, international financial organisations, in particular the Bank for International Settlements (BIS) have devised guidelines for prudential investment. It is clearly unwise to be imprudent. The world economy is unlikely to benefit if international capital markets severely miscalculate the risks of lending. But there is a downside to a more informed approach to risk assessment. In any market where views on risk differ, there will be both buyers and sellers, which will stabilise the market. However, if all market participants hold similar views, or are following the guidelines driven by the market valuation of assets, they are likely to act in similar ways, with the consequence that the market will be more unstable. From this perspective, the increasing adoption of uniform systems of risk management across different categories of investors may increase international capital volatility. Overly optimistic or pessimistic judgements on risk may then become self-fulfilling, and international capital movements are likely to become procyclical.

The adoption of uniform risk assessment techniques may undermine the differences that would otherwise exist across different types of international lender. They may also enhance contagion between assets. Generally speaking, for example, banks may be attracted by a higher interest rate. At the same time, a high interest rate could discourage portfolio investment and foreign direct investment if it carries with it the prospect of economic recession, and financial and corporate failure – although multinational companies contemplating direct investment in a foreign country may be more concerned about long-term economic prospects and domestic wage levels and policies towards the repatriation of profits. Even short-term investors could be concerned that a high domestic interest rate increases the risk of default so that expected return in fact diminishes. At the very least, a sharp increase in the domestic interest rate may be taken as a signal that the economy is in crisis; foreign investors may not want to lend to such an economy.

The long and short of this is that, as yet, we do not have a particularly good general theory of capital movements. Moreover, empirical studies have done little to point to the important determinants, other than suggesting that capital moves internationally in response to both 'push' and 'pull' factors. An inflow of capital may therefore, in part, be 'pushed' towards the country or region receiving it by events elsewhere, and to this extent it is exogenous. It may simply be that interest rates or investment opportunities in the rest of the world have declined, and that investors are looking to diversify. On the other hand, countries may also be able to 'pull' in capital from abroad by enhancing their own attractiveness to foreign investors. This could involve them in improving overall economic policy and performance (although there will be ambiguities about exactly what this means), or pursuing particular policies aimed specifically at potential foreign investors. Of course, from a policy point of view, and in an attempt to moderate instability in international capital movements, it is important to know what causes them. Are they 'hot' and influenced by short-term factors and, if so, what factors? Or 'cool' and largely affected not by short-term factors but by longer-term ones? Can policy-makers manipulate not only total capital inflows and outflows, but also the composition of the flows?

A more fundamental question is whether international capital mobility is basically a good thing that may from time to time become excessive, or a bad thing that systemically should be discouraged?

Capital Mobility: Good or Bad?

The problem with answering this question is that the answer is probably 'both'. In other words, there may simultaneously be good and bad aspects to capital mobility. Whether it is good or bad overall involves weighing up the opposing arguments. Why might it be a good thing? First, it may allow scarce global capital to be allocated efficiently across the world, going to where the rate of return is highest. Second, it may help to remove external financing constraints on economic development, particularly in relatively poor countries. Third, it may be a conduit for the transfer of technology, bringing about increases in productivity in the receiving countries. Fourth, it may discipline countries that are anxious to attract foreign capital to pursue sound economic policies. Finally, and as noted above, it allows investors to diversify risk.

But, it may be bad for the following reasons. First, capital markets may be inefficient. Capital may be allocated globally on the basis of short-term cosmetic factors, or simply on the basis of what others are doing. There may be a herd element. Capital markets may fail, which in turn means that market-driven risk management techniques will also fail. It is certainly unsafe to assume the markets will ensure that capital goes to where its marginal productivity is highest. Second, capital inflows may be used to finance consumption or unproductive investment. They may then result in higher inflation rather than economic growth. They may have undesirable consequences in terms of driving up the domestic money supply or the real exchange rate. There may then be a Dutch disease effect as international competitiveness is lost.[1] Strength in the capital account may weaken the current account. Third, reliance on private international capital markets may mean that low-income countries are starved of external finance, with another equity issue being that, in the case of some forms of capital flow, borrowers may carry a disproportionate share of the risks.[2] Finally, and as noted in the previous section, capital flows tend to be volatile, and this creates additional problems for macroeconomic management. It is to these problems that we turn in the next section.

The Macroeconomic Effects of Capital Flows

Capital Inflows

Capital inflows lead to an increase in the demand for the domestic currency. With no government intervention to prevent it, the nominal exchange rate will appreciate. But governments (and domestic monetary authorities) may be reluctant to allow this to happen, since they may fear the consequences for the current account of the balance of payments. The authorities may therefore seek to offset the effect of the inflow of capital on the exchange rate by buying the foreign exchange being supplied by foreign investors and supplying the domestic currency they are demanding. While this will neutralise the effects of the capital inflow on the value of the domestic currency, it will also have other consequences. The domestic money supply will increase, as too will the country's holdings of foreign exchange. The problem is that the increase in the money supply may cause inflation, with the result that the real exchange rate still appreciates, albeit as a consequence of inflation rather than an appreciation in the nominal exchange rate. In order to prevent inflation, the government may attempt to sterilise the effects of its intervention in the foreign exchange market by issuing bonds in order to absorb excess liquidity. But even this is not the end of it. The bond market may be thin. Selling bonds will depress their prices and keep the rate of interest high, thereby encouraging additional inflows of capital. In any event, issuing bonds increases government debt and the government may have to pay a higher rate of interest on this debt than it is receiving on its additional foreign exchange reserves. This will weaken its fiscal position and the government may lack the fiscal flexibility to compensate for it by reducing other forms of government expenditure or by increasing tax revenue. On top of this, there is the danger that banks hold excess reserves such that conventional open market operations fail to reduce monetary growth. Given the list of problems, it may seem difficult to imagine anything much worse than a sudden inflow of capital. But what about a sudden capital outflow?

Capital Outflows

Capital outflows involve foreigners (and nationals) selling the domestic currency. As a consequence, the exchange rate will depreciate. If the authorities want to avoid this depreciation they will have to supply the foreign exchange that is being demanded, by running down their foreign exchange reserves. Of course, the problem is that this is not a long-term solution, since reserves are finite. There is also the fact that the selling of foreign exchange and the related buying of the domestic currency will lead to a fall in the domestic money supply, and this may have contractionary macroeconomic consequences that the government is anxious to avoid. If it attempts to sterilise the effects of its intervention in the foreign exchange market by pursuing expansionary monetary policy, two things may happen, or perhaps more accurately, fail to happen. First, the domestic rate of interest will be kept relatively low, and this may encourage further capital outflows. Second, the two mechanisms for strengthening the current account – which will be necessary if capital is no longer flowing in to finance the deficit – will have been interrupted; these are the devaluation in the currency that would have encouraged exports and discouraged imports, and the macroeconomic contraction that would have reduced imports. Where capital inflows have been financing a current account deficit, the stark reality is that either international reserves will have to be used to pay for net imports, or the deficit will have to be eliminated.

Policy Options

There is no neat policy solution to deal with the volatility of capital flows; not least because our understanding of what causes capital to move internationally is rather limited. Rather empty policy platitudes therefore tend to stand in place of a firm policy direction and agenda. What can we say about policy?

When faced with a sudden *inflow* of capital, governments need to decide whether it is temporary or permanent. If it is temporary, a policy of sterilised intervention may be appropriate. But this will not work in the long run. If the capital inflow is more permanent, the exchange rate needs to be allowed to reflect the change in fundamentals. Although some sorts of capital inflow may be 'hotter' and more footloose than others, unfortunately, from a policy point of view, capital does not flow into a country with a label on it saying 'temporary' or 'permanent'. There are immense practical problems, therefore, in determining the appropriate policy response.

Similarly, when faced with a capital *outflow*, the temporary/non-temporary distinction needs to be made; although, of course, in these circumstances there are limits on how much capital can flow out. Indeed, perhaps the best way of preventing a sudden and massive outflow of capital is to have prevented massive inflows of capital in the first place. A period of 'bust' can be avoided by avoiding periods of 'boom'. Where the capital outflow is temporary, it may be best to allow international reserves to fall, but where it is not temporary, it may be best to allow the exchange rate to adjust rather than fight a battle to try to protect it. Again, however, the policy problem is to know whether capital outflows can be stopped by raising the domestic rate of interest and by exchange-rate depreciation. Moreover, it is not just a matter of the direction of change, but also of how big the changes need to be. But even in terms of direction, we saw in the previous section that respectable, though not necessarily accurate, arguments can be made that raising the rate of interest and devaluing the currency may merely lead to further capital outflows.

It is in this context of policy uncertainty that governments may decide to resort to 'taxing' capital movements, with differential rates of tax perhaps being used to try to discriminate between short-term and long-term capital. Short-term capital inflows may be seen as potentially volatile and 'bad', while long-term capital inflows are seen as enhancing economic growth and as being 'good'. Policy may therefore focus on trying to switch the composition of capital inflows towards the long-term end. Otherwise, direct controls on capital movements may be adopted, to prevent both capital inflows and outflows. In the case of a sudden capital outflow, the appealing logic of capital controls is that they allow governments to pursue macroeconomic policies that they perceive as being most appropriate to the domestic economic circumstances, as opposed to those designed to keep foreign investors happy. This is likely to mean a lower rate of interest than would otherwise be the case.

But capital controls raise other issues that conventionally are associated with any debate over controls versus the market. We shall not explore them here, except to note that a broad consensus would probably form around the view that direct controls do not offer a long-term permanent solution to the problem of capital volatility. Having said this, the IMF which had, at the beginning of the 1990s, strongly encouraged countries to liberalise their capital accounts and allow free capital mobility, modified its position later in the 1990s, as capital account crises occurred. Although capital account liberalisation remained a long-term objective, the IMF acknowledged that some types of capital control could be useful in the short term to deal with excess capital volatility.

A final policy issue relates to whether capital volatility needs to be addressed at the level of the individual countries experiencing it, or whether it needs to be handled globally. In part, of course, international policy involves the attitude of the IMF and other international agencies to capital account liberalisation and capital controls. But it could also involve proposals to introduce a global tax on short-term international currency transactions – the so-called Tobin tax – and enhanced prudential regulation to minimise the chance that international lending becomes excessively risky.

It turns out that there are no easy answers at the global level either. There are serious doubts as to whether low rates of Tobin tax would be enough to discourage short-term capital instability. At the same time, high tax rates would probably prove potentially unacceptable, and would encourage avoidance. Stricter prudential regulation may rob international capital markets of the diversity of view that assists in generating stability. Short-term, market-driven risk management systems may end up exacerbating rather than moderating volatility, and the challenge is to find acceptable schemes of risk management that allow long-term investors to 'look through the cycle'. Generally speaking, then, the policy challenge associated with capital volatility remains to be met. For international macroeconomics, this is 'work in progress'.

11 | The International Co-ordination of Macroeconomic Policy

Introduction

In Chapter 8 we saw how the choice of macroeconomic policy is influenced by openness. Moreover, where economies are open, the choice of policy in one country will have implications for other countries. A question therefore arises as to whether these externalities should be internalised in some way at the international level. The danger is that, by ignoring them, countries may pursue costly and ultimately ineffective policies. The 1930s are cited frequently as a period when countries adopted beggar-thy-neighbour policies in an attempt to strengthen their own economic performance at the expense of others, but these policies resulted in recession and shrinking world trade. This provided a backdrop to international monetary reform, leading to the setting up of the Bretton Woods system and the International Monetary Fund.

At a regional level, the Eurozone involves a co-ordinated monetary policy designed to best serve the joint interests of member states. In the mid-2000s, the apparent inconsistencies between balance of payments policy in the USA, and in China and elsewhere in Asia, reawakened the idea of additional international co-ordination of macroeconomic policy. But what is meant by co-ordination, and what form might it take? What are the arguments for and against it? This chapter addresses these questions.

Terminology

The loose use of words normally gives rise to loose analysis. In the debate over policy co-ordination, three terms have frequently been used: co-operation, co-ordination and convergence. Although related, these terms remain analytically distinct.

1. *Co-operation* is a broad concept that can cover almost anything. At one extreme, it may involve merely the selective provision of information; while at the other it may involve almost complete economic integration. Such broad concepts – though very useful to politicians, since it allows them to sound as if they are agreeing when in fact they vehemently disagree – tend to be of little use to economists.
2. *Co-ordination* is a narrower concept, and occurs where national policies are modified in order to reflect international economic interdependencies. Through policy co-ordination, countries attempt to maximise some notion of 'joint' welfare; although policy co-ordination will rely on countries seeing it as a way of raising their own welfare.
3. *Convergence* is the process of becoming more similar, and is normally thought of as a consequence of co-ordination. However, care needs to be exercised in establishing clearly what it is that is converging: policies or performance? The difficulty here is that the convergence of one of these may lead to divergence in the other. The co-ordination of policy in order to achieve greater convergence in economic performance may therefore require the pursuit of divergent policies. Furthermore, it is unwise to assume that convergence of performance is the ultimate objective. Who wants to converge towards uniformly high levels of unemployment and low levels of economic activity? The ultimate objective is to raise social welfare. While at the world level this may be undermined if economic performance in individual countries diverges too acutely, the central issue remains that of whether international policy co-ordination facilitates or improves the maximisation of welfare.

Forms of Policy Co-ordination

Rules

Broadly speaking, co-ordination can take two forms. One involves establishing a set of rules or guidelines for the conduct of economic policy. Once the rules have been agreed, countries do not need to discuss the details of policy but merely have to comply with the rules. An example of such an arrangement is to have a rule for maintaining exchange rates at a specific value. Exchange-rate targets impose constraints on domestic economic management and therefore imply a measure of co-ordination.

However, just having an exchange-rate target may be inadequate, and there may need to be supplementary rules covering the ways in which fiscal and monetary policies are to be used. Imagine, for example, a situation where a government's expansionary fiscal policy has led to deficit financing, which has in turn pushed up interest rates. This results in a capital inflow that more than offsets the deterioration in the current account. The exchange rate appreciates. To keep the value of the currency at its predetermined level, the government pursues expansionary monetary policy to lower the rate of interest, but this compounds the original policy error. It would have been more appropriate to reduce the fiscal deficit, or possibly to have encouraged other countries to pursue a greater measure of fiscal expansion. This suggests that a rather thicker rule book will be needed!

Discretion

The second form of co-ordination involves the discretionary use of policy. Under this system, the performance of the world economy and of individual countries in it would be closely monitored. There would be an ongoing collection of data covering performance indicators such as gross national product (GNP), domestic demand, inflation, unemployment, trade and the current account of the balance of payments, monetary growth, the fiscal balance, the exchange rate, the interest rate, and international reserves. Where global or individual performance is deemed to be unsatisfactory, a co-ordinated programme of policies would be undertaken. Here the constraint that co-ordination brings comes from joint decision-making, rather than from compliance with specified guidelines as it does in the 'rule' case. An example of the discretionary approach was the Bonn Economic Summit in 1978, which attempted to co-ordinate policy in a way that sought to overcome the recession of the mid-1970s. The strong economies were encouraged to act as a 'locomotive' to pull the world economy out of recession.

As presented above, the discretionary approach to co-ordination attempts to improve the *general* macroeconomic performance of the world economy. However, in principle, it may also be directed towards specific problems and may operate on a more *ad hoc* basis. Thus the international co-ordination of macroeconomic policy may attempt to offset the perceived contractionary effect of a global stock market crash or a major terrorist attack. The more general and ambitious the discretionary approach, the more problematic it tends to become. This implies that, from a practical point of view, policy co-ordination should be limited to a small number of countries and key areas of policy – although neglected countries may then claim that the process is illegitimate and unrepresentative. Before going on to examine some of the problems with the international co-ordination of macroeconomic policy, let us discuss briefly the main arguments for and against it. Although, as we shall see, part of the argument against it is that it is too difficult to implement in any effective form.

Arguments For Policy Co-ordination

The basic argument for policy co-ordination is that a better outcome in terms of world economic welfare may be achieved than would result from independent and uncoordinated policy. To the extent that there is scope in the process for all countries to benefit, or at least some to benefit without others losing, policy co-ordination is Pareto efficient.

Many of the economic problems that individual countries encounter in terms of inflation, unemployment, recession, the balance of payments and the environment are shared. There is a common-sense appeal to the idea that shared problems require shared solutions. Consider the following example to illustrate the superiority of a shared solution: imagine a country that is anxious to expand domestic demand in an attempt to counter recession and rising unemployment at home, but at the same time is concerned that independent demand expansion will result in balance of payments problems. It therefore accepts a lower level of domestic economic activity than it would ideally prefer. Fear of the balance of payments consequences means that uncoordinated policy results in a suboptimal outcome. If, on the other hand, expansion could be co-ordinated across countries, its balance of payments consequences would be neutralised, since individual countries would experience an increase in their exports as well as their imports. In this set of circumstances, uncoordinated policy has a demand deflationary bias which may be avoided through policy co-ordination. On the other hand, failure to co-ordinate could conceivably lead to uniform expansion across countries, which is excessive in respect of its global inflationary impact. Here, again, closer co-ordination of policy could confer benefits on all parties.

As another sample, take the case of a country that is anxious to strengthen the current account of its balance of payments. In an attempt to do this it supports an undervalued currency and deflates domestic demand. The purpose behind currency undervaluation is to create price incentives, which have the effect of expanding exports and contracting imports (depending on the values of key foreign trade elasticities). The deflation of aggregate domestic demand may be necessary to generate spare capacity, which is then used to meet the additional demand for home-produced goods; but it will also have the effect of lowering the demand for imports. If exports are regarded as given, the reduced demand for imports will translate into a strengthened current account. But can exports be regarded in this way? As we saw in Chapter 2, since the imports of one country are the exports of others, a decline in one country's imports will mean a decline in the exports of other countries. Such a decline will, via the multiplier process, lead to a fall in national income in the exporting countries, and an induced fall in their imports. Some of these imports may come from the country that initiated the decline in demand, with the result that the desired improvement in the balance of payments will not be achieved.

Furthermore, if countries share the desire to 'strengthen' their own balance of payments and endeavour to achieve this by managing domestic demand and depreciating exchange rates, the policies will be doomed to fail. As noted in Chapter 7, there is a 'fallacy of composition' in the sense that what may work for one country on its own will not work for all countries together. All that will happen is that world economic activity and trade will fall, and world unemployment will rise. In the zero sum world of the balance of payments, the current account deficit of some countries may only fall if the surplus of others also falls, and this is likely to require the international orchestration of policy.

Lurking behind the above discussion of policy co-ordination are some fundamental features of the world economy in which we live. First, economies in the world are increasingly interdependent, both through trade and through financial markets; they are, in other words, increasingly 'open'.

Second, but leading on from this, what happens in one country (especially if it is economically important), or one group of countries, has an impact on other countries; overspill effects and feedback effects therefore need to be taken into account in the design of policy. Where externalities do not exist and an economy is completely closed, independent policy formulation is appropriate; but where they do exist, policy may need to be co-ordinated to allow for them. In modern societies, where the actions of one person affects others, we have rules that constrain our behaviour in order to comply with agreed norms; our behaviour is thereby co-ordinated. While some advocates of flexible exchange rates argued that they allow such interdependencies to be eliminated and would allow countries to pursue independent policies, experience has shown that this represented a false prospectus. Although the details of interdependence change with the nature of the exchange-rate regime, it still exists. Appreciation in the value of one major currency such as the US dollar implies depreciation in the values of other currencies such as the euro, which in turn has an impact on both economic performance and economic policy.

Third, economics suggests that the quality of decisions tends to improve as we have more information upon which to base them. Indeed, one of the problems with atomistic competition relates to inadequate information about the behaviour of competitors. Even if international policy co-operation were to be limited to the spread of information among governments concerning economic objectives and intentions, this could show up instances where domestic policies were *unsustainable* (as in the case where the build-up of debt via a fiscal deficit could not be financed internationally); *incompatible* (as in the case where balance of payments targets did not sum to zero, or all countries hoped to generate a counter-inflationary effect through currency appreciation); or would result in policy *overkill*, because global multipliers are higher than individual country multipliers.

The earlier reference to market structure is particularly apposite to a discussion of policy co-ordination, since analysis of the latter has drawn heavily on the theory of oligopoly and related game theory. Oligopoly is characterised by a few large sellers between whom there are significant interdependencies. Ignoring such interdependencies tends to result in what is a generally inferior Nash equilibrium. Similarly, in a world dominated by a few large interdependent countries or country groupings there will be scope for improving on the Nash solution via policy co-ordination, with the distribution of the gains depending on the bargaining skill and strength of the participants in the game.

Arguments Against Policy Co-ordination

Opponents of international policy co-ordination often start by stressing their support for international economic co-operation, and may even go as far as to accept that there are benefits to be gained from the greater sharing of economic information. Beyond that, however, their case incorporates a blend of practical and theoretical concerns, and ranges from the general to the specific.

At a general level, the argument is that the increased bureaucratisation of decision-making will inevitably slow down necessary policy changes, and will therefore impose (avoidable) welfare losses. Moreover, there is concern that the internationalisation of policy will shift attention away from domestic policy and will encourage governments to claim that the solution to domestic problems lies elsewhere, and often beyond their direct control. It will enable governments preoccupied with re-election to avoid, or at least to postpone, necessary but unpopular policies. More broadly, it is argued that the economics of public choice provides little reason to believe that collusion by governments will result in increased economic welfare. Competition in policy formulation, as elsewhere, is seen as the preferred solution, since this will help to ensure that counter-inflationary policies are pursued and sustained.

While, in principle, critics claim that it would be misguided for them to do so, they also claim that in practice it is difficult for governments to deliver the necessary commitment with respect to policy co-ordination. This lack of ability to co-ordinate policy (as contrasted with a lack of willingness) follows in part from the fact that an individual country's own policy preferences may themselves represent the fragile consequence of domestic trade-offs and coalitions, which could be undermined by the additional international dimension to policy formulation. Moreover, critics, with particular reference to the USA, have argued that there may be constitutional problems where an administration cannot commit the USA to fiscal policy independently of approval by Congress.

Even where the international co-ordination of policy could be implemented and would have some advantages, critics argue that the benefits will, at best, be small in relation to the costs of co-ordination, which include the high opportunity cost of the administrative time spent in negotiating any agreement.

A final argument against policy co-ordination is in fact a general argument against any attempt to manage aggregate demand through governmental policy, irrespective of whether it is co-ordinated or uncoordinated. New classical macroeconomics (NCM) maintains that demand management policies will fail because they will induce off-setting changes in behaviour in the private sector and will therefore be crowded out. What is worse, according to NCM, is that while attempts to influence aggregate demand will turn out to be futile, they may still have an adverse effect on the supply side of the economy via the set of incentives (or disincentives) they create. For this reason as well, the international co-ordination of policy, which is usually presented as favouring demand management (even though in principle it could relate to supply-side measures), is seen as being ill-conceived and, if anything, counter-productive.

Issues for Further Consideration

What are the central questions that need to be examined further in the debate over the international co-ordination of macroeconomic policy?

First, we need to improve our knowledge of how the world economy operates. What, for example, is the precise nature of the mechanisms through which economies are interrelated, and what are the lags involved? For as long as different governments believe in different models, agreement on the effects of policies, and therefore on what policies are needed, will be difficult to secure. However, whether *model uncertainty* eliminates any chance of gaining from co-ordination is more doubtful. Indeed, it may be suggested that it is precisely in conditions of uncertainty that co-ordination will be most beneficial. In addition, there may be disagreement not only over the right model, but also over the objectives to be achieved. Co-ordination will be made easier where there are uniform objectives amongst the participants.

Second, what is to stop a government reneging on an agreement to pursue particular policies if it believes such action to be in its own best interests? The economics of international policy co-ordination raises the related questions of *free-riding, time inconsistency* and *reputation*. Free-riding will be possible if governments can avoid domestic policy changes and yet still benefit from policy changes elsewhere. Time inconsistency results where there is an incentive for governments not to implement policies they have announced, since the mere announcement of the intention to implement them has in fact generated the ultimately desired response. Of course, if governments are expected to renege on commitments, or regularly fail to implement the policies they announce, they will not be believed; and they will lose credibility and reputation. In conducting economic policy, governments therefore have to bear in mind their reputations. Although reneging may give short-run gains, the associated loss of reputation may impose long-run costs. However, rather than relying on governments choosing to honour commitments in order to defend their reputations, it may be better to have a system for monitoring compliance and for penalising non-compliance. Clearly, policy co-ordination will tend to work only where participants act in a way that maintains their reputations.

Third, it may be easier to have monitoring and penalty arrangements within a rule-based system of co-ordination than within a discretionary one; it may be easier to identify countries that comply or break the rules. However, rules not only need to be uncomplicated and clearly understood, they also need to be flexible enough to accommodate change and to result in a relatively symmetrical distribution of any adjustment burden; it was the lack of flexibility within both the gold standard and the Bretton Woods system, as well as an asymmetry in adjustment, that led to their eventual demise. Moreover, the pursuit of simplicity can be taken too far. As noted earlier, it is unlikely that a rule-based system that relates only to exchange rates will be adequate.

Fourth, while a system of rule-based co-ordination may on some counts be superior, a discretionary approach may still be needed to deal with global economic crises. Furthermore, a discretionary approach may accommodate a broader agenda of co-ordination than would a rule-based system.

Institutional Arrangements

Even if it was determined that closer co-ordination of macroeconomic policy is, on balance, a good idea, there is still a fundamental problem in terms of designing the best institutional arrangements for organising it. Do the appropriate global institutions already exist or are new ones needed, and on what principles should they be designed? There will be difficult trade-offs relating to representativeness and effectiveness. At one level it may be felt that co-ordination should take place within a new global institution possessing full global membership and terms of reference that give it the objective of maximising global economic welfare. But the practical problems would be legion. Apart from the difficulty of defining global economic welfare and of identifying the macroeconomic policies that would maximise it, the operations of global institutions, as well as the chances of the institutions being established in the first place, will always be constrained by the willingness of member countries to give up national sovereignty. The political limits to international macroeconomic policy co-ordination are therefore likely to exert a strong, and perhaps binding, constraint on its future evolution.

Part III

Applications

12 The Oil Crisis of the 1970s and the Debt Crisis of the 1980s

Introduction

Although memory fades, the 1970s and 1980s were dominated by two global economic events. The first, in 1973/4, was associated with a sharp increase in the price of oil, and the second, coming to the fore in 1982, was the so-called Third World debt crisis. The purpose of this brief chapter, as with the other chapters in this part of the book, is to see whether the analysis we have worked through is useful in helping to understand what was going on. We do not set out to provide a detailed examination backed up by sophisticated empirical evidence, but rather to offer a broad analytical overview based on the concepts and ideas we have acquired.

The Oil Crisis of the 1970s

Oil prices quadrupled between 1973 and 1974. Given the importance of oil to the world economy, a natural question to ask is what effects this had. What actually happened was that global inflation rates rose to post-war record levels and at the same time the world economy moved into sharp recession. Simultaneously therefore, both the rate of inflation and the rate of unemployment rose. Economists at the time were more familiar with an inverse relationship between inflation and unemployment as shown by the Phillips curve, and the question therefore arose as to how an increase in oil prices could have such apparently counter-intuitive effects.

Fortunately the global macroeconomic effects of the rise in the price of oil may be conveniently analysed within the framework of the global *IS–LM* model shown in Figure 12.1. The rising oil price redistributed income from oil-consuming and importing countries to oil-producing and exporting countries. On the basis that the latter had a higher mar-

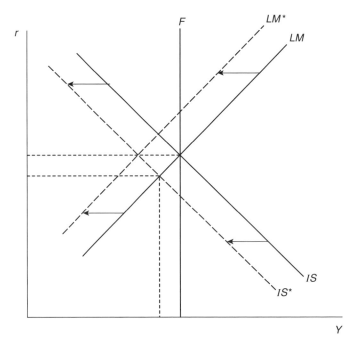

Figure 12.1

ginal propensity to save than the former, the effect of such redistribution was to increase the global average propensity to save and to shift the global *IS* schedule to the left. The uncertainty caused by the large rise in the price of oil also had a detrimental effect on expectations. The global investment schedule therefore shifted to the left thus causing a further leftward shift in *IS*.

With no change in the location of a positively sloped global *LM* schedule, such a leftward shift in *IS* causes both output and the rate of interest to fall. Assuming that the world economy is initially at full employment, the leftward shift in *IS* also causes unemployment and capacity under-utilisation.

Of course, it is also possible that increasing uncertainty strengthens liquidity preference. The related increase in the demand for money might then shift *LM* leftwards. Such a leftward shift endorses the impact on output and income but causes the interest rate to rise. Falling real interest rates during the 1970s would, however, seem to suggest that it was the leftward shift in *IS* which dominated.[1]

So far the analysis shows how the increase in oil prices had a demand deflationary impact on the global economy. Is this inconsistent with

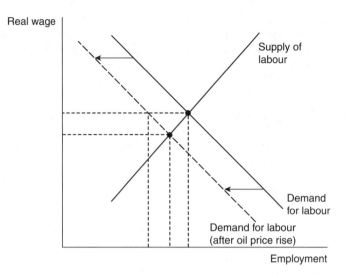

Figure 12.2

the fact that, following the rise in the price of oil, global inflation accelerated? The answer is 'not necessarily'. For although global aggregate demand was deflated, the increase in oil prices also exerted a cost inflationary effect.[2] While, in principle, a once and for all increase in the price of oil will lead to a once and for all increase in the price level, it may also lead to expectations of further price increases. Besides, what if wage earners resist the implied cut in real wages? In these circumstances there will be secondary effects, and a more general and persistent tendency for prices to rise. Where the nominal money supply is fixed, inflation will reduce the real supply of money, and the real *LM* schedule will shift leftwards, thus emphasising the demand deflationary effects.

Real wage resistance has further implications. For, to the extent that workers are successful in protecting their real wages in circumstances where the equilibrium real wage has fallen, profits will tend to fall and unemployment will rise. The process is illustrated in Figure 12.2. Here it is seen that an increase in the price of oil shifts the demand curve for labour to the left thus reducing both the equilibrium real wage and the equilibrium level (or so called natural rate) of employment. If real wages are maintained at their former equilibrium level the increase in unemployment is more marked, rising above the already higher 'natural' rate of unemployment.

The balance of payments implications of the oil price rise were perhaps rather more complex than might at first be thought. Not only did the rise in the price of oil create current-account disequilibria, it also served to generate both a demand for and a supply of international capital. Many developing countries borrowed heavily to finance current account deficits.

The Developing Country Debt Crisis of the 1980s

If the 1970s were dominated by the oil crisis, the 1980s were dominated by the Third World debt crisis which broke when Mexico announced in 1982 that it was unable to meet its outstanding debt obligations. The nub of the crisis was reflected by the rapid rise in the debt service ratios (DSR) that faced indebted nations. This ratio expresses debt service payments as a percentage of export earnings. A rising debt service ratio can therefore be associated with either increasing debt service payments or falling export earnings. But what caused the crisis, and what in particular brought it about in the early 1980s?

Although it is unwise to ignore the role of domestic factors such as over-expansionary fiscal and monetary policies which led to currency over-valuation within the indebted nations, and contributed to the crisis, it is helpful to examine the global economic environment in which they found themselves.[3]

The trade functions introduced in Chapter 3 show a country's exports as depending on income levels in importing countries. Since developing countries sell most of their exports to industrial countries, the level of economic activity in the richer economies exerts an important influence over the export performance of developing countries.

Debt service payments depend on the amount of debt and the rate of interest. Although developing countries can influence the amount of debt they acquire, they have to take world interest rates as given, since these are largely determined by the monetary policies of industrial countries. Interest rates will rise and fall as monetary policy becomes more and less restrictive. To explain rising debt service ratios we are therefore looking for a combination of circumstances that led to falling national income and rising interest rates in the industrial countries.

The early 1980s were indeed a period of economic recession and rising interest rates in industrial countries, but why?[4] Newly elected governments in the US and UK were preoccupied with reducing inflation, which had accelerated towards the end of the 1970s. The governments were influenced by monetarist modes of thought and therefore put the control of monetary aggregates at the centre of their macroeconomic strategy. As Figure 12.3 illustrates, contractionary monetary policy shifted the industrial countries' *LM* schedule to the left. With a fixed *IS* schedule, the rate of interest r rises from r^1 to r^2 and income falls

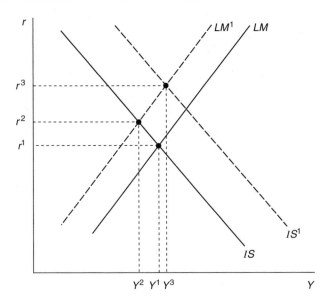

Figure 12.3

from Y^1 to Y^2 and we have a simple (albeit partial) explanation of the debt crisis. Perhaps without this bout of monetary contraction in industrial economies the debt crisis could have been averted.

In the mid 1980s, the US began to relax fiscal policy and its *IS* schedule shifted rightwards. This was a mixed blessing for indebted developing countries. For those, such as Mexico, that sold their exports mainly in the US market, export earnings rose, and this served to reduce their debt service ratios. But, as Figure 12.3 reveals, fiscal expansion (with *IS* shifting to *IS^1*) which is accompanied by monetary tightness (with no accommodating shift in *LM*) leads to rising interest rates (r^2 to r^3) that then increase DSRs.

Moreover, the heavily indebted developing countries had most of their debt denominated in dollars. The last thing that they wanted to see in the early 1980s was a sharp appreciation in the value of the dollar, but this was exactly what happened. At first glance the dollar appreciation was counter-intuitive since the US was running a large fiscal deficit. Fiscal deficits are normally associated in people's minds with balance of payments current account deficits, indeed there is talk of the 'terrible twins'. Surely a current account deficit should have led to depreciation in the value of the dollar and not appreciation? Again, the *IS–LM–BP* model comes to our rescue. Given the configuration of schedules shown in Figure 12.4, it can be seen that fiscal expansion leads to an overall

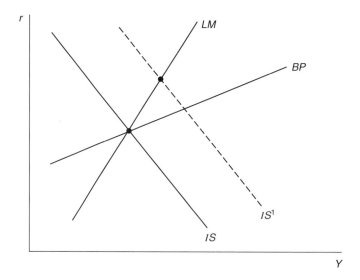

Figure 12.4

balance of payments surplus and exchange-rate appreciation, for, while the increase in national income weakens the current account, the increase in the interest rate induces capital inflows to such an extent that the capital account effect overpowers the current account effect.[5]

The way in which the course of the Third World debt crisis was affected by economic developments in advanced economies, and particularly the USA, provides an example of the transmission mechanisms we discussed briefly in Chapter 2 and again in Chapter 6. These spillover effects were also to be associated with subsequent crises in the world economy.

13 Monetary Integration in Europe: The UK and the Euro

Introduction

Every so often a sequence of events occurs in the real world that seems custom-made to illustrate basic economic principles. The UK's flirtation with the European Exchange Rate Mechanism (ERM) at the beginning of the 1990s – joining in October 1990 and leaving in September 1992 – represents just such a sequence. It is difficult to imagine a better designed case study of the international macroeconomics developed throughout the earlier chapters of this book.

The travails of the European Monetary System over 1992–93, with immense foreign exchange uncertainty affecting a number of currencies, provided a real 'humdinger' of a crisis. Not only did key dates get written into the economic history books (16 September 1992, when the UK withdrew from the ERM became known as 'Black Wednesday'), but five years later the debacle of Britain's dramatic reversal of the principal plank of its macroeconomic strategy – the commitment to a pegged exchange rate against other European currencies – was being seen as the beginning of the end of the Conservative administration, opening the way for the Labour Party's landslide victory in 1997. So why did Britain join the ERM in the first place, and why did it leave it? What went wrong? If errors were made, were they of the UK's own making or were they external and outside the Government's control?

Britain's Entry into the ERM

For many years prior to its eventual entry into the quasi-fixed exchange rate element of the European Monetary System, the UK had agonised about the issue, saying that it would join when the 'time was ripe'. This stance failed to hide deep disagreements within the government which resulted in the resignation of senior ministers, including a Chancellor of the Exchequer, a Foreign Secretary, and ultimately the Prime Minister. What finally tipped the balance in favour of entering the ERM was a belief in its counter-inflationary benefits. It was assuredly not the advantages emphasised by optimum currency area (OCA) theory, as explained in Chapter 9, that were persuasive. Indeed, the government clearly believed that Europe (with Britain included) did not constitute an optimum currency area on the basis of the criteria identified in OCA theory.

However, the government was in something of a dilemma towards the end of the 1980s. The centrepiece of its macroeconomic policy in the early to mid-1980s, namely the tight control of monetary aggregates, had been largely discredited and abandoned, and it was therefore keen to find an alternative anti-inflationary policy 'rule' to which it could commit itself.[1] The defence of a pegged exchange rate offered one alternative; 'new' OCA theory emphasised the credibility and counter-inflationary benefits of adopting a peg and tracking the monetary policy of a lower inflation partner (Germany). A cynic might argue that the desire to control inflation took precedence over the government's natural preference for unregulated markets (including foreign exchange markets), and its dislike of the speed with which Europe was integrating. The government acted as if it disliked inflation more than it was sceptical of Europe! This, in part, also explains why the UK entered the ERM at what many observers believed to be an overvalued exchange rate, since about the only argument for currency overvaluation is as a counter-inflationary device. In 1990 the UK government was anxious to reduce interest rates for domestic reasons. Entering the ERM with a high value for sterling seemed to provide an offsetting disinflationary effect.

In this narrow sense joining the ERM seemed to deliver its promise, and the UK's inflation rate, that had been accelerating up until 1989, when it reached over 7 per cent, began to decline thereafter. There was some evidence that, as new OCA theory predicted, the UK had been able to improve its 'sacrifice ratio'. The credibility gains seemed to have enabled inflation to be reduced at a lower cost in terms of lost output and unemployment than if Britain had continued to stay outside the ERM. So what went wrong?

Britain's Exit from the ERM

As explained in Chapter 9, one of the dangers of an exchange-rate union between countries is its exposure to asymmetrical shocks, which affect different countries in different ways. Such shocks or disturbances create macroeconomic disequilibria, and such disequilibria put strains on fixed exchange rates. The ERM was hit by just such a shock in 1990 when East and West Germany unified. German monetary policy, which had been a strength of the ERM in the second half of the 1980s, was destined to become a fundamental weakness in the early 1990s.

The need to rebuild the East German economy resulted in German fiscal expansion; Germany's *IS* schedule shifted to the right. With an independent and inflation-averse central bank (the Bundesbank), German monetary policy remained tight. Germany's *LM* schedule remained static, and did not shift to the right to monetise the fiscal deficit. Expansionary fiscal policy therefore increased German national income (Y), but it also drove up the interest rate as the German government borrowed heavily to finance the fiscal stimulus.

This was something of a mixed blessing for Germany's European partners. The good news was that there was now greater scope for exporting to Germany and enjoying an element of export-led growth in their own economies. It is no coincidence that as the German current account balance of payments moved from surplus in 1990 into deficit in 1991 and beyond, the current account deficits in France and the UK diminished. German expansion to some extent therefore spilled over to partner countries. However, given European trading patterns, this benefit was not large enough to off-set overall balance of payments problems.

More significantly, the bad news was that in order to defend fixed exchange rates and avoid the pressures put on them by capital moving to Germany attracted by higher German interest rates, other European economies had to increase their own interest rates. Germany acted as if it had the degree of freedom to determine its own monetary policy independently. Other European economies without this freedom followed suit. What had originally been a counter-inflationary benefit of ERM membership consequently became counter-inflationary overkill.

It is interesting that events seemed to be inconsistent with intertemporal optimising models of the balance of payments. These would have had forward-looking agents anticipating future fiscal surpluses in Germany to pay for contemporary fiscal deficits. The behaviour induced by this – that is, increases in current private saving to pay for future tax hikes, should then have ameliorated pressures on the value of the Deutschmark (DM) to rise. In fact, the DM appreciated against the US dollar and this reinforced the recessionary tendencies in Germany's European partners.

While high interest rates made sense in a German context they did not make sense in other European economies, including the UK. The rate of economic growth in the UK was a mere 0.4 per cent in 1990; but in 1991 and 1992 it was −2.0 per cent and −0.5 per cent, respectively. Unsurprisingly in these circumstances, unemployment had risen from 5.8 per cent in 1990 to nearly 10 per cent in 1992. These were politically significant economic problems.

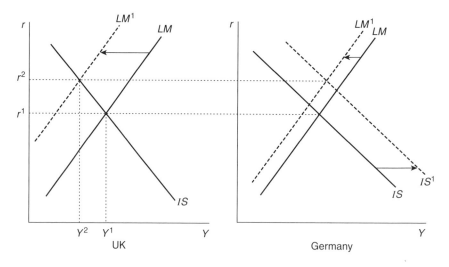

Figure 13.1

But there was worse to come. Increased spending in Germany was threatening German price stability. The rate of inflation in Germany rose from 1.5 per cent per annum in 1988 to 5.5 per cent per annum in 1992, a rate deemed unacceptable by the Bundesbank. Its reaction was to pursue contractionary monetary policy, shifting the German *LM* schedule to the left. German short-term interest rates, that had been below 4 per cent in 1988, rose to 9.5 per cent by 1992.

Germany's European partners now had a stark choice. Capital controls had been removed in the late 1980s, so they could not prevent interest rate differentials from leading to capital flows. The choice was therefore to match German interest rates in order to defend agreed exchange rates, or set lower interest rates that were seen as being more appropriate for achieving domestic targets, and abandon fixed exchange rates. The system simply did not allow them to have fixed exchange rates, free capital mobility and monetary autonomy. Initially they followed the high interest rate route as shown in Figure 13.1. Here the UK is seen as shifting its *LM* schedule sufficiently far to the left to create macroeconomic equilibrium (a point of intersection between the UK's *IS* and *LM* schedules) at an interest rate level determined by the intersection between German *IS* and *LM* schedules. The consequence is that national income in the UK falls from Y^1 to Y^2 and unemployment, by implication, rises. This is exactly what happened.

There is one important further twist to the story. The whole point of joining the ERM was to make a *credible* commitment to a fixed exchange rate and to overcome time consistency problems associated with expected policy reversals. However, credibility does not depend on what governments say, but on whether private agents believe that economic and political circumstances will enable them to do what they say. Although in the run up to the 1992 crisis the UK government repeated its commitment to the ERM, with rising unemployment and recession in the UK, foreign exchange speculators found the commitment to a fixed exchange rate to be literally incredible, especially when the government was publicly admitting its dislike of high interest rates. Anticipating that the UK government would eventually be forced to renege on its commitment and devalue, they started to sell sterling, and sell it heavily. The die was cast.

Now if speculators were selling sterling and a fall in its value was to be avoided, someone had to buy it to offset market forces. In such a situation it was the UK government that bought sterling by running down its foreign exchange reserves. But, by definition, this is not a policy that can be pursued for ever, since reserves are finite. For as long as it does continue, the domestic money supply falls and the *LM* schedule shifts further leftwards.

Furthermore, once speculators expect a devaluation, they have to be offered yet higher interest rates in the form of a risk premium in order to encourage them to hold the currency that they believe will be devalued. There has to be an additional interest rate incentive to hold the currency. Thus once the crisis had begun – triggered by referendum results in Denmark and France that called into question whether EMU was politically feasible and whether exchange rates would be realigned – the UK authorities had to increase interest rates still further, even though speculators knew that the government believed that they were already too high for domestic purposes. It is in this way that exchange-rate crises feed on themselves, with the eventual outcome assuming an air of inevitability, unless something happens to strategically alter speculators' expectations. There were the makings of a second generation currency crisis as described in Chapter 6.

As in the crisis in emerging economies to be discussed in the next chapter, the UK government found itself in a situation where it was losing reserves in an almost certainly unsustainable attempt to defend an overvalued exchange rate. There was a clear inconsistency between internal and external targets at the then given exchange rate. Prolonging the agony would have wiped out Britain's reserves and simply handed more profits to private speculators. By the time Black Wednesday dawned there was little option other than to devalue sterling. As shown in Figure 13.2 the UK simultaneously shifted both *LM* and *BP* downwards and to the right, ensuring that equilibrium was attained with a lower rate of interest, (r to r^1), a lower value for sterling, and a higher level of national income (Y to Y^1).

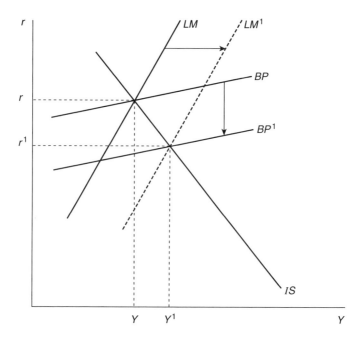

Figure 13.2

When it came to a contradiction between the internal objectives of economic growth and lower unemployment and the external object- ive of defending the exchange rate, it was demonstrated that a point is reached at which economic growth and fuller employment take pri- ority. This challenged the time consistency of exchange-rate commit- ments. Was there any merit in 'tying your hands' to a fixed exchange rate if you could untie them when it became awkward to have them tied? This question reverberated through the subsequent discussions of monetary union in Europe.

But what happened to inflation after Black Wednesday? Did aban- doning the ERM have a cost for the UK in terms of lost reputation in the effort to control inflation? Did inflation accelerate? Significantly, this was not the case. Inflation continued to fall even after the UK had withdrawn from the ERM, dipping below 2 per cent per annum in 1994 and hovering around 2.5 per cent per annum up to 1997. If nothing else, the ERM experience seemed to have persuaded people that the government was serious about inflation.[2] Indeed, most of the princi- pal macroeconomic factors beyond 1992 performed quite well. Economic growth began to accelerate and unemployment began to fall. To the extent that it is economic performance that determines the outcome of elections, the British experience seems to suggest that there can be a lengthy lag. Strong contemporary macroeconomic indicators in 1997 were apparently insufficient to expunge the electorate's memory of the events surrounding Black Wednesday.

Monetary Integration in Europe After the Crisis

As the above account demonstrates, the crisis in the Exchange Rate Mechanism (ERM) of the European Monetary System (EMS) in 1992 was an archetypal example of a second-generation currency crisis (as analysed in Chapter 6). There was a shock in the form of German unification that created disequilibrium at the original set of exchange rates. In many of the other economies belonging to the ERM, apart from Germany, there were inconsistencies between internal and external targets. There were doubts about the commitment of some governments to maintaining their currency pegs, and this stimulated private capital markets to speculate about devaluation. The response of private markets therefore helped to determine the outcome (multiple equilibria). And, once devaluation had occurred, the prioritisation of economic growth and employment was reflected by a reduction in the rate of interest in devaluing countries.

But what was the longer-term response to the crisis? One interpretation was that it reflected the fundamental problem with fixed exchange-rate regimes: that they do not offer enough flexibility to deal with shocks. This interpretation suggested that national governments will always eventually behave in ways that they see as benefiting their own national interests. Private markets understand this and, as a result, any pegged rate regime is going to be vulnerable. Even if partner countries' economies are initially synchronised, shocks will occur that lead to disequilibria. This interpretation raised doubts about the movement towards Economic and Monetary Union (EMU) in Europe.

The second interpretation was in sharp contrast. This suggested that the crisis only happened because the commitment to defending pegged exchange rates in some countries lacked credibility. This interpretation argued that, for as long as governments retained the option of devaluation, there would always be suspicions that in some circumstances they might use it. The answer was to eliminate the possibility by adopting a single currency in Europe. Indeed, advocates of fast-track EMU argued that prior convergence, as incorporated in the Maastricht Treaty, was only necessary in the case of a fixed exchange-rate system in order to avoid the possibility that non-convergence would lead to expectations of currency realignment. Once realignment was ruled out by the adoption of a single currency, prior convergence was no longer of central importance.

The debate over EMU during the 1990s reflected, in applied fashion, many aspects of the theoretical debates amongst economists over international macroeconomics. Economists who believe in a non-vertical short-run Phillips curve tend to argue that giving up the exchange rate as a policy instrument can carry a real cost in terms of unemployment. Whereas those who believe that Phillips curves are vertical in the short run as well as the long run see the only cost as being that of being unable to choose a domestically-optimal inflation rate – and this may be only a relatively small cost. Economists who believe that nominal exchange-rate changes lead to real changes are reluctant to give up the exchange-rate instrument, whereas those who believe that devaluation is ineffective because it leads to offsetting inflation see no problem. Economists who believe that goods and labour markets work inefficiently are reluctant to give up being able to adjust the exchange rate, whereas those who believe in efficient markets have no such reservations because they see labour and goods markets adjusting instead of foreign exchange markets.

Economists who argue that with highly mobile private capital, limited official reserves, and asymmetric shocks, there can never be any such thing as *immutably* or *irrevocably* fixed exchange rates, claim that the real choice is between flexible exchange rates on the one hand, and full monetary union on the other. This choice is often couched as being as much a political as an economic one, since it largely depends on the scope for regional transfers within the union.

Those economists who believe that it is possible to calculate equilibrium exchange rates argue that there is a third option involving managed exchange-rate flexibility. To them the 1992–3 crisis in the ERM reflected the eventually dramatic but essentially fairly basic refusal to allow exchange rates to adjust prior to 1992 in order to reflect the changed economic fundamentals associated with German unification.

It is because of these debates over the macroeconomics of single currencies, alongside the uncertainties about the microeconomics of international money which we have not discussed in this book, that economists appear frustratingly unable to speak with a common voice about such an important issue as monetary union in Europe. Indeed it is this lack of economic consensus that has helped to make monetary integration a political issue. Where the economics is unclear the politics dominates. But, as implied above, the economics and politics are connected, since some economic policies, such as regional transfers, require a high degree of political cohesion. It is in this sense that an economic union can only survive in the context of a political union.

The Euro Arrives: To Join or Not to Join?

When the stage was reached in 1999 at which the euro was being introduced with a view to becoming Europe's single currency by 2002, those countries that opted in were either convinced by the economic advantages of single currencies, as explained in Chapter 9, or were persuaded by the political arguments for still closer monetary integration. Those that stayed out, including the UK, remained unconvinced by either or both sets of arguments. The formal line in the UK was that the timing was not appropriate, since the UK economy was out of step with many countries that were joining the Eurozone but, once convergence had happened, the UK would probably join. The reality was that significant divisions existed within the government. Europhiles favoured Britain's entry on political grounds, arguing that to be at the centre of Europe required membership of the Eurozone. Sceptics were reluctant to cede national sovereignty over the design of monetary policy, and were concerned that the heralded advantages of membership were outweighed by the inability to choose interest rates to meet national needs and to allow the value of sterling to change to facilitate economic adjustment. What is certain is that the decision to join or not to join the Eurozone hardly reflected the dictates of optimum currency area theory.

The Downs and Ups of the Euro

What happened to the value of the euro following its introduction, and does the theory examined in Chapter 5 help to explain the variations that occurred? Initially, the euro's value fell, but it recovered strongly towards the mid-2000s. The theory of purchasing power parity implies that the explanation may be found in the Eurozone's inflation rate. However, inflation in Eurozone countries in comparison to the USA does not seem to be consistent with this explanation. It is not the case that Eurozone inflation was relatively high in the early years and relatively low later on. The evidence is therefore broadly consistent with the general observation that PPP theory is not well equipped to explain short-term movements in exchange rates.

Other suggestions, that the initial fall in the value of the euro reflected fundamental weaknesses in the Eurozone economies and was indicative of 'Eurosclerosis', were also rather unconvincing, particularly as many performance indicators showed little change between the periods of euro decline and euro recovery. This could also be said of the stance of fiscal policy. Perhaps more persuasive was the argument that the European Central Bank (ECB) started out without a positive reputation; indeed, it had no reputation. As a new institution there was a degree of uncertainty about its commitment to controlling inflation. Moreover, the Eurozone interest rate was set slightly below that of the USA. With uncertainties about monetary policy in Europe, and with enduring European economic stagnation, international capital gravitated to the USA. Movements in currency values tend to feed on themselves – at least for a time. A depreciating euro led to expectations that its value would depreciate further, providing another reason for capital to move to the USA, into the dollar and away from the Eurozone and the euro.

Certainly, the evidence is at odds with the claim that the value of the euro – or the dollar, for that matter – was dictated by the current account. The Eurozone's current account balance of payments was in surplus over the entire period from 1999 to 2005, and yet it was only in the second half of this period that the euro's value rose. The answer would therefore seem to lie in the capital account, where early on, doubts about the durability of the euro and about the policies of the new European institutions, combined with relatively slow economic growth and low interest rates, made Europe a less attractive place in which to invest than the USA. Later on, declining confidence in the dollar and in the sustainability of the US current account – to be examined in Chapter 15 – coincided with increasing confidence in the euro. There were therefore factors both pushing capital away from the USA and pulling it towards Europe. If dollars became less attractive, what other options were available, given the economic problems in Japan? Once the dollar began to depreciate and the euro to appreciate, short-term expectations changed in ways that were self-fulfilling.

Experience with the euro would suggest that, while there is indeed a tendency for short-term exchange rates to overshoot their long-run equilibrium levels, this may be more to do with the elasticity of expectations in private capital markets, where a movement in the value of a currency in one direction is taken as an indication that there will be a further movement in the same direction, than with the pursuit of unstable monetary policy, as the model of overshooting summarised in Chapter 5 implies. Experience with the euro and the path taken by the euro's value in foreign exchange markets informs us that we still have much to learn about the short-run determinants of exchange rates.

In the short run, exchange rates seem able to deviate significantly from their long-run equilibria. There is little even to suggest that the probability of further short-run deviation depends on the size of the initial deviation. Thus, while it might have been suggested that the initial fall in the euro's exchange rate had driven it below its long-run equilibrium value, exchange-rate models struggled to predict the timing of the recovery.

With problems engulfing European integration in the mid-2000s it is premature to argue that the euro's recovery will be sustained. Evaporating confidence could once again depress its value. There are even those who suggest that the whole single currency experiment will unravel; only time will tell.

14 Currency and Economic Crises in Emerging Economies

Introduction

While the crisis in the Exchange Rate Mechanism (ERM) of the European Monetary System (EMS) dominated the early 1990s, the rest of the decade and the first half of the 2000s was more associated with currency and financial crises in a number of emerging economies. The sequence of crises began in Mexico in 1994, followed by further crises in East Asia in 1997–8, Russia and Brazil at the end of the 1990s, and Argentina and Turkey at the beginning of the 2000s. In this chapter we focus on Mexico, East Asia and Argentina. Again, the purpose is not to provide in-depth analyses of the crises – time and space rule this out. Instead, it is to use these global events to allow us to apply relatively simple international macroeconomics and to illustrate how this analysis provides us with insights into what was going on.

The Mexican Peso Crisis of 1994

In Chapter 12 we saw how economic developments in the USA spilled over and affected Latin America. In the early 1990s, US economic growth was slow, and US interest rates relatively low. International capital was, as a result, 'pushed' south of the border to Mexico and elsewhere in Latin America. It was not, however, only that this capital was being pushed away from the USA. It was also being 'pulled' in by the Latin-American economies, where both economic performance and policy seemed to be improving significantly after the 1980s. The conversion of high levels of external debt from short-term to long-term debt contributed to easing their debt difficulties; the adoption of more market-based policies, such as privatisation, seemed to be having a pay-off in terms of economic growth; trade liberalisation and a more outward-looking trade orientation, allied with closer trade integration with the

USA – particularly in the case of Mexico via the North American Free Trade Area – offered brighter prospects for exports; a more relaxed attitude to inward foreign direct investment hinted at greater chances of technology transfer and further productivity growth; the control of fiscal deficits seemed to be receiving more attention; and, as a consequence, monetary expansion and inflation were falling. Furthermore, many Latin-American economies were using their exchange rates as a 'nominal anchor' and were pursuing exchange-rate-based stabilisation. In short, and according to our simple analysis of capital movements in Chapter 3, it is relatively easy to see why capital was attracted to countries such as Mexico.

But capital inflows carried their own problems. In Mexico, for example, they drove up the real value of the peso, and this fairly rapidly undermined the Mexican current account balance of payments which moved into substantial deficit as imports increased sharply. Capital inflows also encouraged the Mexican government to allow domestic consumption to rise; increasing absorption put pressure on the balance of payments.

Overvaluation of the currency eventually led to expectations that the peso would have to be devalued. The authorities were reluctant to do so for fear of the inflationary consequences; but defending the exchange rate rapidly depleted reserves which further endorsed expectations that the government would have to devalue. A sharp rise in US interest rates in 1994 and 1995 made matters worse by further encouraging capital to move back to the USA. Capital was now no longer coming into Mexico to finance the current account deficit. The Mexican authorities resisted pressures to raise domestic interest rates for fear of the effects on the domestic financial sector and economic growth, and expanded domestic credit to offset the effects of capital outflows on the domestic money supply. This again weakened the balance of payments and, with the enduring attempt to avoid devaluation, led to losses of international reserves.

A self-perpetuating speculative crisis resulted, the nature of which eventually forced Mexico to devalue and raise interest rates, as well as to turn to the IMF for historically large amounts of financial assistance.

The course of events outlined above is illustrated by Figures 14.1a and 14.1b. In the early 1990s (shown by Figure 14.1a), the Mexican *IS* and *LM* schedules intersected above the *BP* schedule, with the Mexican interest rate inducing capital inflows which were more than adequate to finance the current account deficit, and which allowed international reserves to be accumulated. By the end of 1994 (shown by Figure 14.1b) the *IS* schedule had shifted across to the right, reflecting increased consumption and lower saving, but the monetary authorities had also expanded the domestic money supply in an attempt to keep interest rates from

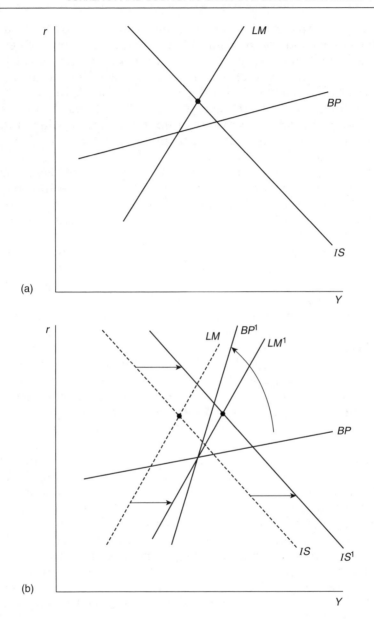

(a)

(b)

Figure 14.1

rising. At the same time the Mexican *BP* schedule had become steeper since an uncertain and unstable political environment in Mexico had increased the risk premium needed to encourage foreign lenders to lend.

Furthermore the interest rate in the USA had risen, thereby reducing the Mexican rate relative to the US rate. The outcome of this combination of factors was that by 1994 and 1995 the Mexican IS and LM schedules (shown by IS^1 and LM^1 in Figure 14.1b) intersected below the new BP schedule (BP^1) showing that capital inflows were no longer adequate to finance the (increasing) current account deficit. Instead the deficit had to be financed by running down reserves. Clearly this was only a short-term possibility since reserves are finite. Ultimately, and faced by a financial crisis, the Mexican authorities had to devalue, shifting the BP schedule downwards, and to adopt contractionary monetary policies, shifting LM to the left.

Given our analysis of currency crises in Chapter 6, the Mexican crisis seems to have been broadly consistent with the first-generation model. Fiscal deficits, in conjunction with high domestic consumption, monetary expansion, relatively rapid inflation (by comparison with the USA, if not previous inflation rates in Mexico), an appreciating real exchange rate, current account deficits, a reluctance to devalue, and a fated attempt to ride out the storm by running down reserves, were key features of the crisis. The policy response was also standard first-generation. The peso was devalued and the domestic interest rate was increased. There was a downside to devaluation, which is no doubt one of the reasons why the Mexican authorities delayed it. To finance their fiscal deficits prior to the crisis, they had borrowed short-term in dollars, in the hope of signalling their commitment to maintaining the value of the peso. Following devaluation, the peso cost of servicing this debt rose. However, while this created problems for fiscal management, the devaluation was also associated with a significant short-term current account response that enabled the Mexican economy to recover from the crisis much more quickly than many observers had forecast. The recovery also helped to mitigate the spillover consequences – the tequila effect – of the Mexican crisis. The crisis did, however, show the difficulties in forming a judgement between the counter-inflationary benefits of a pegged exchange rate, and the costs of sticking to it once the currency becomes overvalued, particularly in a global environment of high capital mobility. As a consequence, the Mexican crisis began to raise questions concerning the design and structure of the international monetary system. A theme throughout the 1990s, and one that gained momentum following the East Asian crisis a few years after the Mexican one, was that fundamental reform was needed to better deal with excessive international capital mobility.

The East Asian Crisis, 1997–8

Whereas Latin America had exhibited a chequered economic history prior to the Mexican crisis and had endured the debt crisis of the 1980s,

East Asian economies had largely bypassed the debt crisis and indeed were heralded as 'miracle' countries in terms of economic growth and development. Their performance may not have been 'miraculous', but certainly the size of the reverse from success to failure made the East Asian crisis a dramatic global event. But why did it happen? Again, it is not possible to do justice to the topic in part of one chapter in a small intermediate textbook, but it is possible to gain some insight from the theory we have assembled.

While, retrospectively, East Asian economies were located in a 'zone of vulnerability', this was not something that was widely perceived at the time, even just before the crisis occurred. Broad macroeconomic fundamentals seemed to be relatively strong. Domestic saving was high, investment was relatively productive (although productivity was falling), fiscal deficits were moderate by international standards, current account deficits were relatively small, and economic growth had been rapid. It is, of course, always easier to be wise after the event. After the occurrence of the initial crisis in Thailand, and in the subsequent transmission from this trigger country to other economies in the region, it became acknowledged that much of the investment was high-risk and speculative, that the current account was weakening because of adverse terms-of-trade movements, and that the policy of pegging domestic currencies, such as the Thai baht, to the US dollar meant that, as the dollar appreciated in the foreign exchange market, so the values of the Asian currencies also appreciated against third currencies, thereby undermining competitiveness. But were these factors enough to cause the crisis? Almost certainly not. So what did cause it?

The broad consensus is that the answer is more appropriately provided by what was happening in domestic financial markets, with their associated impact on capital flows. Here, policies of repression were replaced by ones of liberalisation. As a consequence, domestic interest rates rose and, with a liberalised capital account, international capital flowed in, especially since the commitment to pegged exchange rates was seen as being strong, and there was little perceived risk of default. However, the inflow of capital was often used to finance speculative investment. There was a boom, or at least a bubble. The boom was maintained since the increased supply of capital from abroad was matched by an increase in the domestic demand for it, and interest rates remained relatively high. But the problem with bubbles is that they burst. Two things happened to burst the bubble in Thailand: first, interest rates in Japan rose amid fears that the economy was moving too rapidly out of recession (as it transpired, it was not). This narrowed the interest rate differential that had previously favoured other countries in the region. Second, failed speculative investments led to corporate and financial weakness, which served to alter perceptions of risk. As the analysis in

Chapters 3 and 6 shows, the likely impact of these changes is that capital will begin to exit, and this is indeed what happened in Thailand; although initially the outflow was in the form of short-term bank loans rather than long-term investment flows.

The best way of dealing with crises is to avoid them. Once beyond a certain point, crises pick up a momentum of their own, and policymakers are faced with a series of unpleasant and difficult choices. Certainly in Thailand, once short-term capital began to exit, the choices were stark. The capital outflow could have been allowed to drive down the value of the baht, but this would have meant abandoning an important strand of macroeconomic policy. The consensus was that devaluation would lead to adverse balance sheet effects. The authorities could instead have decided to buy bahts and sell foreign exchange, but this would have led to a domestic credit crunch and a fall in reserves. The credit crunch could be offset by relaxing domestic monetary policy, but this would push interest rates lower, and stimulate further capital outflows. And, in any case, running down reserves is not a long-term option.

How did things turn out? Initially, reserves were used to buy the Thai baht and to prop up its value. But when there was little indication that the capital outflow would abate, and with reserves imploding, the baht was allowed to depreciate in July 1997. However, this did not avert the crisis. Capital flows did not respond positively to the increases in the interest rate. The devaluation resulted in significant balance sheet effects that further weakened the financial and corporate sectors and led to an additional erosion of confidence. There is a two-way causal relationship between financial and currency crises. Furthermore, the fall in the value of the baht opened the eyes of foreign investors to an exchange-rate risk that they had previously tended to ignore.

Although not ideally designed to capture its financial causes or the problems of inappropriate sequencing (where the capital account is liberalised alongside the domestic financial sector and before adequate domestic financial regulation is in place), Figure 14.2 gives a broad graphical exposition of what happened. During the boom period prior to the crisis, speculative investment fostered a rightward shift in Thailand's IS schedule from IS^1 to IS^2. Meanwhile, capital inflows brought with them monetary expansion, and LM shifted from LM^1 to LM^2. The strong capital account more than offset a current account deficit and allowed reserves to be accumulated. IS^2 and LM^2 intersected above BP^1. However, with the rise in global interest rates and with increased perceptions of risk, the BP schedule shifted upwards and became steeper, moving from BP^1 to BP^2. However, LM did not shift to the left, since the Thai authorities relaxed monetary policy to offset the effect of capital outflows on the domestic monetary sector. IS and LM now intersected

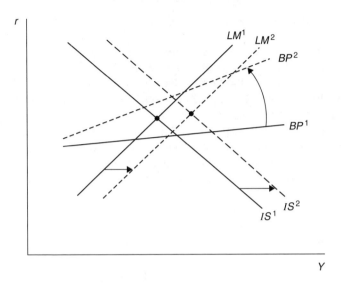

Figure 14.2

below BP^2, and devaluation, although initially resisted, eventually proved irresistible. The devaluation, perhaps rather more than contractionary monetary and fiscal policy, contributed to economic recession which, in addition to its relative price effects, subsequently created a large current account surplus.

The East Asian crisis is aptly described by the third-generation model. It was driven by the capital account rather than by the current account. But even so, it was domestic financial and corporate weakness that was the root cause. Contagion occurred. But some countries in the region survived this better than others. Hong Kong's currency board and China's large reserve holdings seemed to insulate them. Malaysia, although affected (or infected) by the crisis, opted for an unconventional policy response, much to the chagrin of the IMF. Controls were introduced to limit capital outflows. The idea was that the domestic interest rate could be kept lower than it would otherwise have needed to be, thus allowing the recessionary effects of the crisis to be neutralised. Critics of globalisation argued, with some admiration, that it was good to see a government putting the interests of domestic residents above those of international capital markets. Supporters of conventional policy wisdom argued that Malaysia would pay the price by adversely affecting its creditworthiness and its long-term access to international capital.

Argentina, 2002

If Mexico in 1994 was an example of a first-generation crisis, and East Asia in 1997–8 an example of a third-generation crisis, then Argentina in 2002 was (as Europe had been a decade earlier) an example of a second-generation crisis; albeit, perhaps, with elements of the other crisis models present as well.

For many years prior to 1991, Argentina had experienced very rapid inflation. This undermined competitiveness and led to frequent devaluations. The cycle of inflation, devaluation and more inflation was politically unpopular, and the breaking of this cycle became a political priority.

The government attempted to do this by pegging the value of the peso to the US dollar and by setting up a currency board, both to increase the credibility of the peg and to constrain monetary policy and therefore fiscal policy. When shocks occurred, such as the Mexican crisis in 1994, Argentina could no longer respond by changing its exchange rate. What happened instead was that the economy experienced recession and rising unemployment.

Immediately following the Mexican crisis, Argentinians seemed prepared to accept this; after all, memories of what had gone before were reasonably fresh, and the recession appeared to be temporary. But by the beginning of the twenty-first century, and certainly by 2001–02, there had been a protracted period of low inflation and exchange-rate stability. Economic growth had been almost non-existent, and unemployment had been high for some time; restoring economic growth assumed a higher political priority. Given the conflict between this priority and the external target of maintaining the pegged exchange rate and the currency board, something had to change.

Argentina's economy was in fundamental disequilibrium. Ever since the setting up of the Bretton Woods system in the mid-1940s, it has been accepted that in such circumstances the exchange rate may need to be altered and, eventually, this is what Argentina's government had to do.

The basic lesson from Argentina's experience is hardly novel; it is impossible to sustain a disequilibrium exchange rate over a protracted period of time. The costs of trying to do so simply become too high in both economic and political terms, making exchange-rate realignment inevitable.

The more interesting issue in Argentina's case, and elsewhere, however, was how to shift away from a peg without the need for a crisis that brings matters to a head, and without the costs associated with crises. Could the transition not have been achieved at a lower cost to Argentina's economic prosperity?

The appeal to Argentina of establishing a firm one-to-one currency peg to the US dollar in 1991, and putting this in the context of a currency board arrangement, is relatively easy to understand. It was not that Argentina came particularly close to meeting the optimum currency area criteria for exchange-rate pegging. Indeed, according to each of these criteria, Argentina was a weak candidate for exchange-rate pegging. Instead, the rationale was much more to use a pegged exchange rate as the centrepiece of a counter-inflationary policy.

Exchange-rate-based stabilisation was popular in Latin America at that time. But Argentina went further than some regional neighbours by instituting a currency board, because its inflation history was even worse than theirs. According to IMF data, inflation in Argentina was running at over 3000 per cent in 1989, and about 2300 per cent in 1990.

The government believed that a currency board arrangement that linked the domestic money supply to variations in the level of international reserves was needed to give the peg credibility. Under this arrangement, much as under the old gold standard of the late 1800s and early 1900s, disequilibrium in the balance of payments automatically induced domestic monetary adjustment. It was also believed that the currency board would discipline monetary and fiscal policy, excesses in which had previously contributed to poor inflation performance.

While pegging was central to the counter-inflationary strategy, pegging to the US dollar as opposed to other forms of peg (to a different anchor currency or a basket of currencies) did not reflect the strength of trading ties between the two countries. Indeed, historically, a relatively small amount of Argentina's trade was with the USA, and Argentina was seeking to expand its trade with its regional neighbours under the Mercosur arrangement, which had been signed with Brazil, Paraguay and Uruguay in 1991. Instead, the reason was more that the USA had a reputation for low and stable inflation, and it was this that Argentina was seeking to import. Moreover, it was believed that pegging to the dollar would encourage capital inflows from the USA. These considerations ruled out pegging to the currencies of regional neighbours.

Furthermore, at the beginning of the 1990s, Argentina lacked the credentials for inflation targeting as an alternative counter-inflationary strategy. Credible currency pegging offered a way of eliminating hyperinflation at a lower cost than would have been incurred using conventional tools of macroeconomic management. A further attraction of the US dollar was its status as an international currency, and the related network externalities associated with pegging to it.

Over the period 1992–7, the decision to institute a currency board appeared to pay off. Inflation fell dramatically and was barely positive by 1996. Economic growth averaged about 8 per cent per annum over the period 1991–4. While this could have had more to do with other policies of economic liberalisation that were being pursued simultaneously, there is little doubt that reducing inflation was a necessary precondition. The strong political commitment to the currency board also enabled Argentina to weather the contagion effects from the Mexican crisis in 1994. Although economic growth turned negative in 1995 and unemployment rose to over 17 per cent, this did not lead to severe political unrest; a stage was never reached where the government's commitment to the currency board appeared to be in serious danger. The benefits of reduced inflation were still politically paramount, and in any case, strong economic growth was restored by 1996.

Critics of exchange-rate pegging and currency boards were now beginning to have second thoughts. However, it was around this time that events began to move against Argentina's currency board. In some measure they were interrelated and it is difficult to quantify their relative importance. Many were external to Argentina.

First, while the peso was pegged to the US dollar, the dollar was itself floating against other currencies. This meant that the peso was also effectively floating against third currencies. However, the value of the peso moved against them in a way dictated by movements in the US dollar, and not in response to Argentina's economic position. This problem with pegging – the so-called 'third currency phenomenon' – had long been recognised. The importance of the problem for Argentina depended on its trade pattern. It would not have been a problem if Argentina had traded exclusively, or even very heavily, with the USA. However, this was not the case.

While its nominal value was pegged bilaterally to the US dollar, in other respects the value of the peso was not pegged at all. The real exchange rate *vis-à-vis* the US dollar depended on the inflation rates in the two countries. The price level in Argentina rose by less than 1 per cent per annum during 1996–8, and fell by about 1 per cent per annum during 1998–2001. As a consequence, Argentina's real exchange rate *vis-à-vis* the US dollar depreciated. However, at the same time, the value of the dollar appreciated strongly in the foreign exchange market towards the end of the 1990s, and this meant that the peso appreciated in real terms against other currencies. Certainly, the sustained fall in the value of the euro after its introduction in 1999, and the sharp fall in the value of the Brazilian 'real', with the devaluation of 1999, severely weakened Argentina's international competitiveness. The appreciation of the peso against these currencies, as well as against the yen, weakened Argentina's current account. The overvaluation of the peso against third currencies made it more difficult for domestic producers to compete, in spite of low domestic inflation. Domestic output fell, and unemployment rose. Economic growth was consistently negative over the period 1999–2001. Thus both the current account deficit and the prolonged recession were associated with the peso's appreciation against currencies other than the US dollar.

Second, but not unconnected with the recession, Argentina's fiscal position weakened in the second half of the 1990s and into the early 2000s. Not untypical for Latin-American economies, Argentina had encountered problems in increasing tax revenue. In the midst of a recession, tax revenues tend to fall. In the absence of equivalent reductions in government expenditure, the fiscal deficit increased, but this was unmatched by an increase in private saving, which has historically been low in Argentina. Given the currency board arrangement, the fiscal deficit could not be monetised and it therefore had to be financed by borrowing. The high interest rates that this implied deepened the recession and built up government debt. Since much of the borrowing was external – it was capital inflows that had financed the current account deficit – the debt was largely denominated in dollars rather than pesos.

The stock of external debt made devaluation less attractive, since it would bring with it an increase in the peso value of the debt that would then accentuate domestic fiscal difficulties. The inclination was therefore to avoid devaluation. Yet avoiding devaluation reduced the chances of eliminating the current account deficit that then needed to be financed by more borrowing and more debt accumulation. Through these developments, Argentina became a crisis waiting to happen.

But there was more. Argentina is a primary product producer. At the end of the 1990s, primary product prices were falling relative to those of manufactured goods, and the terms of trade therefore moved against Argentina. In these circumstances, the equilibrium exchange rate fell while the real value of the peso was appreciating. A bad situation was thus made worse.

However, perhaps the worst matter as far as the currency board was concerned, was the unwillingness of Argentinians to accept its implications for the domestic economy: high unemployment and prolonged recession. Moreover, the prospects for economic recovery seemed slim. Faced with a trade-off between inflation and unemployment, Argentina had in effect moved too far in the direction of low inflation and high unemployment.

High interest rates in Argentina – made higher in real terms by deflation – were in part a consequence of the currency board arrangement and were needed to attract the capital inflows that were required to finance the current account deficit. However, in conditions of recession and high unemployment, high interest rates hardly seemed appropriate domestically.

Devaluation eventually came to be accepted as the only way of resolving the conflict. However, it was not a policy without dangers, which is why the decision to devalue was deferred until it could in practice no longer be avoided. What were the dangers?

The first was that it would reignite inflation and wipe out the hard-won gains of the previous ten years. There was less confidence in inflation targeting than in exchange-rate targeting as a counter-inflationary strategy. Just as unemployment and recession were politically unpopular, the government's fear was that devaluation and inflation would be just as unpopular. Moreover, to the extent that the fear of an inflationary backlash was justified, devaluation could have proved to be an ineffective way of lowering the real exchange rate.

The second danger was that devaluation would have (as it had in East Asia) a recessionary rather than expansionary impact through its balance sheet effects. In Argentina's case, and as noted above, it was the government as well as the private sector (both central and provincial) that held liabilities in dollars.

Combined with these concerns about devaluation, and as in any set of circumstances where a risky and potentially unpleasant course of action is contemplated, there was the hope that something would turn up. In Argentina's case the hope was that with a sizeable current account deficit in the USA, the value of the dollar would fall, and that of the euro would rise. This would have provided Argentina with the adjustment it needed in its real effective exchange rate without it having to abandon its peg to the dollar. However, the dollar's value did not fall in time, and Argentina was not allowed to escape from its policy dilemma.

Whereas the UK had been forced to withdraw from the ERM because its commitment was not believed by speculators, and reserves were rapidly being erased in an attempt to defend the currency, in Argentina it was the adverse political response to the policies needed to sustain the currency board, as much as the loss of confidence by international investors who anticipated the abandonment of the peg, that led to devaluation. Over a ten-year period, Argentina had come full circle. A policy designed to reduce the output and unemployment costs of reducing inflation was only being sustained by means of generating recession and high unemployment. From a political point of view, the policy calculus had changed fundamentally, and it was therefore hardly surprising that the government's policy choice changed as well.

15 The US Current Account Deficit and Global Economic Imbalances

Introduction

The US current account balance of payments was in deficit for the entire period from 1995 to 2005. Indeed, the size of the deficit increased fairly remorselessly throughout that period. Over this time, the value of the dollar both rose and fell, and the US fiscal deficit got bigger, then smaller and then bigger again. What explains the US current account deficit, and why was it sustainable over such a lengthy period of time? Had it become unsustainable by the mid-2000s, and what were the policy options? Moreover, to what extent was the deficit just one part of a broader picture of global economic imbalances? If the USA was exhibiting a current account deficit, where was the matching surplus, and to what extent did these imbalances create problems for the world economy?

Explaining the US Current Account Deficit

A convenient place to start looking for an explanation of the US current account deficit is the theory of the balance of payments presented in Chapter 4. The absorption approach suggests that the answer lies in an increase in US aggregate domestic demand comprising consumption, investment and government expenditure relative to aggregate domestic supply. This approach may be reformulated using the open economy framework discussed in Chapter 2 and in which (with a government):

$$X - M = (S - I) + (T - G)$$

This equation points to a number of factors that may have been at work. It implies that, with other things being constant, an increasing fiscal deficit will be associated with a weakening current account. Yet it also shows, if other things change, why a shrinking fiscal deficit need not guarantee a strengthening current account. An increase in T relative to G will fail to deliver an improvement in the current account if, simultaneously, S falls relative to I. In the USA it appears to have been the private sector imbalance between saving and investment that has dictated the course of the US current account. Relative to investment, there was simply deficient saving (or excessive consumption). Increasing fiscal prudence in the late 1990s was dominated by private sector laxity. The effect of these changes on the current account was exaggerated by the fact that private sector expenditure in the USA has a much higher import content than public sector expenditure, so a fall in private sector saving has a particularly pronounced effect on the current account.

The message also comes through from the simple import and export functions introduced in Chapter 2: where a country's economic growth exceeds that in the rest of the world it is likely that its current account will weaken. Throughout much of the 1990–2005 period, the US economy was growing more rapidly than either Europe or Japan. While US imports rose alongside increasing US income, US exports that depended on income levels elsewhere grew less rapidly. However, some care needs to be shown in equating rapid economic growth with a deteriorating current account, since much depends on the sources of the growth. The effect will be particularly pronounced when the growth is consumption-led and there is a high propensity to import.

Low private sector saving, often combined with fiscal deficits, had the effect of shifting the US's IS schedule to the right, as depicted in Figure 15.1. The current account weakened in association with the increase in national income, Y. But what were the implications of the rightward shift in IS for the rate of interest, and for the capital account and therefore for the sustainability of the current account deficit? We return to this question later in the chapter.

The monetary approach to the balance of payments reviewed in Chapter 4 shows how monetary expansion may, in principle, be a potential cause of balance of payments deficits. Was this a factor in the USA? The Federal Reserve did not oversee policies that were particularly expansionary over 1990–2001, but thereafter monetary policy loosened. So in terms of Figure 15.1, the US's LM schedule did not shift significantly to the right until the early 2000s. In developing economies, by contrast, where there is less opportunity to finance fiscal deficits by borrowing, or indeed to finance private sector deficits by borrowing, governments have been more inclined to relax monetary policy. In these countries, monetary policy has been subject to fiscal dominance; fiscal deficits have been monetised and expansionary monetary policy (a rightward shift in LM) has augmented and enhanced the effects of rightward shifts in IS on the current account of the balance of payments.

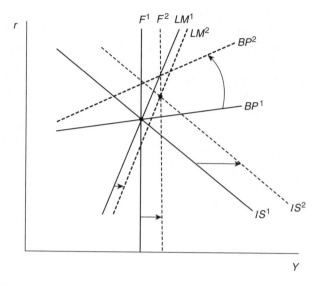

Figure 15.1

But in the USA, monetary policy does not appear to have played a great part in explaining the increasing current account deficit. It is certainly not the case that expansionary monetary policy led to inflation and a loss of competitiveness.

Rather, without full monetary endorsement, increasing expenditure resulted in relatively high interest rates, certainly in real terms (since inflation remained low throughout the 1990s and 2000s). Indeed it was the capital inflows attracted by the appeal of US assets that sustained the current account deficits. An explanation of current account deficits based on rapid inflation and a related appreciation in real exchange rates did not apply to the USA. To the extent that the real exchange rate appreciated over certain periods, this was more to do with an appreciating nominal exchange rate. But why would the nominal exchange rate appreciate if the current account of the balance of payments was in deficit? We have already hinted at the answer. In spite of the current account deficit, US financial assets remained attractive to foreign investors.

Figure 15.1 again illustrates what may have been happening. With a rightward shift in *IS* and a stable but relatively steep *LM* schedule, the rate of interest rises. This attracts capital from abroad and pushes the capital account into surplus. If this surplus exceeds the current account deficit, macroeconomic equilibrium, as shown by the intersection between *IS* and *LM*, lies above *BP*. There will be an overall balance of payments surplus and the exchange rate will appreciate. If, however, macroeconomic equilibrium lies below *BP*, the implication is that any capital account surplus falls short of the current account deficit; there is then an excess supply of dollars in foreign exchange markets and the value of the dollar falls. Herein lies an explanation of why the dollar appreciation of the late 1990s was followed by depreciation in the early 2000s. The US BP schedule shifted upwards and may have become steeper (BP^2 compared to BP^1 in Figure 15.1).

But why did the depreciation of the dollar at the beginning of the 2000s fail to have a discernible impact on the US current account? Was it that US foreign trade price elasticities were simply too low to make depreciation an effective balance of payments instrument? Other explanations seem more likely. First, of course, it is uncertain what the current account would have been in the absence of a depreciating dollar in the early 2000s. The current account deficit might have been even larger. Second, other factors might have changed in a way that negated the impact of dollar depreciation on US competitiveness. In principle, devaluation may stimulate inflation so that real exchange-rate depreciation is much less than nominal depreciation. But, as noted above, in practice there did not appear to be significant inflation pass-through in the US case. More likely is the possibility that foreign producers changed their pricing policies to offset the effects of dollar devaluation. They may have maintained the price of their exports to the USA in terms of dollars and been prepared to reduce their profits in terms of their own currencies in order to protect their market share in the USA. Third, countries in competition with the USA may have sought to maintain a currency peg against the US dollar so that, as the dollar depreciated, they also depreciated against other currencies, but retained the value of their currencies in terms of the dollar. This was certainly an explanation that found favour with the US administration as it became critical of exchange-rate policy in Asian economies. Finally, it may simply be that foreign trade price elasticities are low in the short run. There may be a J-curve, which implies that devaluation will not have an immediate effect, but may have a delayed one. Perhaps dollar depreciation in the early 2000s had not had time to exert its effects on the current account by 2005.

Can structural explanations of the balance of payments contribute to our understanding of the US current account deficit? At first sight this may seem implausible, since the structural approach is usually employed to explain the secular weakness of the current account balance of payments in those developing countries that concentrate heavily on exporting primary products with a low income elasticity of demand, and that import manufactured goods with a higher one. But, even for the USA, it is feasible that the income elasticity of demand for imports exceeds that of its exports. This would compound the effect on the US current account of low income growth in the markets in which the USA seeks to sell its exports.

A structural explanation may seem yet more relevant when one observes the degree of concentration within the USA on producing services. Generally speaking, trade in services has been less liberalised globally than trade in manufactured goods. This implies that, even if the income elasticity of demand for services is relatively high, this was not allowed to have its full impact on US exports. At the same time, continued trade liberalisation in terms of the goods in which the USA does not have a comparative advantage enhanced the growth of US imports. The structural approach may therefore have something to tell us about the US current account deficit, and rather more than might initially be thought.

The Current Account Deficit and Sustainability

The sustainability of a current account deficit depends on a country's ability to finance it externally. A loss of external financing can quickly transform a deficit from one that appears sustainable into one that is not. This was the situation for the capital account crisis countries in the 1990s, as explained in Chapter 14. Low-income countries tend to rely on foreign aid to enable them to sustain trade deficits. Periodically for them as well, their access to external finance declines, or it becomes insufficient to cover increasing deficits; this normally leads to their turning to the IMF for financial assistance, while they attempt to re-create balance of payments sustainability. Re-creating sustainability may involve substantial balance of payments adjustment.

For much of the 1990s and 2000s it was the attractions of investing in the USA that enabled the current account deficit to be sustained. The US economy was growing. The productivity of capital was relatively high. Interest rates were at least comparable to those elsewhere, and the dollar was appreciating for much of the time, with apparently little chance of an immediate depreciation. At the same time, Japan was trapped in a recession.[1] The European economy appeared to be stagnating and the value of the euro was falling. The situation was much as depicted in Figure 15.1. A buoyant US capital account sustained a weak current account.

By the mid-2000s, however, the question was how long could this continue? The dollar had been weakening in the early 2000s, the euro had been appreciating, the US current account was getting bigger, and an increasing US fiscal deficit seemed to offer little prospect that the current account would decline in the near future, especially when combined with a persistently low US savings rate. As much as anything else, sustainability seemed to rely on the reluctance of foreign holders of US assets to sell them and depress both the value of the other US assets they held and the value of the dollar in which the assets were denominated. There was an uneasy equilibrium in which Asian economies in surplus were prepared to use their excess export earnings to buy US assets and thereby sustain both the US current account deficit and the value of the dollar. But this hardly suggested that they would be prepared for ever to provide the finance necessary to cover a persistent and growing US deficit. By the mid-2000s, the US current account deficit seemed to be becoming of concern not only to the rest of the world but also to the US authorities themselves. What did this mean for policy?

Policy Options in the USA

The first policy option was to suggest that no adjustment was needed. The argument made was that, with the continued growth of international capital markets and the enduring relative attractiveness of US assets, capital would continue to flow into the USA. Indeed, attempts to eliminate the current account deficit, it was claimed, would destabilise both the USA and the world economy.

A second policy option also involved a passive approach. But here the argument was that adjustment would occur automatically. According to this view, a weakening US capital account would lead to dollar depreciation that would then eliminate the current account deficit. The threat of inflation, if not the inflation itself, would lead to tighter monetary policy and higher US interest rates, which would slow down growth in the US economy and therefore the growth of imports, and would also, alongside the dollar devaluation, begin to attract capital inflows again. Interest rates would, in any case, rise as asset prices fell. Moreover, the 'no need to worry' school of policy thought pointed out that dollar devaluation in the US does not have the adverse balance sheet effects that currency devaluation had exhibited in the emerging market crisis countries during the 1990s. Indeed, the reverse tends to be the case, since US assets are denominated in other currencies while its liabilities are denominated in dollars. Overall, the argument was that the current account is driven by the capital account. Capital inflows drive up the value of the dollar, and this causes the current account to weaken. Lower capital inflows drive down the value of the dollar, and the current account strengthens. What is there to worry about? Why is a proactive policy needed?

The 'worriers', by comparison, argued that there could be a 'hard landing'. The concern here was about the size and speed of devaluation once confidence in the USA and the dollar diminished or even evaporated. With a large devaluation, the threat of inflation becomes more significant and the concern is that, to counter this, a pronounced recession will have to be endured at a high real cost. Moreover, the 'worriers' doubted the long-term effectiveness of dollar devaluation in strengthening the current account, arguing that the fundamental cause of the deficit was deficient domestic saving combined with a growing fiscal deficit.

The current account would only be put right in the long run, according to this view, if these fundamental imbalances were corrected. If it is difficult to increase private saving, then at least governments can increase public saving by raising taxes. The 'worriers' were concerned that a lack of action on fiscal policy would lead to mounting pressures to reintroduce protectionist measures as a way of reducing US imports, without having to accept a large dollar devaluation and/or a deep recession. Even so, it was acknowledged that closing a fiscal deficit is particularly difficult when demographic changes lead to higher public spending on pensions and health care, there are significant security issues and there is strong political resistance to increasing taxes.

In principle, an increase in the US interest rate associated with capital outflows and with sales of US assets might stimulate saving, but empirical evidence suggests that in practice the effect is unlikely to be strong or even discernible. Worriers were instead concerned that higher interest rates and falling asset prices would lead to a severe recession, and that the savings rate could then fall as people attempted to protect their standard of living. A severe recession in the USA could then spill over to other countries and plunge the world economy into recession.

Global Economic Imbalances and Policy Co-ordination

As seen above, global economic interrelationships become an important part of the story. Where a significant proportion of the demand for US assets is coming from Asia, asset prices and interest rates in the USA can be affected by the changing behaviour of Asian investors. A strong demand for US assets by these investors keeps US interest rates low, and in this way helps to maintain US economic growth (although it may also maintain a high demand for real estate). The economic growth sustains the demand for US imports, which in part may be met, at relatively low cost, by Asian exporters. In any case, by sustaining an 'overvalued' dollar, the price of US imports is kept low, further restraining US inflation. In a sense, everyone gets what they want. The USA has low inflation, relatively low interest rates, and economic growth. Asian economies experience export-led economic growth and are able to build up their international reserves – which they were keen to do after the Asian economic crisis of 1997–8. However, the equilibrium is uneasy – as noted earlier – inasmuch as it relies on both parties remaining content with the status quo. If either the Asian appetite for US assets diminishes, or the USA becomes concerned about the size of its current account deficit, and its vulnerability to capital account shocks, the related changes in behaviour run the risk of leading to a substantial depreciation in the value of the US dollar, higher US inflation, higher US interest rates, and economic recession in the USA, that then spreads to other countries. Asian economies may then face much slower export growth that has, in part, been the engine of their economic success. At the same time, they may be reluctant to expand domestic demand for fear of inflation and the effects on their balance of payments.[2] If these interrelationships exist, should they not be taken into account in the formulation of policy?

The observation that, by the mid-2000s, countries might begin to make globally inconsistent choices about balance of payments policy, and that this threatened global economic prosperity made increasing protectionism more likely, led some to conclude that a greater degree of co-ordination internationally was required in the design of macro-economic policy (see Chapter 11 for a discussion of the issues involved). This then touched on many other questions relative to 'globalisation' and the adequacy of existing international institutions. As important as these issues are, they are beyond the scope of this chapter, except to note that an underlying dilemma was that, although it was keen to encourage policy change elsewhere, the USA was generally rather unenthusiastic about ceding more influence to those international organisations that might seek to orchestrate macroeconomic policy at the global level.

16 Macroeconomic Policy and the International Monetary Fund

In neither the case of the crisis in the ERM in 1992 (reviewed in Chapter 13) nor that of the current account deficit in the USA (reviewed in Chapter 15) did the countries concerned ever come close to turning to the International Monetary Fund (IMF) for assistance. In the former case, and although the situation proved unsustainable, policy was designed without a significant input from the IMF (of course, this is not to claim that the IMF did not have a point of view about appropriate policy). In the latter case, and up to the time of writing, the USA was able to sustain its current account deficit because of its access to private capital; it did not need to borrow from the IMF. However, in the case of the emerging market crisis countries (reviewed in Chapter 14), the IMF played an important role; Mexico, Thailand (and most of the other East Asian economies apart from Malaysia, Singapore and Hong Kong), as well as Argentina and Turkey have all had programmes with the IMF. The design of these programmes has not only been an issue for debate between the governments concerned and the IMF, but it has also been the subject of considerable disagreement among economists. In particular, some economists have argued that the policies favoured by the IMF in the aftermath of the Asian crisis were ill-advised and resulted in a recession that could have been avoided. Other economists have argued that the policies were well designed and entirely appropriate. How do such disagreements arise? We can answer this question by drawing on the analysis presented throughout this book.

The Classic Current Account Case and Conventional IMF Policy Wisdom

In circumstances where, historically, international private capital markets were relatively ill-developed, and controls over capital movements were common, balance of payments problems were usually associated

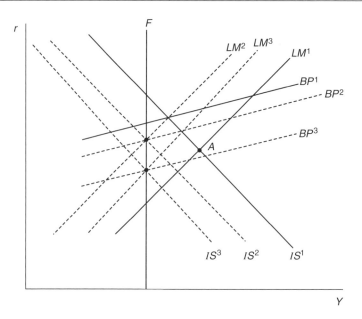

Figure 16.1

with the current account. In many instances the explanation for them lay in over-expansionary fiscal policy, with the resulting fiscal deficits then being monetised and leading to monetary expansion and inflation. In the context of the *IS–LM–BP* model, the *BP* schedule was relatively steep, and rightward shifts in *IS* and *LM* caused large current account deficits which could not be sustained by borrowing from private capital markets or by running down reserves. Enter the IMF. This was the 'classic' case. The policy remedy was relatively straightforward; it involved fiscal and monetary contraction combined with exchange-rate devaluation. The devaluation was needed to reverse the effects of past inflation on the real exchange rate. The fiscal and monetary contraction was needed to prevent the problem from reasserting itself and to negate the inflationary effects of the devaluation. Problem solved! Well, up to a point. To the extent that there was a debate over policy in this classic case it was about the quantitative size of fiscal and monetary retrenchment and the size of devaluation, rather than about the broad direction of policy.

The classic case is illustrated in Figure 16.1. Point *A* depicts the situation when the IMF becomes involved. There is a current account deficit, currency overvaluation and inflation (since *IS* and *LM* intersect below *BP* and to the right of *F*). Fiscal policy shifts IS^1 to IS^2. Monetary policy shifts LM^1 to LM^2, and devaluation shifts BP^1 to BP^2. Both the current

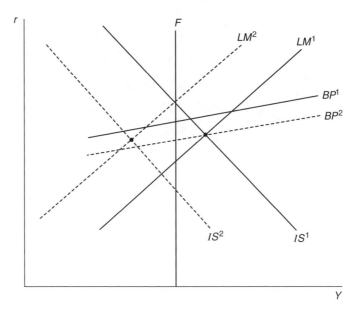

Figure 16.2

account deficit and inflation are eliminated. The question is, how big these shifts should be relative to each other. As configured in Figure 16.1, the rate of interest rises, the rate of inflation falls, there is no adverse effect on real output (as shown by the real output schedule, F) and the current account is strengthened. But the decline in inflation and the improvement in the current account could have been achieved by, for example, bigger shifts in BP (to BP^3) and in IS (to IS^3) and a smaller shift in LM (to LM^3), with the result that the rate of interest falls. Moreover, there is a danger of overkill. In Figure 16.2, the leftward shifts in IS and LM are such that the new equilibrium occurs to the left of F. There is now unemployment and an overall balance of payments surplus. Macroeconomic retrenchment has gone too far. The 'classic' case also reveals an emphasis on managing aggregate demand. It is the mismanagement of aggregate demand that caused the problem, and it is the restoration of appropriate macroeconomic policies that resolves it. The supply side does not enter the story.

Low-income Countries and Structural Adjustment

In the case of low-income countries, aggregate supply may be much more central. Not only is economic growth the means through which

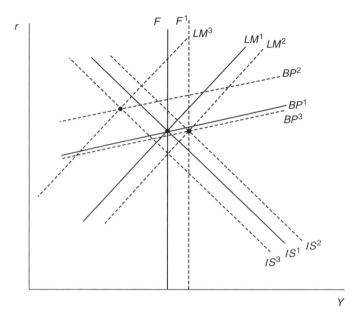

Figure 16.3

poor countries can seek to improve their living standards, but, with living standards low, it becomes particularly attractive to explore ways of improving the current account by raising domestic output rather than by compressing aggregate domestic demand. For low-income countries that focus on producing and exporting a narrow range of primary products, structural explanations of their current account deficits (as explored in Chapter 4) may be as important as the absorption and monetary explanations.

Take the case illustrated in Figure 16.3. Here, the balance of payments problems that bring the country to the IMF are associated only in part with over-expansionary fiscal and monetary policy (see the rightward shifts in *IS* and *LM*). A greater part of the explanation is the adverse terms of trade movement reflected by the upward shift in *BP* from BP^1 to BP^2. Balance of payments equilibrium could, in principle, be restored along BP^2 by shifting *IS* and *LM* leftwards to IS^3 and LM^3, respectively. But these policies would lead to recession and a decline in living standards. More desirable might be to leave IS^2 and LM^2 where they are, shift *BP* down to BP^3 via devaluation and other policies designed to improve export performance, and shift *F* to the right, to F^1. More desirable, yes, but far from easy.

The difficulties may be illustrated by reintroducing the basic open economy equation discussed in Chapter 2:

$$X - M = Y - [C + I + G]$$

The objective is to increase $(X - M)$ by raising Y relative to $[C + I + G]$. But for future period Y to rise it is probably necessary to raise current period I. Investment helps to bring about economic growth. Moreover, increased capital expenditure by the government on improving physical and social infrastructure may be needed to increase I. This type of government expenditure may crowd in private investment. The problem is that an increase in current period I and G, with no change in current period Y, will cause the current account deficit to deteriorate. Does this not simply mean that consumption and the current component of government expenditure need to be cut? But now – and as we observed in Chapter 6 – there is another problem. Reducing current consumption as well as government subsidies and welfare payments will be unpopular politically, and in any case will not be an appealing option in countries where living standards are already low.

The IMF encounters yet further difficulties in its dealing with low-income countries. First, identifying policies that will encourage economic growth is non-trivial. Second, if policies to encourage economic growth have an adverse effect on the current account in the short run, how is this current account deficit to be financed? If the IMF does not have sufficient resources itself, can it persuade aid donors to provide them? Third, some economists argue that fiscal policy, monetary policy and devaluation will be least effective in low-income countries, and may even have perverse effects. The fiscal balance may be affected by exogenous factors, such as a shortfall in exports, leading to a decline in the revenue from export taxes, or by an increase in government expenditure resulting from an appreciation in the currencies in which sovereign debt is denominated, or an increase in world interest rates. Contractionary monetary policy may increase the cost of borrowing to firms that rely heavily on bank credit, and this may be cost-inflationary. Devaluation may have a contractionary effect on both aggregate supply and aggregate demand through the routes examined in Chapter 9. The suggestion is that, as with monetary policy, devaluation may be simultaneously cost-inflationary and demand-deflationary.

In circumstances where the emphasis is on increasing aggregate supply, it is not hard to see why some economists have argued that the policies conventionally supported by the IMF may be the least appropriate; although whether this means that the IMF should change its policies in these countries, or extricate itself from lending to them is a moot point.

Capital Account Crises and Discontentment with IMF Policy

Fewer observers contend that the IMF does not have a role at all in emerging economies facing currency crises. But there is considerable disagreement over what policies the IMF should support. The conventional wisdom follows directly from the analysis of capital movements in Chapters 2 and 3. If the problem is that there has been a capital reversal, policy must raise domestic interest rates (to improve the return to capital) and eliminate any expected depreciation in the value of the currency by means of devaluation. Critics of the conventional wisdom claim that an increase in the domestic rate of interest will also increase the risk of corporate and financial default, so that risk-adjusted returns in fact decline, and that depreciation in the currency will foster the belief that the value of the currency will fall further, increasing exchange-rate risk. In conjunction, the conventional policies may lead to further capital outflows, making the situation worse rather than better.

Discontentment with conventional IMF policy also maintains that the Fund has tended to treat capital account crises in the same way as it has treated current account crises. It has opted for contractionary fiscal policy, when fiscal deficits have not been a cause of the problem. It has underestimated the negative effect that crises themselves have on business confidence, and has therefore overstated the need for fiscal prudence. According to those who are discontented, an increase in $(S - I)$ has offset the need to raise $(T - G)$. As a consequence, fiscal austerity causes an excessive turnaround in the current account, which moves quickly from a relatively modest deficit into a large surplus. The recessionary effects of fiscal and monetary policy are exacerbated by the contractionary balance sheet effects of devaluation. Again, the consequence is contractionary overkill, which does little to attract portfolio investment and foreign direct investment. Discontents claim that IMF advice has severely damaged living standards.

What should the response be to these discontents? It should not be for the IMF to reverse its policy advice. It would surely be unwise for countries in the middle of a balance of payments crisis to opt for larger fiscal deficits, rapid monetary expansion and currency revaluation. Instead, it is more a matter of moderating the conventional policy wisdom in the light of circumstances, and being prepared to be flexible both over time and case by case. For example, in a situation where foreign direct investment is more important than bank lending, capital flows may be less sensitive to increasing domestic interest rates. Where there has been a great deal of external borrowing and there is a currency mismatch between the domestic financial and corporate sectors' assets and liabilities, the balance sheet effects of devaluation will be more significant than if borrowing had been more modest and no mismatch existed. When domestic saving is high and exceeds investment, there will be less need for sharp fiscal contraction, especially if there is a reasonable presumption that private investment will fall. Where unemployment is above the natural rate and there is scope to increase domestic output, there is much less need to be preoccupied with inflation; indeed, there may be an argument for maintaining interest rates at a relatively low level in order to stimulate economic activity. While there are no simple textbook answers, even a simple textbook can highlight the issues. The problem remains easy to express. Graphically, it is to manipulate the positions of the *IS*, *LM*, *BP* and 'full' employment lines so as to ensure low inflation, low unemployment and high levels of capacity utilisation, along with a sustainable balance of payments. It is also to achieve economic growth, so that full employment output increases over time. The challenge is in designing a combination of fiscal, monetary and exchange-rate policies that deliver the desired outcomes. In this context, the IMF has demonstrated that it does not possess a magic wand. But then, nobody else does either.

Notes

1 Introduction

1. Although open-economy macroeconomics is the fashionable title, most traditional textbooks in international economics contain an analysis of similar issues.
2. Views differ about the usefulness of the *IS–LM* construct employed in this book. Those who dislike it will tend not to like the book. The justification for using it here is that it provides a fairly simple way of presenting and analysing quite complex problems. Not only that, but, as the case studies reveal, the model does seem to stand up quite well against observed facts. For the undergraduate anxious to find an analytical framework within which to work, the *IS–LM* model has much to be said for it.

2 An Open-economy Macroeconomic Model

1. These models are adequately described in most introductory economics textbooks.
2. In a closed economy, the 'paradox of thrift' occurs where the desire by individuals to increase their saving fails to lead to any increase in aggregate savings, since the very act of saving reduces the level of national income, which then induces saving to fall.
3. A more rigorous and mathematical presentation of the process described here may be found in many intermediate or advanced texts in international economics.
4. There are numerous books available which survey the various theories of inflation. Readers of this book are encouraged to glance through at least one of these surveys in order to appreciate just how narrow is the analysis of inflation presented here.

3 Trade Functions and Capital Movements

1. A fairly wide-ranging selection of empirical evidence is available on the import function. The independent variables usually include, in one form or another, relative prices and terms of sale, the level of domestic income and/or

212

the internal pressure of demand and a time trend. Some pieces of research take a broad look at the determination of imports as a whole, while others concentrate on the determination of one specific category or type of import.

Some empirical work, instead of taking actual imports as the dependent variable, takes import share, which allows attention to be focused on determinants such as relative prices and capacity utilisation. Although estimations using import share carry with them certain underlying assumptions; for example, that there are identical income elasticities of demand for both home and foreign produced goods, the main advantage of using it is that the problem of multicollinearity is reduced.

A major problem involved with empirical estimation of the import function is that the independent variables may not be directly observable. We are, therefore, forced to look for suitable proxies. Some determining variables may simply not be suited to quantitative estimation at all. It is, for example, *ex ante* waiting time which is of significance, and this has been variously estimated from delivery lag, inventory level and capacity utilisation data. Actual waiting time may be a less satisfactory proxy since it may be far removed from the quoted waiting time and may fail to reflect the producers' willingness to seek and accept new orders which will influence the supply of imports. It is very difficult, however, to derive any series at all that represents clearly the enthusiasm with which suppliers pursue the sale. Lags are also likely to be significant in attempting to explain import performance, though the precise structure of these may be difficult to ascertain.

Different empirical studies have come up with different results, some have found relatively high price elasticities whereas others have found relatively low ones. In many studies, the internal pressure of demand appears to be important, not least because it affects aspects of non-price competitiveness. Furthermore, there is some empirical support for a cyclical ratchet effect.

2. Empirical studies of the export function tend to have adopted a disaggregated approach. Such an approach may be viewed as being substantially legitimate since different industries exhibit different market structures and technologies, as well as different elasticities of demand and supply, both long-run and short-run.

No clear conclusions emerge from the empirical evidence. Price variables get a mixed reception, while perhaps the majority of studies find that exports are negatively related to domestic demand pressure, although the evidence is by no means unanimous.

3. Almost all good introductory texts in macroeconomics contain an analysis of investment and of the capital stock adjustment principle. Interested readers should refer to one of these.

4. Again analyses of the demand for money are available in most introductory texts.

4 Balance of Payments Theory

1. Readers are again reminded that the treatment given to inflation in this book is extremely superficial and they are encouraged to look at other texts

which focus more fully on this phenomenon. Similarly scant treatment is given to unemployment. Again, as unemployment has become more of a problem, there has been a growing number of texts produced which focus on it, and one of these should be consulted in order to fill the gaps left here.

2. A deficit on current account implies a net inflow of goods and services and, in the short run at least, this will tend to increase the domestic standard of living. The problem, of course, is to finance and sustain such an inflow.

3. Again, most introductory texts in macroeconomics contain analyses of monetary policy and open-market policy.

5   Theories of Exchange-rate Determination

1. This chapter concentrates on factors that influence the exchange rate, it does not examine alternative generalised exchange-rate regimes. Readers interested in the arguments for and against different exchange rate systems should consult a textbook in international financial economics.

2. In the former case, the location of *LM* does not alter and the size of the increase in the interest rate depends on the slope of *LM*, which itself in large part depends on the interest elasticity of the demand for money, becoming steeper as the elasticity falls. In the latter case, *LM* shifts to the right thus offsetting the impact of the rightward shift in *IS*, reflecting the increase in government spending, on the rate of interest.

3. More is said about this important theorem in a later section of this chapter.

4. PPP may still hold even if there is a significant non-traded goods sector, provided there is a fixed price relationship between traded and non-traded goods. This may exist if changes in the prices of traded goods are transmitted to non-traded goods through factor markets or through changes in the pattern of demand induced by relative price changes.

   A related problem is to identify which price index to use in testing the PPP theorem or in predicting exchange-rate movements on the basis of differences in inflation rates across countries. The consumer price index, for example, may be unsatisfactory precisely because it includes the prices of non-traded goods.

5. The question of the way in which expectations are formed is also relevant to, for example, the discussion of investment, inflation and the demand for money.

6. As with other parts of this book, readers are encouraged to experiment with the analysis for themselves. Here, for example, the basic thought processes that are run through in the text can be used to analyse a situation where *LM* is non-vertical.

7. There has been a great deal of debate in the literature concerning whether speculation stabilises or destabilises exchange rates. Much depends on the way in which speculators form their expectations. Where they have a fixed view of the long-run equilibrium rate, profit-making behaviour will tend to stabilise the exchange rate around this level. With 'elastic' expectations, however – where a movement in the rate is taken to suggest a further movement in the same direction – speculation will destabilise exchange rates,

while speculators will still make a profit. If speculators possess rational expectations, possessing perfect foresight of the future, they will exploit every opportunity to make a profit and their profits will therefore be maximised. This is linked to the idea of 'efficient markets', where directly new information becomes available it will be fully incorporated into the spot rate thus eliminating unexploited opportunities for profit through speculation. Another aspect of efficient markets is that expectations affecting the future spot rate will be incorporated into the forward rate which then becomes the best predictor of the future spot rate.

The empirical evidence does not provide a great measure of support for rational expectations and efficient markets in the context of the exchange rate. Unexploited profit opportunities do seem to exist. Speculation may sometimes be dominated by uncertainty and high risk premia, and by bandwagon effects. Furthermore, the forward rate does not appear to be an accurate predictor of the future spot rate, suggesting that things that occur after the forward contract is signed are not foreseen. There appears to be little bias in the errors made, with differences between forward rates and actual future spot rates averaging out to zero over time.

8. Where real disturbances are more significant than monetary ones PPP is unlikely to hold even in the long run. It is generally accepted that PPP provides an inadequate explanation of short-run variations in exchange rates, with these normally being much more volatile than aggregate price levels.

6 Theories of Currency Crisis

1. Because of its emphasis on fundamental disequilibrium, the second-generation currency crisis model has some resonance with the Bretton Woods international monetary system, which in principle allowed countries to alter exchange rates in circumstances where fundamental disequilibrium existed.

2. To a large degree the sustainability of a current account balance of payments deficit depends on the availability of capital inflows in one form or another. A country with poor access to international capital may therefore be less able to sustain a current account deficit that is smaller (normalised for country size) than that in another country with better access to international capital.

3. For a brief review of alternative approaches see, for example, Graham Bird and Ramkishen Rajan (2003) 'Too Much of a Good Thing? The Adequacy of International Reserves in the Aftermath of Crises', *The World Economy*, vol. 26, no. 6, pp. 973–91.

4. This is discussed more fully in Chapter 16.

7 Balance of Payments Policy

1. Whereas structural adjustment in developing countries may in this way be linked to increases in some types of government expenditure, 'supply side

economics' has usually been taken to imply measures to reduce the role of government and to reduce marginal tax rates as a means of creating incentives which lead to higher output.

8 Stabilisation Policy in an Open Economy

1. These are all important issues. Fortunately most introductory macroeconomics textbooks discuss them and readers are advised to consult one of them.
2. In preference to the fixed targets approach it may be better to think in terms of a social welfare function with targets being arguments in this function. Here the policy-makers' objective is to maximise the welfare function subject to certain policy constraints, allowing for the fact that certain targets may be seen as being more important than others and that there may be trade-offs between them.
3. For clarification of this see an intermediate macroeconomic textbook. The basic idea behind Say's Law is that supply creates its own demand, while with the gold standard mechanism, flows of gold, which reflect payments disequilibria, cause changes in money supplies which automatically eliminate the disequilibria. Thus in a deficit country the domestic money supply falls as gold flows out to finance the deficit. Prices fall and the deficit is eliminated.
4. See J. Tinbergen, *On the Theory of Economic Policy* (Amsterdam: North-Holland, 1952).
5. See R. A. Mundell, 'The Appropriate Use of Monetary and Fiscal Policy for Internal and External Stability', *IMF Staff Papers*, 1962.
6. Again most conventional textbooks in macroeconomics have a section on the balanced budget multiplier theorem. Resting as it does on a series of restrictive assumptions, the theorem shows that if government expenditure and taxation are raised by the same amount, national income will increase by an amount equal to the increase in government expenditure. Furthermore, it has been suggested that indirect taxes have a greater deflationary effect than equal yielding direct taxes, since direct taxes may be partially offset by a fall in saving while indirect taxes will not be, and because indirect taxes tend to increase the price level and reduce the real supply of money.
7. Cost based theories of inflation have over the years became less popular.
8. Readers may wish to note at this stage that these conclusions change if *LM* is drawn steeper than *BP* implying a relatively higher degree of capital mobility. Here contractionary monetary policy will restore payments equilibrium at some cost in terms of unemployment. But contractionary fiscal policy will only widen the payments deficit. Those sufficiently interested may confirm this by redrawing Figure 8.4 for themselves. We return to the question of different degrees of capital mobility later in the chapter.
9. Criticisms of *IS–LM* range from a relatively minor debate over the values of certain elasticities or the specification of underlying functional relationships to a fairly root and branch rejection of the entire framework.
10. Again most standard macroeconomics textbooks contain an analysis of aggregate demand and supply schedules.

11. See Trevor W. Swan, 'Longer Run Problems of the Balance of Payments', in R. E. Caves and H. G. Johnson (eds), *Readings in International Economics* (London: Allen & Unwin, 1968).

9   Exchange Rate Management and Policy

1. The issues raised here can be presented in a more rigorous fashion mathematically. Many books provide just such an analysis of the so-called Marshall–Lerner conditions for successful devaluation.

10   Dealing with International Capital Volatility

1. Dutch disease refers to a situation where strength in terms of the capital account (perhaps associated with the discovery of a natural resource, as it was in the case of the Netherlands with natural gas) induces weakness in terms of the current account as a consequence of appreciation in the real exchange rate.
2. Different types of capital involve different distributions of risk, as between debtors and creditors. In the case of portfolio investment, those buying equity shares carry a risk that the price of the shares may fall. Multinational enterprises engaging in foreign direct investment carry the risk that it may turn out to be unprofitable. In the case of short-term international bank lending, where the parameters of the contract are defined *ex ante*, borrowers tend to carry the risks, except of course in circumstances where they decide to default on their obligations (although this also carries risks).

12   The Oil Crisis of the 1970s and the Debt Crisis of the 1980s

1. Short-term real interest rates for the major industrial countries were, for example, −0.3 per cent in 1976, −0.5 per cent in 1977 and −0.3 per cent in 1978.
2. However, there remains some debate concerning just how inflationary was the increase in oil prices. A counter-argument is that the increase in oil prices simply reflected a response to increasing global aggregate demand and was not a cost-push phenomenon at all.
3. The overvaluation will arise as domestic inflation causes the real exchange rate to appreciate. The real exchange rate is sometimes presented as the relative price of non-tradable and tradable goods. An increase in the relative price of non-tradable goods represents real exchange rate appreciation.
4. Readers may conveniently check the data by consulting the IMF's *World Economic Outlook*. For the G7 industrial countries' economic growth, which had been running at about 4 per cent in the second half of the 1970s, fell

to little over 1 per cent in 1980 and 1981 and to − 0.4 per cent in 1982. Short-term real interest rates rose to over 4 per cent in 1981 and 1982, from the negative rates of the late 1970s.

5. The analysis abstracts from the fact that changes in the exchange rate will have implications for the location of *IS* and *LM*. Currency depreciation will, for example, shift *IS* to the right if a net expansionary effect is assumed.

13   Monetary Integration in Europe: The UK and the Euro

1. Emphasis on monetary aggregates had been discredited by the fact that it proved difficult to define and control these aggregates, and that financial innovation seemed to provide considerable scope for increasing the efficiency with which money was used, effectively increasing the velocity of circulation. Furthermore, the view that inflation could be reduced without an increase in unemployment seemed to be inconsistent with the facts and this made a 'monetarist' approach less attractive politically. While the UK probably stuck with the monetarist experiment for rather longer than the USA, the government's response to the stock market crash of 1987 was essentially Keynesian, suggesting that a macroeconomic strategy based solely on controlling monetary aggregates had been abandoned.

2. Of course, it does not follow that joining the ERM was the best counter-inflationary policy. Moreover, it is difficult to disentangle the extent to which it was membership of the ERM *per se* which brought a counter-inflationary pay-off, or merely the high interest rates that were necessary to sustain this membership.

15   The US Current Account Deficit and Global Economic Imbalances

1. Japanese recession could itself be a worthy case study of the analysis contained in this book. Why did it seem so difficult for Japan to break out of its recession? First, while nominal interest rates were extremely low and near zero, falling consumer prices meant that real rates were positive. Monetary policy was largely impotent. Even expansionary fiscal policy was relatively ineffective, since private sector saving was high, such that although $G > T$, this was offset by $S > I$. Meanwhile, the recession kept the demand for imports relatively low and contributed to a current account surplus. This in turn militated against a fall in the value of the yen and prevented Japan from pursuing a policy of export-led growth based on an undervalued currency. To a large extent, Japan therefore avoided the ire of the USA which instead tended to be directed towards China.

2. The global imbalances did not affect only the USA and Asia. In Europe, where the euro had appreciated in the early 2000s, the legacy of currency appreciation appeared to be economic stagnation and unemployment. But the European Central Bank remained reluctant in the mid-2000s to reduce

interest rates any further. In any case, this was difficult to achieve while inflation was low. Furthermore, Europe's Growth and Stability Pact imposed constraints – at least formally – on relaxing fiscal policy. At the same time, many European economies would have been concerned about an unorchestrated free fall in the value of the US dollar for the reasons discussed in the main body of this chapter.

Index